AF840233

AN EXPRESSIVE THEORY OF POSSESSION

Possession is a foundational concept in property law. Despite its undoubted importance, it is poorly understood and a perennial source of confusion. Indeed, there is a widely held view amongst lawyers that possession is an irredeemably ambiguous and amorphous concept. This book aims to challenge this conventional wisdom and to demonstrate that possession is in fact far simpler than generations of lawyers have been led to believe.

In viewing possession as a knotty problem for the philosopher or legal theoretician, scholars are apt to overlook the important truth that possession is a concept that laymen routinely and, for the most part, effortlessly apply as they navigate through the countless property interactions that shape everyday life. The key to understanding the nature and function of possession in the law is to appreciate that the possession 'rule' is, first and foremost, a spontaneously emergent phenomenon. Possession describes those acts that, as a matter of an extra-legal convention, constitute the accepted way in which members of a given population stake their claims to tangible things.

Fusing traditional legal analysis with insights from philosophy and economics, *An Expressive Theory of Possession* applies this central claim to both theoretical and doctrinal problems in property law and, in doing so, provides a coherent explanation of possession and its role in law and life.

An Expressive Theory of Possession

Michael JR Crawford

•HART•
OXFORD • LONDON • NEW YORK • NEW DELHI • SYDNEY

HART PUBLISHING

Bloomsbury Publishing Plc

Kemp House, Chawley Park, Cumnor Hill, Oxford, OX2 9PH, UK

1385 Broadway, New York, NY 10018, USA

HART PUBLISHING, the Hart/Stag logo, BLOOMSBURY and the Diana logo are trademarks of Bloomsbury Publishing Plc

First published in Great Britain 2020

Copyright © Michael JR Crawford, 2020

Michael JR Crawford has asserted his right under the Copyright, Designs and Patents Act 1988 to be identified as Author of this work.

All rights reserved. No part of this publication may be reproduced or transmitted in any form or by any means, electronic or mechanical, including photocopying, recording, or any information storage or retrieval system, without prior permission in writing from the publishers.

While every care has been taken to ensure the accuracy of this work, no responsibility for loss or damage occasioned to any person acting or refraining from action as a result of any statement in it can be accepted by the authors, editors or publishers.

All UK Government legislation and other public sector information used in the work is Crown Copyright ©. All House of Lords and House of Commons information used in the work is Parliamentary Copyright ©. This information is reused under the terms of the Open Government Licence v3.0 (http://www.nationalarchives.gov.uk/doc/open-government-licence/version/3) except where otherwise stated.

All Eur-lex material used in the work is © European Union, http://eur-lex.europa.eu/, 1998–2020.

A catalogue record for this book is available from the British Library.

Library of Congress Cataloging-in-Publication data

Names: Crawford, Michael J.R. (John Rooke), author.

Title: An expressive theory of possession / Michael J. R. Crawford.

Description: Oxford ; New York : Hart, 2020. | Based on author's thesis (doctoral – Melbourne Law School, 2017). | Includes bibliographical references and index.

Identifiers: LCCN 2020005274 (print) | LCCN 2020005275 (ebook) | ISBN 9781509929924 (hardcover) | ISBN 9781509929931 (Epub)

Subjects: LCSH: Possession (Law)—Philosophy. | Right of property.

Classification: LCC K726 .C73 2020 (print) | LCC K726 (ebook) | DDC 346.04—dc23

LC record available at https://lccn.loc.gov/2020005274

LC ebook record available at https://lccn.loc.gov/2020005275

ISBN: HB: 978-1-50992-992-4
ePDF: 978-1-50992-994-8
ePub: 978-1-50992-993-1

Typeset by Compuscript Ltd, Shannon

To find out more about our authors and books visit www.hartpublishing.co.uk. Here you will find extracts, author information, details of forthcoming events and the option to sign up for our newsletters.

FOREWORD

Whether or not it is nine-tenths of the law, possession accounts for a much lower proportion of the law library. This is a shame. The concept remains crucial in property law and in many areas both within and beyond the law. Moreover, it has a distinguished pedigree, having attracted the attention of international legal heavyweights such as Savigny, Holmes, and Pollock. Part of the problem stems from the realist contention that such foundational concepts are mere deceits, empty vessels good only for concealing judges' unarticulated preferences: for example, Dias, in his *Jurisprudence*, concluded that 'possession' is 'no more than a device of convenience and policy'.

Yet concepts such as possession persist and are employed by practitioners, judges, and legislators without any great embarrassment. Recently, indeed, there has been a renewal of scholarly interest in the content and detail of these classic doctrines. This 'New Private Law', however, does not merely seek to turn the clock back to a pre-realist era; rather, it brings new perspectives to the challenging task of understanding the legal principles, drawing not just on standard economics, but also on ideas drawn from disciplines such as behavioural economics, psychology, and social theory. This is not a one-way process, whereby the law is the passive recipient of insights from elsewhere; rather, the great resource of the common law can be mined for lessons which will allow us better to understand not only the law, but also other areas of life.

I therefore warmly welcome Dr Crawford's important contribution, as this excellent book successfully performs at least three valuable functions. First, it provides a rigorous and nuanced account of the role of possession within private law. Second, it draws on other disciplines, such as work in game theory, not to impose an ill-fitting external model, but to draw out key features of the law's operation. Third, in doing so, it develops a theory which can help us to understand the nature of possession not only within the confines of the law library, but in the wider world too. This book certainly deserves the salience it identifies in its subject.

Ben McFarlane
April 2020

ACKNOWLEDGEMENTS

This book is a revised and expanded version of a thesis successfully submitted for the degree of Doctor of Philosophy at the University of Melbourne in October 2017. It was my good fortune to be supervised by Professor Elise Bant and Professor Matthew Harding and I thank them for their guidance, support and unwavering enthusiasm throughout my candidature. I would also like to thank my PhD examiners, Professor Lisa Austin and Professor Ben McFarlane. I could not have hoped for two more rigorous examiners, and I am grateful to them for their detailed, thoughtful and encouraging comments. This book owes much to them and their outstanding contributions to property theory. As ever, responsibility for any and all errors lies with the author.

I also owe a debt of gratitude to my friend, Marco Paoletti, and my father, Kerry John Crawford, for reading the manuscript in its entirety and to Rosie Rand for her outstanding research and editorial assistance. Finally, thanks are also due to Kate Whetter, Linda Staniford and the entire team at Hart Publishing who made the process of transforming the manuscript into a finished book so smooth and enjoyable.

This book is dedicated to my wife, Lisa Burton Crawford, and to my son, Charles Fox Crawford.

Michael JR Crawford
Sydney
December 2019

TABLE OF CONTENTS

TABLE OF CASES

UK

Australia

US

Canada

NZ

TABLE OF STATUTES

UK

Australia

Introduction

I. The Possession Puzzle

Possession is universally regarded as one of the most important concepts in the law of property. Holmes commenced his famous treatment of the subject by remarking that, '[p]ossession is a conception which is only less important than contract'.[1] Likewise, the first sentence of Pollock and Wright's seminal work, *An Essay on Possession in the Common Law*, reads:

> [p]ossession is a term of common occurrence and no mean significance in the law. It imports something which at an earlier time constantly made the difference between having the benefit of prompt and effectual remedies, or being left with cumbrous and doubtful ones; which in modern times has constantly determined and often may still determine the existence or non-existence of a right to restrain acts of interference with property, the relative priority of the claims of competing creditors, or the incidence of public burdens; and which for centuries has been, and is still capable of being, of critical importance in defining the boundary between civil wrongs and crimes.[2]

Despite its undoubted significance, possession is notoriously poorly understood and a perennial source of confusion in the law. As Pollock went on to remark:

> [y]et, as the name of Possession is in these and other ways one of the most important in our books, so it is one of the most ambiguous. Its legal senses (for they are several) overlap the popular sense, and even the popular sense includes the assumption of matters of fact which are not always easy to verify.[3]

Nor has the possession mystery been solved in the years since Pollock penned those lines. As a leading modern work on the law of personal property reminded its readers, it is more or less mandatory to commence any discussion of the concept with Earl Jowitt's lament that '[i]n truth, English law has never worked out a completely logical and exhaustive definition of possession'.[4] Lord Parker complained that, '[t]he term "possession" is always giving rise to trouble'.[5]

[1] Oliver Wendell Holmes, *The Common Law* (Boston, Little, Brown and Company, 1948) 206.

[2] Frederick Pollock and Robert Samuel Wright, *An Essay on Possession in the Common Law* (Oxford, Clarendon Press, 1888) 1. Because this work is a compilation of three sole-authored essays, all references are to the author of the relevant part.

[3] Ibid, 1.

[4] *United States of America v Dollfus Mieg et Compagnie SA* [1952] AC 582 (HL), 605, quoted in Michael Bridge et al, *The Law of Personal Property* (London, Sweet & Maxwell, 2013) 55 [2-035].

[5] *Towers & Co Ltd v Gray* [1961] 2 QB 351, 361.

Such dicta are ubiquitous in the case law.[6] The feeling of despair aroused by the concept is captured by Hickey's remark that:

> [g]enerally, possession is thought to be a hopelessly vague concept, continually changing its content and import with the exigencies of legal practice. Textbook writers have considered it unsusceptible to satisfactory definition, and even the most positive statement of possession in the law retains some sense of apology for its ambiguity.[7]

There is no consensus, for example, on whether possession is simply a fact which, when proven by evidence, creates a property right, or whether it also describes a species of legal right in an object of property that is different from ownership. Even amongst those who agree that possession is a fact and not a right, there is no agreement on whether it describes a simple, observable fact about physical control or a more complex, and uniquely legal, concept concerned with the particular intention displayed by the possessor. And this is to say nothing of the broader philosophical mystery about why the unilateral act of possession should create non-consensual duties *in rem* at all.

II. Scope of the Book

Given the persistent ambiguity and confusion that has surrounded the concept, one may be forgiven for concluding that the best solution to the 'possession puzzle' is simply to abandon the concept altogether. However, this would be a false step. As will become apparent in the analysis that follows, possession is so deeply rooted in our system of private property rights that any attempt to extirpate it from the law of property would be doomed to fail. Given the timeless importance of possession and the now relative antiquity of Pollock and Wright's famous work, there is a need for an account that, unlike briefer treatments in works on personal property law, land law and tort, focuses exclusively on possession.[8]

Before describing the book's methodology and arguments, it is important to articulate its limits. The term 'possession' is ubiquitous within the law.[9] In the law of landlord and tenant, the question of whether someone has a leasehold or a

[6] *National Safe Deposit Co v Stead* 232 US 58, 67–68 (Lamar J) (1914).

[7] Robin Hickey, *Property and the Law of Finders* (Oxford, Hart Publishing, 2010) 162.

[8] In personal property law see, eg, Andrew P Bell, *Modern Law of Personal Property in England and Ireland* (Oxford, Butterworths, 1989) 33–65; Michael Bridge, *Personal Property Law*, 4th edn (Oxford, Oxford University Press, 2015) 32–43; Bridge et al (n 4) 55–66 [2-035]–[2-060]; Royston Miles Goode and Ewan McKendrick, *Goode on Commercial Law*, 4th edn (London, Penguin, 2010) 45–49; Duncan Sheehan, *The Principles of Personal Property Law*, 2nd edn (Oxford, Hart Publishing, 2017) 10–19. In land law see, eg, EH Burn and J Cartwright, *Cheshire and Burn's Modern Law of Real Property*, 18th edn (Oxford, Oxford University Press, 2011) 48–51; Kevin Gray and Susan Francis Gray, *Elements of Land Law*, 5th edn (Oxford, Oxford University Press, 2009) 150–79 [2.1.2]–[2.1.54]; Mark Wonnacott, *Possession of Land* (Cambridge, Cambridge University Press, 2006).

[9] DR Harris, 'The Concept of Possession in English Law' in AG Guest (ed), *Oxford Essays in Jurisprudence* (Oxford, Oxford University Press, 1961) 69, 70–71.

mere contractual interest in land depends upon whether they have been granted 'exclusive possession'.[10] Possession is also integral to the transfer of legal rights. As Holroyd J stated in *Irons v Smallpiece*, '[i]n order to change the property by a gift of this description, there must be a change of possession'.[11] A 'delivery' of goods under the various iterations of the *Sale of Goods Act* is defined as a 'voluntary transfer of possession from one person to another'.[12] In the criminal law, the offence of larceny has historically been understood in terms of violations of 'possession'. As Wright explained, '[t]he ordinary conception of theft is that it is a violation of a person's ownership of a thing: but the proper conception is that it is a violation of a person's possession of a thing accompanied with an intention to misappropriate the thing'.[13] In most jurisdictions it is an indictable offence to be in 'possession' of a drug of dependence.[14]

This huge diversity in the use of the term has led Harris to write that, '[w]e should therefore study the way in which the word "possession" is used in English rules of law; we cannot study the legal concept of possession in the abstract, for the word has no legal meaning apart from these particular rules'.[15] Others have concluded that possession is best viewed as a 'lump concept'.[16] Although there is no in-principle reason why the meaning of possession should be so context-dependent,[17] the consensus is otherwise. As Dawson J remarked of its use in criminal statutes, 'the technical doctrines of the civil law which separate proprietary and possessory rights in chattels are generally irrelevant for the purposes of the criminal law'.[18]

The question of whether there is, or should be, a uniform conception of possession across all areas of the law is not, however, the question to be answered in this book. The account developed below concentrates on possession's core role as a 'root of title'[19] or way of creating an original property right in an object of property. Although this enquiry raises cognate issues, they are only addressed to the extent that they are raised by the central question. It may well be that the conception of possession developed in this book explains, for example, the role of possession in larceny or the transfer of legal rights. Alternatively, it may reveal that, contrary to Harris's position, the concept of possession is not context-dependent and that many purported instances of 'possession' in the law are, in fact, unnecessary fictions. However, whether such things are true is a question for another work.

[10] *Street v Mountford* [1985] AC 809 (HL), 816.
[11] *Irons v Smallpiece* (1819) 106 ER 467, 468; 2 B & Ald 551, 553.
[12] See, eg, *Goods Act 1958* (Vic) s 3; *Sale of Goods Act 1979* (UK) s 61.
[13] Pollock and Wright (n 2) 118.
[14] See, eg, *Drugs, Poisons and Controlled Substances Act 1981* (Vic) s 73(1); *Misuse of Drugs Act 1971* (UK) s 5.
[15] Harris (n 9) 70.
[16] Bridge et al (n 4) 55 [2-036].
[17] Sheehan (n 8) 10.
[18] *He Kaw Teh v R* [1985] HCA 43; (1985) 157 CLR 523, 599.
[19] Pollock and Wright (n 2) 22.

Nevertheless, because this is not a treatment of possession in the context of a larger work on personal property law, land law or tort, the account offered below is not constrained by other taxonomical boundaries in property law, in particular that between real and personal property. Indeed, the conceptual uniformity of possession across this traditional boundary is an important element of the account presented in this book. So far as the objects of property are concerned, the only relevant distinction is that between tangible and ideational things, the latter of which cannot be possessed in any meaningful sense of the word.

Two final limits must be briefly articulated. First, despite the extensive use of interdisciplinary materials, this is not a book about legal theory or game theory per se. Theoretical and inter-disciplinary insights are deployed to illuminate a concept that is of fundamental importance in property *law*. Secondly, while it is argued that possession is a fundamentally social, rather than a legal, fact, no attempt is made to exhaustively catalogue those particular relationships between people and things that amount to acts of 'possession' in different interpretive communities. This is an empirical task that is beyond the scope of this work. Nevertheless, it is hoped that some of the arguments presented in this book might be of use to, in particular, 'law and society' scholars who may choose to undertake this work.

III. Methodological Divergence in Private Law Scholarship

There has long been a growing methodological divide in Anglo-American private law scholarship.[20] While many English writers have remained faithful to a generally 'doctrinal' tradition, American scholars have enthusiastically applied inter-disciplinary methods to the study of law. While this diversity in methodology has enriched our understanding of private law, the gap between the various methodological camps has at times become so wide that one wonders whether members of each are engaged in the same field of intellectual enquiry.

A prime illustration of this divergence is furnished by the occasionally intemperate, yet curiously overlooked,[21] debate between Simpson, an eminent legal historian, and Coase, an eminent economist, played out in the pages of the *Journal of Legal Studies*.[22] Simpson criticised Coase's seminal article 'The Problem

[20] On this issue see Andrew Burrows, 'Challenges for Private Law in the Twenty-First Century' in Kit Barker, Karen Fairweather and Ross Grantham (eds), *Private Law in the 21st Century* (Oxford, Hart Publishing, 2017) 29, 34–40; Richard A Posner, 'The Deprofessionalization of Legal Teaching and Scholarship' (1993) 91 *Michigan Law Review* 1921, 1923. On the continued importance of doctrinal scholarship in property law see Martin Dixon, 'A Doctrinal Approach to Property Law Scholarship: Who Cares and Why?' in Susan Bright and Sarah Blandy (eds), *Researching Property Law* (London, Palgrave Macmillan, 2015) 1.

[21] David Campbell and Matthias Klaes, 'What Did Ronald Coase Know About the Law of Tort?' (2016) 39 *Melbourne University Law Review* 793, 795–96.

[22] AW Brian Simpson, 'Coase v. Pigou Reexamined' (1996) 25 *Journal of Legal Studies* 53; Ronald H Coase, 'Law and Economics and AW Brian Simpson' (1996) 25 *Journal of Legal Studies* 103; AW Brian Simpson, 'An Addendum' (1996) 25 *Journal of Legal Studies* 99.

of Social Cost'[23] on the ground that he had misunderstood the nineteenth-century nuisance cases on which he purported to rely.[24] Coase, for his part, responded that Simpson's criticisms were irrelevant because Coase's argument was economic, not legal,[25] and Simpson, as a lawyer, failed to understand the economic concepts discussed in the paper.[26]

As Campbell and Klaes have recently argued, the better view seems to be that both men were right and wrong. Coase did misunderstand the law, but his misunderstanding did not undermine the validity of his ingenious economic argument.[27] Perhaps what is most striking about the exchange was Coase's intemperate remark that:

> [n]otwithstanding the many references to my work in the literature on the economic analysis of law in the last 35 years, I have never attempted to contribute to it … my unwillingness to take part in the discussions of this subject is a result of … my lack of knowledge of the detailed working of the legal system and my very superficial knowledge of the legal literature. I admit that this lack of knowledge is a deficiency. But it is surely a virtue not to write on a subject of which one is ignorant. I wish Professor Brian Simpson had shown a similar prudence. He writes about economics and economists from the point of view of an historian and a lawyer. It is not surprising to find that his article contains so many misunderstandings of my position and misstatements about me and my work.[28]

Coase was almost certainly wrong to say that Simpson failed to follow his economic argument. In any case, what is most significant about this exchange is that it reveals that two eminent scholars, though writing in the *Journal of Legal Studies*, appeared to regard themselves as pursuing entirely different intellectual endeavours.

This issue of 'continental drift' in Anglo-American private law scholarship is not merely one of general interest. It is of central importance to this book because possession is a topic that has consistently straddled this transatlantic methodological divide.

Beginning most prominently with Pollock and Wright's *Essay on Possession*, published in 1888, English accounts of possession have tended to be rigorously doctrinal in approach and have attempted to solve the enduring riddle of possession by closely analysing the cases in which it has figured prominently. Quite apart from the strongly doctrinal bent in much English private law scholarship, the predominance of this approach must, at least in part, be attributable to the long shadow that the arcane concept of 'seisin' has cast over English law. By contrast,

[23] RH Coase, 'The Problem of Social Cost' (1960) 3 *Journal of Law & Economics* 1.

[24] Simpson, 'Coase v Pigou' (n 22) 88–91. In particular, Simpson argued that Coase failed to appreciate the import of the seminal nuisance case, *Sturges v Bridgman* (1879) LR 11 Ch D 852.

[25] Coase, 'Law and Economics' (n 22, 104).

[26] Ibid, 104–5.

[27] Campbell and Klaes (n 21) 813–23.

[28] Coase, 'Law and Economics' n 22, 105. Simpson replied that, 'I am sorry to hear that I appear to have made Professor Coase so cross by raising what seem to be some difficulties in his celebrated article, not all of which he addresses in his reply.' See Simpson, 'An Addendum' (n 22) 99.

leading American accounts of possession have tended to approach the issue from a higher level of theoretical abstraction, focusing on fewer cases and discussing them in light of insights drawn from fields of enquiry other than law.[29]

Neither of these methodologies is either 'right' or 'wrong'. Each has its own particular advantages and deficiencies. For present purposes, doctrinal accounts have two important virtues. First, in contrast to broad arguments about efficiency, moral justifiability or distributive fairness, doctrinal arguments about the law *are* legal arguments. As McFarlane has observed:

> an important aspect of the doctrinal approach ... is that it not only examines property law, it also *is* property law: in the sense that it shares its method with that of a judge seeking to interpret a line of cases or statutory provision.[30]

Secondly, lawyers who make arguments about the doctrinal architecture of the law are playing to their strengths by harnessing a form of technical expertise that is unique to those who have undertaken formal training in the law.[31] On the question of the role of high theory in property law, Smith is surely correct to observe that, 'talking about ultimate ends is more glamorous than asking the more engineering-like question of how to serve them. But if there is anything legal scholars do better than economists, social-scientists, and philosophers, it is institutional design'.[32]

Nevertheless, doctrinal accounts are limited by the fact that there are circumstances in which the law raises questions that it cannot answer by application of its own unique form of reasoning. In these situations, conventional legal analysis simply 'runs out'. Appreciating the limits of doctrinal analysis is particularly important in the present context because possession is an instance in which the utility of conventional legal analysis is soon exhausted. As is argued throughout this book, the possession *rule* cannot be understood in isolation from the spontaneously emergent *convention* that operates quite independently of the positive law. As a consequence, doctrinal analyses of possession can only ever reveal a part of the larger picture.

Theoretical explanations are not without their deficiencies either. While moving up the ladder of abstraction may enable one to give a coherent and elegant explanation of the nature and function of possession, it can also obscure anomalies in the substantive rules that can only be appreciated at ground level. As the discussion of the 'bona fide purchaser rule' in Chapter 7 illustrates, legal rules are often ad hoc and approximate solutions to pressing practical problems. Inconvenient as

[29] Two very influential accounts are Richard A Epstein, 'Possession as the Root of Title' (1979) 13 *Georgia Law Review* 1221; Carol M Rose, 'Possession as the Origin of Property' (1985) 52 *University of Chicago Law Review* 73.

[30] Ben McFarlane, 'Book Review: Researching Property Law' (2017) 133 *Law Quarterly Review* 167, 168.

[31] On this issue see Harry T Edwards, 'The Growing Disjunction between Legal Education and the Legal Profession' (1992) 91 *Michigan Law Review* 34.

[32] Henry E Smith, 'Mind the Gap: The Indirect Relation between Ends and Means in American Property Law' (2009) 94 *Cornell Law Review* 959, 970.

this might be for the formulation of an overarching theory, it cannot be ignored in any account that purports to explain the role of possession in the *law*.

What is thus required is an account of possession that uses theoretical and interdisciplinary insights as a means of augmenting traditional doctrinal analysis. This sort of approach is not without precedent in property scholarship. Harris's work *Property and Justice*[33] provides a template. Likewise, Penner's *The Idea of Property in Law*[34] has been highly influential amongst both property theorists and doctrinal scholars. Despite these precedents, recent contributions to the literature on possession demonstrate an ongoing absence of cross-pollination between those occupying either side of this methodological divide.[35] A substantial aim of this book is thus to attempt to combine the theoretical and interdisciplinary insights of American scholars with the rigorously doctrinal analysis that has characterised English writing on the topic. It is hoped that this methodological approach will lead to a more satisfactory explanation of possession and its role in the law.

IV. Central Arguments

Broadly speaking, this book aims to answer a '*What?*' question and a '*Why?*' question. It attempts to explain, first, the nature of possession in the law and, secondly, why possession, as opposed to some other mechanism, fulfils the function of creating original property rights in tangible things.

In answer to the first, '*What?*' question, it is argued that the concept of possession in the law is far simpler than generations of lawyers have been given to believe. Possession does not describe some distinct form of right, or jural interest, in an object of property. Rather, it describes those relations between people and tangible things which, as a matter of social fact, constitute accepted ways of claiming some form of entitlement to them. Contrary to standard accounts, the significance of those relationships is not to be found in the extent of the putative possessor's control. While it might be that the higher the degree of control, the clearer the 'signal', the significance of those relationships lies in the fact that, within particular populations, they constitute legitimate ways of announcing one's claim to an object that is capable of being owned. In short, in a society that habitually respects property rights, the role of possession is purely *expressive*.

Philosophers and jurists have long sought to explain why the unilateral act of taking possession of some object has the effect of creating original property rights to it. The claim defended in this book is that there is no meaningful answer to this

[33] JW Harris, *Property and Justice* (Oxford, Clarendon Press, 1996).

[34] JE Penner, *The Idea of Property in Law* (Oxford, Clarendon Press, 1997).

[35] Compare, for example, the contributions in Eric Descheemaeker (ed), *The Consequences of Possession* (Edinburgh, Edinburgh University Press, 2014) with those in James Penner and Henry E Smith (eds), *Philosophical Foundations of Property Law* (Oxford, Oxford University Press, 2013) and Yun-chien Chang (ed), *Law and Economics of Possession* (Cambridge, Cambridge University Press, 2015).

second, '*Why?*', question. There is no quality, either moral or instrumental, peculiar to the fact of possession that explains why it, as opposed to some other mechanism, came to fulfil the essential function of allocating property rights to those capable of holding them. The important insight of the 'spontaneous order' tradition, which commenced with Hume, is that the possession rule is not a product of conscious design but arose, quite unconsciously, through the repeated interaction of self-interested individuals. Possession triumphed as the dominant allocative rule, not because it was regarded as uniquely desirable by those whose behaviour was guided by it, but instead because it was 'salient'. For largely inscrutable psychological reasons, the fact of possession was, and continues to be, prominent to those who must decide which objects belong to whom. While moral and rights-based arguments can be deployed in support of the possession convention, they cannot explain why possession, as opposed to some other mechanism, came to fulfil the vital function of assigning property rights to particular people.

Perhaps most importantly, the argument presented in this book challenges the tendency of jurists to view possession as an intractable *legal* problem in need of a *legal* solution. While the possession rule raises legal and philosophical questions that do not admit of simple answers, it should never be forgotten that, beneath the legal rule, lies a convention that countless people, without legal or philosophical training, effortlessly adhere to as they successfully navigate the countless coordination problems generated by everyday life.[36]

V. Chapter Outlines

Chapter 1 provides an analytical overview of a property right. Following the 'property as exclusion' model, it is argued that the essence of a property right is to be found in the duty that forbids anyone but the owner from physically interfering with its subject matter. For present purposes, the value of the 'property as exclusion' model is that, by distinguishing 'possession' from 'exclusion', it makes clear that possession does not describe the content of a property right. Contrary to standard formulations, liability in the property torts has nothing to do with interferences with 'possession'.

Chapter 2 provides a summary of both the divergent academic views on the concept of possession and the byzantine nomenclature that has become such a feature of this area of the law. The argument presented in this chapter is that the mistaken tendency to conceive of possession as a species of 'right' is attributable to both a failure to distinguish between 'jural' and 'non-jural' concepts and to appreciate the constrained nature of ownership in a system in which rights are relative and not absolute. Consistently with the argument offered in Chapter 1, it is argued

[36] For a similar observation see Thomas W Merrill, 'Possession as a Natural Right' (2015) 9 *New York University Journal of Law and Liberty* 345, 358.

that there is no reason to regard possession in the law as anything other than a fact that creates a property right.

Chapter 3 gives some conceptual substance to the fact of possession. It argues that possession describes any act that, within a particular population, is an accepted way of conveying one's intention to stake a claim to an object of property. This 'expressive' account of possession challenges the standard 'control plus intention' explanation offered by jurists such as Holmes and Pollock. In particular, it rejects the notion that actual control, in the sense of an ability to exclude others, is ever necessary in order to establish 'possession'.

Chapter 4 takes a theoretical turn and investigates the 'conventional' origins of the possession rule. It argues that the possession rule is not an example of conscious design but is, instead, a spontaneously emergent convention that has been adopted, seemingly without modification, by the positive law. It follows that all attempts to explain the possession rule by reference to some rationale that is peculiar to the fact of possession fall victim to the same 'constructivist' trap; namely, the failure to appreciate that there is no such rationale. The existence of the possession convention cannot be explained by, for example, the inherent moral significance of acts of possession. The convention prevailed at the expense of other potential methods of allocating 'names to things' because it is 'salient' and, importantly, there is no necessary connection between the salience of a solution to a 'coordination problem' and its desirability, as judged by any exogenous standard.

Chapter 5 argues that, while the moral desirability of a convention is immaterial to its ability to spread throughout a population, it does not follow that any given convention is therefore unfair. In other words, that a convention is amoral does not mean that it is also immoral. The claim defended in this chapter is that the possession rule, and the convention on which it is based, satisfies a minimum standard of fairness. The arbitrariness of the possession convention, which appears to make it so morally suspect, in fact turns out to be its strength.

Chapters 6 and 7 apply the insights of the expressive theory of possession to particular doctrinal issues. Chapter 6 considers the implications of applying the theory to the so-called 'finders' cases', a group of decisions that has been famously resistant to coherent analysis. It is argued that, while no one has proposed a compelling reason for departing from the possession rule in cases of finding, it is nevertheless true that the modern cases cannot be explained as examples of the possession rule in action. Because one cannot can signal her intention to stake a claim to an object of which she is entirely ignorant, the better view is that most cases of finding are resolved by the application of a *sui generis* set of rules that are not possessory, but instead turn on the factual circumstances of the find.

Finally, Chapter 7 applies the expressive theory of possession to two particularly difficult issues in the law of property; the acquisition of property rights through acts of theft and the treatment of the good faith purchaser at common law. The argument advanced in this chapter is that these very practical problems reveal the inherent limitations of rules that are, at base, spontaneously emergent conventions.

VI. A Note on Nomenclature

As a final introductory matter, a brief note should be made about the way in which the terms 'property right' and 'ownership' are used throughout this book. In legal analysis, the hallmark of a 'property right' is that, unlike a 'personal right', it binds 'strangers to its creation'.[37] Leases, mortgages, easements and *profits à prendre* thus all qualify as 'property rights' at common law. However, because this book is concerned with possession as a means of announcing that 'this thing is *mine*', security rights, servitudes and estates less than freehold are only of tangential relevance and are seldom discussed in any detail. The term 'property right' is thus used exclusively to denote an 'ownership' interest in an object of property which, following Honoré, can be satisfactorily defined as 'the greatest interest in a thing admitted by a mature legal system'.[38]

Honoré commenced his famous essay by remarking that, '[o]wnership is one of the characteristic institutions of human society. A people to whom ownership was unknown … would live in a world that is not our world'.[39] Despite the central role that ownership plays in both life and the law, it remains a vexed concept amongst lawyers. As discussed in Chapter 2, it is often said that the common law does not recognise the concept of ownership and, for that reason, many legal scholars actively discourage its use. Nevertheless, quite apart from the contestable truth of such claims,[40] there are at least two practical reasons to continue to use it. First, because English law does not recognise a system of estates in goods,[41] one cannot describe the greatest possible interest in a chattel as a 'fee simple absolute in possession'. There is simply no alternative but to describe such an interest as 'ownership'.[42] Secondly, even where it is appropriate, to insist upon the use of the technical language of estates is to invite tedious prolixity that is not justified by a commensurate payoff in clarity. In the vast majority of instances, to describe someone as an 'owner' concisely captures their status within the system without transgressing doctrinal taboos of any consequence.[43] For these reasons, the term 'ownership' will be used throughout this book.

[37] William Swadling, 'Property: General Principles' in Andrew Burrows (ed), *English Private Law*, 3rd edn (Oxford, Oxford University Press, 2013) 173, 174 [4.03].

[38] AM Honoré, 'Ownership' in AG Guest (ed), *Oxford Essays in Jurisprudence* (Oxford, Oxford University Press, 1961) 107, 107. For the avoidance of doubt, this restrictive usage of 'property right' is not a claim about the sorts of rights that ought to qualify as 'property', but an attempt to minimise the necessary nomenclature.

[39] Ibid.

[40] Harris, for instance, is surely correct to argue that the doctrine of estates in English real property law does not displace the importance of ownership as an organising idea. See Harris (n 33) 68–70.

[41] ELG Tyler and Norman Palmer, *Crossley Vaines' Personal Property*, 5th edn (London, Butterworths, 1973) 43–44; Swadling (n 37) 267 [4.130].

[42] Hickey is correct to argue that personal property law would become much simpler if common lawyers reclaimed ownership as a technical term. See Hickey (n 7) 164. Rostill has recently suggested the term 'general property interest'. See Luke Rostill, 'Terminology and Title to Chattels: A Case Against "Possessory Title"' 134 *Law Quarterly Review* 407, 424.

[43] This point it also made by McFarlane. See Ben McFarlane, *The Structure of Property Law* (Oxford, Hart Publishing, 2008) 342.

1

'Exclusion' and 'Possession'

An Introduction to Property Rights

I. Introduction

According to Bentham, the institution of property has achieved no less a feat than to give 'to man the empire of the earth'.[1] Yet, despite its undoubted importance, property remains ambiguous and contested.[2] Depending on the context, the appellation 'property' may describe a tangible thing, a right to a tangible thing, an abstract 'bundle of rights', an 'ideational thing', a 'conclusory term'[3] or, to the sceptical, a 'magic solving word'.[4] Even doctrinal treatments of property law routinely cover both 'things in possession' and 'things in action', though the latter category includes shares, debts and other assets that are essentially promises which, having no corporeal form, can only be vindicated by judicial action.[5]

Fortunately, the purpose of this chapter is not to attempt the impossible task of defining 'property'. Its more limited objective is to introduce the basic elements, or 'ontology',[6] of property and to begin to explain the role that possession plays within its formal architecture. Following the 'property as exclusion' model, it is argued that the law of property describes a system in which the imposition of a strict *in rem* duty of non-interference confers upon the right-holder the exclusive ability to choose, subject to property limitation rules, between an essentially limitless

[1] Jeremy Bentham, *The Theory of Legislation* (London, Kegan Paul, 1931) 114.

[2] JW Harris, *Property and Justice* (Oxford, Clarendon Press, 1996) 6.

[3] Arnold S Weinrib, 'Information and Property' (1988) 38 *University of Toronto Law Journal* 117, 121.

[4] Felix S Cohen, 'Transcendental Nonsense and the Functional Approach' (1935) 35 *Columbia Law Review* 809, 820.

[5] *Colonial Bank v Whinney* (1885) 30 Ch D 261 (CA), 285 (Fry LJ); *Your Response Ltd v Datateam Business Media Ltd* [2014] EWCA Civ 281; [2015] QB 41, 48 [13] (Moore-Bick LJ). The inclusion of 'things in action' within many standard treatments of personal property law is attributable to the fact that, in Roman law, the category of 'things' included debts and other contractual rights. See Barry Nicholas, *An Introduction to Roman Law* (Oxford, Clarendon Press, 1976) 98–100. Nevertheless, as Swadling writes, 'a property right in a car and a right to be paid £100 are fundamentally different. Title to car can be acquired by taking possession of the car, while it is impossible to take possession of a debt': William J Swadling, 'Book Review: The Law of Personal Property' [2015] *Lloyd's Maritime & Commercial Law Quarterly* 595, 596.

[6] For this usage of 'ontology' see, eg, Henry E Smith, 'The Elements of Possession' in Yun-chien Chang (ed), *Law and Economics of Possession* (Cambridge, Cambridge University Press, 2015) 65, 74.

number of uses in respect of an object that counts as a 'thing' for the purposes of the system.

What is emphasised in both this chapter and those that follow is that if we are to understand possession's role within property law, we must uncouple the concept of 'property', which describes a right to exclude others from an object of property, from that of 'possession', which describes a fact that creates such a right. For present purposes, the power of the 'property as exclusion' model is that it discards the inaccurate, but widely held, notion that the content of a property right is a right to 'exclusive possession'. While an owner is certainly in a better position than anyone else to exercise effective control of some thing, property rights do not and cannot protect an owner's right to 'possess' in this sense. Rather, property rights correlate to a duty that forbids duty-owers from interfering with the object of the right. The core of the 'property strategy'[7] is to afford an owner the exclusive ability to choose between alternative uses by the simple expedient of obliging everyone else to 'keep off'.

II. What is a 'Thing' and How Do I Get One?

A. Tangible and Intangible Things

Amongst other elements, every system of property law must have rules about what constitutes a 'thing', or object of property, and how rights to such things are acquired and lost.[8] The things of property law are, for the most part, relatively simple. A chair, a parcel of land and a coat are all objects of property. Although Rahmatian is correct to argue that the tangibility of some thing does not, without more, make it an *object of property*,[9] there is, as McFarlane observes, a strong presumption that any tangible thing can become the object of a property right.[10] As far as tangible things are concerned, difficulties only arise in penumbral cases, such as those involving sperm samples, in which the law must weigh its traditional moral aversion to characterising human tissue as a chattel against the desirability of invoking 'property' as a vehicle for imposing legal duties that promote its responsible handling and storage.[11]

[7] Thomas W Merrill, 'The Property Strategy' (2011) 160 *University of Pennsylvania Law Review* 2061, 2066–67.

[8] Smith (n 6) 74. For a similar observation see also Emily Sherwin, 'Two- and Three-Dimensional Property Rights' (1997) 29 *Arizona State Law Journal* 1075, 1084.

[9] Andreas Rahmatian, 'Intellectual Property and the Concept of Dematerialised Property' in Susan Bright (ed), *Modern Studies in Property Law: Volume 6* (Oxford, Hart Publishing, 2011) 361, 368.

[10] Ben McFarlane, *The Structure of Property Law* (Oxford, Hart Publishing, 2008) 135.

[11] See, eg, *Yearworth v North Bristol NHS Trust* [2009] EWCA Civ 37; [2010] QB 1. For a discussion of this case see James Lee, '*Yearworth v North Bristol NHS Trust* [2009]: Instrumentalism and Fictions in Property Law' in Simon Douglas, Robin Hickey and Emma Waring (eds), *Landmark Cases in Property Law* (Oxford, Hart Publishing, 2015) 25. As Lee remarks, the Court invoked 'property' as a 'hook on which to hang claims in tort and bailment': at 26.

A more difficult question is whether non-corporeal things such as debts, shares and copyrights can properly be described as objects of property. In large measure, the answer to this question depends on the purpose for which it is asked. There is no doubt that 'intangible' assets both should be and are considered 'property' for the purposes of powers of compulsory acquisition that are subject to just terms requirements. The High Court of Australia, for instance, has made it clear that the concept of property in section 51(xxxi) of the Australian Constitution[12] is 'not to be confined pedantically'[13] and includes various 'innominate and anomalous interests'[14] such as statutory entitlements to healthcare benefits.[15] Nevertheless, Douglas and McFarlane are correct to argue that the intangible subject matter of a copyright, for instance, makes it analytically different from an ownership right in a car.[16]

Likewise, whilst *in personam* rights such as contractual promises are clearly valuable assets, to transform them into what Harris has called 'ideational things'[17] is to overlook an important distinction between promises and pottery. The difference is that, unlike in the case of a chattel, one cannot generally be deprived of a contractual right by a third party. Any attempt to render performance to someone other than the promisee will simply fail to discharge the duty. Take *OBG Ltd v Allan*,[18] which concerned improperly appointed receivers who took control of OBG Ltd, a failing engineering firm. Among other acts, the receivers compromised outstanding contractual obligations on terms that appeared to be very favourable to OBG's clients.[19] OBG subsequently went into liquidation and the liquidator brought proceedings against the receiver. While there was no doubt that the receiver was liable in conversion for any dealings with OBG's chattels, the question was whether it could also be liable for converting the benefit of contractual

[12] Section 51(xxxi) provides that Parliament may make laws with respect to 'the acquisition of property on just terms from any State or person …'. Unlike the Fifth Amendment to the United States Constitution, s 51(xxxi) is both a grant of and limitation on the legislative power of the Commonwealth. See George Williams, Sean Brennan and Andrew Lynch, *Blackshield and Williams: Australian Constitutional Law and Theory*, 7th edn (Alexandria, Federation Press, 2018) 1298 [28.82].

[13] See *Bank of New South Wales v Commonwealth ('Bank Nationalisation Case')* [1948] HCA 7; (1948) 76 CLR 1, 349 (Dixon J).

[14] Ibid. See also *Victoria v Commonwealth ('Industrial Relations Act Case')* [1996] HCA 56; (1996) 187 CLR 416, 559 (Brennan CJ, Toohey, Gaudron, McHugh and Gummow JJ).

[15] *Health Insurance Commission v Peverill* [1994] HCA 8; (1994) 179 CLR 226, 235 (Mason CJ, Deane and Gaudron JJ). The Court has largely managed to avoid confronting questions about the penumbra of property by adopting a correspondingly narrow definition of 'acquisition'. See *Mutual Pools & Staff Pty Ltd v Commonwealth* [1994] HCA 9; (1994) 179 CLR 155, 185 (Deane and Gaudron JJ). It has also taken the view that, whether they amount to 'property', certain statutory rights are inherently fragile and, consequently, their extinguishment does not constitute an acquisition. See, *Health Insurance Commission v Peverill* [1994] HCA 8; (1994) 179 CLR 226, 237 (Mason CJ, Deane and Gaudron JJ). See also *JT International SA v Commonwealth* [2012] HCA 43; (2012) 250 CLR 1, 27 [29] (French CJ).

[16] Because the object of the right is the literary work, not the book as a chattel, there is, in their words, no 'physical thing around which the general duty owed by the rest of the world can coalesce'. Simon Douglas and Ben McFarlane, 'Defining Property Rights' in James Penner and Henry E Smith (eds), *Philosophical Foundations of Property Law* (Oxford, Oxford University Press, 2014) 219, 240.

[17] Harris (n 2) 45–46.

[18] *OBG Ltd v Allan* [2007] UKHL 21; [2008] 1 AC 1 ('*OBG*').

[19] Ibid, 65 [211]–[212] (Lord Nicholls).

promises. By a majority, the House of Lords held that conversion did not extend to 'intangible property', such as the benefit of a contractual right.

The reasoning of the majority was essentially constitutional. They argued that, whilst there may be an argument for extending conversion to contractual rights, the restriction of the tort to interferences with chattels was so entrenched that expanding its scope was beyond the Court's competence.[20] The minority argued, with particular reference to negotiable instruments evidencing a debt, that the 'tangible/intangible' dichotomy is a distinction without a difference.[21] According to Lord Nicholls, confining conversion to interference with tangible things was to return to the dark days of the forms of action when the substance of the law was determined by procedure.[22] Prominent commentators have agreed.[23]

The minority judges were clearly right to stress that a legal system which extended greater protection to tangible than intangible sources of wealth would be irrational, if not seriously defective. As Pound observed long ago, '[w]ealth, in a commercial age, is made up largely of promises'.[24] However, the minority position is only compelling if restricting the ambit of conversion to corporeal objects of property actually creates a lacuna in legal protection. It is here that the purely ideational nature of a contractual right as a 'thing' makes a difference.

What is insufficiently stressed about *OBG* is its peculiar facts. Green has written of the decision that, '[s]ince settled debts no longer exist as items of property, the receivers, in acting as they did, deprived the rightful owners substantially of the value of those assets'.[25] The statement that someone has been deprived of a debt *because* it no longer exists is, of course, circular. The relevant anterior question is why the debt no longer exists. The assumption underpinning Green's position is that the receivers were able give good discharge of the obligations owing to the company. This, however, cannot be correct. As a matter of first principles, it must be that, due to their invalid appointment, any attempt by the receivers to discharge outstanding contractual obligations was ultra vires and of no legal effect. The liquidator was only forced to raise its novel argument about extending the scope of conversion because it unwisely chose to accept the validity of the settlements that the receivers had negotiated with OBG's clients.[26] But for this poor strategic decision, the contractual liability of those clients would have remained undischarged and, contrary to Baroness Hale's claim,[27] *OBG* would have neatly illustrated why

[20] Ibid, 43 [99]–[100] (Lord Hoffmann), 75 [271] (Lord Walker), 92 [321] (Lord Brown).

[21] Ibid, 67 [221], 69 [232]–[242] (Lord Nicholls), 88–89 [309]–[311] (Baroness Hale).

[22] Ibid at 67 [223] (Lord Nicholls).

[23] See, eg, Sarah Green and John Randall, *The Tort of Conversion* (Oxford, Hart Publishing, 2009) 131–32.

[24] Roscoe Pound, *An Introduction to the Philosophy of Law* (Urbana, Project Gutenberg, 2010) 236.

[25] Sarah Green, 'To Have and to Hold? Conversion and Intangible Property' (2008) 71 *Modern Law Review* 114, 118.

[26] *OBG* (n 18) 45 [107]. See also Simon Douglas, 'The Scope of Conversion: Property and Contract' (2011) 74 *Modern Law Review* 329, 340 n 57.

[27] *OBG* (n 18) 89 [311].

the difference between 'owning and being owed something'[28] actually matters. The point is well made by Douglas, who observes that:

> [t]he legal nature of a contractual right makes it generally impossible for the holder of such a right to be deprived of it. Whereas an agreement between two parties may, of itself, create moral rights and obligations, a contractual right, a right enforceable in court, is a purely legal construct. It is something which depends upon a legal system for its existence. As such, it is for the legal system to determine when such a right comes into existence and … when the holder of such a right is deprived of it. As a matter of law it is clear that, under normal circumstances, the holder of a contractual right only loses his right when the other contracting party performs his contractual duty.[29]

Whilst a thief can steal chattel money, he cannot steal 'bank money' because payment by the bank on the direction of someone other than its customer does not constitute a good discharge of the debt owed by the bank.[30] Likewise, if a mischievous third party manages to dupe a promisor into rendering performance to the wrong person, that is a problem for the promisor, who must perform again, not the promisee, who retains the right to performance.[31]

By contrast, if someone steals a painting from my wall and throws it into a fire, no legal system can pretend that, despite the immolation, the pile of ashes in the grate remains a Matisse. To borrow Birks's phrase, '[a] right *in rem* cannot survive the extinction of its *res*'.[32] As a purely intellectual construct, the law is not subject to, for instance, the second law of thermodynamics. Nevertheless, contrary to the view that '[c]lassifying property according to its tangibility or intangibility creates false categories unrelated to significant legal distinctions',[33] the materiality of tangible things imposes structural limitations that cannot be ignored and that dictate the contours of the right.[34]

B. Defining Legal Things

There is another reason why, for the purposes of a book on possession, the discussion of 'things' can be limited to tangible things. As is discussed in detail in Chapter 3, possession describes a simple and observable relationship between a person and an object of property, the purpose of which is to publicise a claim to it.[35] Unlike placing a bag in a prominent position on a library desk or hanging a

[28] Nicholas (n 5) 99.
[29] Douglas, 'The Scope of Conversion' (n 26) 340.
[30] *Rogers v Kelly* (1809) 2 Camp 123, 123–4; 170 ER 1102, 1102 (Lord Ellenborough).
[31] Although the law cannot turn back time to guarantee timely performance.
[32] Peter Birks, *An Introduction to the Law of Restitution* (Oxford, Clarendon Press, 1985) 49.
[33] Juliet M Moringiello, 'False Categories in Commercial Law: The (Ir)Relevance of (In)Tangibility' (2007) 35 *Florida State University Law Review* 119, 120.
[34] See also JE Penner, 'The "Bundle of Rights" Picture of Property' (1996) 43 *UCLA Law Review* 711, 727.
[35] For a different view see Green, 'To Have and to Hold?' above n 25, 115–17.

'keep out' sign on a fence, one cannot enter into an easily observable relationship with a promise to, for instance, deliver a dozen eggs on a certain date.

Even if one's right to an intangible thing is evidenced by a chattel, such as a share certificate, possession of the certificate simply creates a relative title to the piece of paper *qua* chattel and does not give the possessor a right to vote in company meetings, to dividends or to the return of surplus capital on winding up.[36] The only exception to this basic truth occurs when an *in personam* right is evidenced by a chattel that qualifies as a negotiable instrument, in which case the law makes the 'intangible thing' and its reifier truly coextensive.[37] In the case of cheques and bills of exchange, for instance, the law 'thingifies' a right to be paid a certain sum of money by treating the piece of paper on which the debt is recorded as a normal chattel,[38] but with the qualification that, for the purposes of an action in conversion, its value is the value of the debt which it evidences, and not the piece of paper on which it is written.[39]

For the purposes of a book on possession, the 'things' of property law are precisely what we think they are. At a deeper level, however, even simple objects of property, from chairs to parcels of land, can be understood, not as monolithic entities, but as collections of attributes that are bundled together in combinations that enable or promote valuable uses. According to Smith's modular account, '[p]roperty clusters complementary attributes – land's soil nutrients, moisture, building support, into the parcels of real estate or tangible and intangible objects of

[36] Green and Randall make much of the fact that, in *Solloway v McLaughlin* [1938] AC 247 (PC), a stockbroking firm that had converted its client's share certificates was liable for the value of the shares, not the piece of paper on which the certificates were printed. See Sarah Green and John Randall, *The Tort of Conversion* (Oxford, Hart Publishing, 2009) 37. Importantly, however, the shares in question were treated as if they were bearer shares. See *Solloway v McLaughlin* [1938] AC 247 (PC), 256 (Lord Atkin). The outcome in *Solloway* would not apply to non-bearer shares because, in the case of non-bearer shares, title to the underlying rights against the company does not pass with title to the share certificate as a chattel.

[37] See *Building & Civil Engineering Holidays Scheme Management Ltd v Post Office* [1964] 2 QB 430 (QB), 445–46 (Roskill J). See also Simon Douglas, 'Converting Contractual Rights' [2008] *Lloyd's Maritime and Commercial Law Quarterly* 129, 131–32. It might be, as Douglas notes, that a plaintiff can recover damages equal to the face value of a non-negotiable instrument if, in the absence of the instrument, he cannot prove the existence of the obligation. Such losses are, however, properly categorised as consequential losses: at 131.

[38] Hence Diplock LJ's observation that the common law has historically treated negotiable instruments as 'goods'. See *Marfani & Co Ltd v Midland Bank Ltd* [1968] 1 WLR 956 (CA), 970; [1968] 2 All ER 573, 577. Unlike goods, those who take negotiable instruments in good faith and for value, known as 'holders in due course', take free of any defect in their transferor's title. See, eg, *Cheques Act 1986* (Cth), s 49(2)(a); *Bills of Exchange Act 1882* (UK) s 38(2). In contrast, the normal *nemo dat* rule applies, subject to limited exceptions, to buyers of goods. See, for instance, *Sale of Goods Act 1923* (NSW) s 26(1); *Sale of Goods Act 1979* (UK) s 21(1).

[39] *Morison v London County and Westminster Bank Ltd* [1914] 3 KB 356 (CA), 379 (Phillimore LJ). Lord Halsbury thus remarked that: '[t]he supposed distinction between the title to the cheque itself and the title to the money obtained or represented by it seems to me to be absolutely illusory': *Great Western Railway v London and County Banking Co Ltd* [1901] AC 414 (HL), 418.

personal property'.[40] If I purchase a violin, I am entitled to the strings. If I purchase a car, I am entitled to the wheels, even though they may be more valuable than the rest of the car and are easily removed from the hubs.

Determining which resource attributes together form a 'thing' finds formal expression in property law through the doctrines of fixtures, accession, manufacture and mixture.[41] When affixed to land, objects from gas engines[42] to tapestries[43] cease to be chattels and become attributes of the parcel of land to which they have been affixed.[44] A button sewn on to a shirt is no longer a discrete chattel but part of the shirt.[45] When combined together in a mixing bowl, flour, eggs and butter lose their independent existence and become components of a new object of property called a 'cake'.[46] When mixed in a silo, individual bushels of wheat become a unitary bulk that is co-owned by the contributors in proportion to their contributions.[47]

The effect of these doctrines is to extinguish property rights. However, unlike rules about limitation periods,[48] judgment debts[49] and abandonment,[50] they do not simply declare that the right is extinguished. Instead, doctrines such as

[40] Henry E Smith, 'Property as the Law of Things' (2012) 125 *Harvard Law Review* 1691, 1703. For a much older, though less developed, version of a similar idea, see Frederick Pollock, 'What Is a Thing?' (1894) 10 *Law Quarterly Review* 318, 318.

[41] See also Smith, 'The Elements of Possession' (n 6) 66–67.

[42] *Hobson v Gorringe* [1897] 1 Ch 182 (CA).

[43] *D'Eyncourt v Gregory* (1866) LR 3 Eq 382.

[44] This is often rendered in the Latin maxim *quicquid plantatur solo, solo cedit*. See *Minshall v Lloyd* (1837) 2 M & W 450, 459; (1983) 150 ER 834, 838 (Parke B). See generally Robert Megarry et al, *The Law of Real Property*, 8th edn (London, Sweet & Maxwell, 2012) 1103 [23–001].

[45] *Appleby v Myers* [1867] LR 2 CP 651, 659–60 (Blackburn J).

[46] Birks argues that the transformation of flour, eggs and butter into a cake is an example of specification whereas the addition of icing is an example of accession. Peter Birks, 'Mixtures' in Norman Palmer and Ewan McKendrick (eds), *Interests in Goods*, 2nd edn (London, Lloyd's of London Press, 1998) 227, 228.

[47] *Spence v Union Marine Insurance Company Ltd* [1868] LR 3 CP 427, 437 (Bovill CJ); *Sandeman & Sons v Tyzack and Branfoot Steamship Co* [1913] AC 680 (HL), 695 (Lord Moulton). If relative contributions cannot be ascertained, the default position is that each party is entitled to an undivided half share. See *Buckley v Gross* (1863) 3 B&S 566, 575; (1863) 122 ER 213, 216 (Blackburn J). Where the mixing is wrongful, any question concerning relative contributions is resolved against the wrongdoer. See *Indian Oil Corp Ltd v Greenstone Shipping SA (Panama)* [1988] QB 345 (Com Ct), 370–71 (Staughton J); *Glencore International AG v Metro Trading International Inc* [2000] EWHC 199, (2001) 1 Lloyds Law Rep 284, 322–23, 330 (Moore-Bick J). For an excellent account see Robin Hickey, 'Dazed and Confused: Accidental Mixtures of Goods and the Theory of Acquisition of Title' (2003) 66 *Modern Law Review* 368.

[48] *Limitation of Actions Act 1958* (Vic) s 6(2); *Limitation Act 1969* (NSW) s 21; *Limitation Act 1980* (UK) s 3.

[49] *United States of America v Dollfus Mieg et Compagnie SA* [1952] AC 582 (HL), 607 (Earl Jowitt); *Torts (Interference with Goods) Act 1977* (UK) s 5(1).

[50] *Arrow Shipping Co Ltd v Tyne Improvement Commissioners* [1894] AC 508 (HL), 521 (Lord Watson), 532 (Lord Macnaghten). Although this point may seem elementary, the authorities are not entirely consistent. See generally AH Hudson, 'Is Divesting Abandonment Possible at Common Law?' (1984) 100 *Law Quarterly Review* 110.

accession and specification indirectly extinguish property rights by altering the package of attributes that together make up the legal 'thing'. The ownership right in the subsidiary chattel is destroyed because the law ceases to recognise it as a subsisting legal 'thing' and, just as importantly, does not grant its erstwhile owner a co-ownership stake in the dominant chattel to which it accedes or the product into which it is transformed. If, for instance, A uses B's resin in the manufacture of chipboard without B's permission, A will be liable to B in conversion. However, B will cease to own the resin, which will no longer exist as a 'thing', and will not become a co-owner in the chipboard created from it.[51] The general principle is neatly encapsulated by Rudden's remark that, '[i]f B feeds his horse with A's hay, A owns neither the hay nor a share in the horse'.[52]

The vital role played by these particular doctrines is to help prevent a manifestation of what Heller has described as the tragedy of the 'anticommons'.[53] Unlike the 'tragedy of the commons', famously described by Hardin,[54] which describes the overexploitation of a common pool resource, the anticommons problem arises when the fragmentation of private rights in a single resource creates high transaction costs that prevent it from moving to its highest valued use. To illustrate with a simple example, whilst a potential purchaser may well value a car more than its vendor, a welfare-increasing sale will be thwarted if a prudent purchaser is forced to incur the cost of verifying that the vendor has good title to each of its components. As with the exceptions to *nemo dat*, extinguishing extant property rights to these components relieves the purchaser of the necessity of incurring these costs. However, unlike exceptions to *nemo dat*, doctrines such as accession do so by redefining the object of property. So far as the law of property is concerned, there are no longer 'wheels', 'seats' and 'doors', only a 'car'.

The significance of the positive law in the present context is not so much that it defines what constitutes accession or specification, but that it specifies the proprietary consequences of those events by denying an erstwhile owner a co-ownership interest in the dominant chattel or resultant product. The law does not, for the most part,[55] define the collection of attributes that together constitute a thing for the purpose of these doctrines. This question of 'what goes with what?' is instead answered by reference to extra-legal knowledge about what combination

[51] See *Borden (UK) Ltd v Scottish Timber Products Ltd* (1981) Ch 25 (CA).

[52] FH Lawson and Bernard Rudden, *The Law of Property*, 3rd edn (Oxford, Oxford University Press, 2002) 52.

[53] Michael A Heller, 'The Tragedy of the Anticommons: Property in the Transition from Marx to Markets' (1998) 111 *Harvard Law Review* 621, 624; Michael A Heller, 'The Boundaries of Private Property' (1999) 108 *Yale Law Journal* 1163, 1165–66.

[54] Garrett Hardin, 'The Tragedy of the Commons' (1968) 162 *Science* 1243.

[55] Although the law of fixtures, for instance, does contain technical rules that, for example, specify the evidence to which a court may have regard in determining the fixer's intention. See, eg, *Melluish (Inspector of Taxes) v BMI (No 3) Ltd* [1996] AC 454 (HL), 473 (Lord Browne-Wilkinson); *Elitestone Ltd v Morris* [1997] 1 WLR 687 (HL), 693 (Lord Lloyd), 698 (Lord Clyde). The formalising effect of such rules does not, however, mean that a court and a layman would arrive at a different conclusion on any given set of facts.

of components or resource attributes together make up particular things. Take Blackburn J's classic statement of accession:

> materials worked by one into the property of another become part of that property. This is equally true, whether it be fixed or movable property. Bricks built into a wall become part of the house; thread stitched into a coat which is under repair, or planks and nails and pitch worked into a ship under repair, become part of the coat or the ship ...[56]

No layman would be surprised to hear that wool cloth and cotton thread together form complementary attributes of a thing called a 'coat', or that an entitlement to a 'ship' includes an entitlement to the planks of wood that together form its deck.

This is not to say that the lay and legal conception of a thing are always coextensive. Take land, as an example. The law defines land, not as a horizontal plane, but as a vertical column that extends from the centre of the earth to the upper reaches of the atmosphere.[57] Once it has defined land in these spatial terms, the law then refines the collection of attributes that together constitute land as a legal thing by altering or removing particular elements. At common law, gold and silver deposits, though they may lie immediately under the soil, are not resource attributes of a freehold interest in land because title to 'royal metals', as the name suggests, is automatically vested in the Crown.[58] Likewise, the entitlement of a riparian owner 'to the water of his stream, in its natural flow, without sensible diminution or increase and without sensible alteration in its character or quality'[59] alters the default package of resources that together make up the 'thing' held by upstream proprietors. Instead of being defined spatially in accordance with the *ad coelum* rule, their entitlement to water flowing through a defined channel is restricted to whatever is required for uses that are 'ordinary' or 'reasonable' in the circumstances.[60] This quasi-commons solution to the problem of fugitive resources and natural flows such as streams and rivers is, as Epstein explains, a recognition of the fact that, 'a flowing river [is] worth more than the entire river water [is] worth in a barrel.'[61]

[56] *Appleby v Myers* [1867] LR 2 CP 651, 659–60.

[57] This is usually captured by the Latin maxim *cuius est solum, eius est usque ad coelum et ad inferos*. This maxim is often treated with scepticism. See, eg, *Commissioner for Railways v Valuer-General* [1974] AC 328 (PC), 351–52 (Lord Wilberforce). See, generally, Kevin Gray and Susan Francis Gray, *Elements of Land Law*, 5th edn (Oxford, Oxford University Press, 2009) 14–15 [1.2.14]–[1.2.17]. However, Lord Hope has recently confirmed that it 'still has value in English law as encapsulating ... a proposition of law which has commanded general acceptance': *Bocardo SA v Star Energy UK Onshore Ltd* [2010] UKSC 35; [2011] 1 AC 380, 398 [26].

[58] *R v The Earl of Northumberland ('The Case of Mines')* (1568) 75 ER 472, 1 Plowden 310. In many jurisdictions, rights to minerals are now vested in the Crown by operation of statute. See, eg, *Mining Act 1992* (NSW) ss 379 and 379AA; *Mineral Resources (Sustainable Development) Act 1990* (Vic) s 9; *Mineral Resources Act 1989* (Qld) s 8; *Mining Act 1971* (SA) s 16; *Mining Act 1978* (WA) ss 8A and 9; *Mineral Resources Development Act* 1995 (Tas) s 6(4).

[59] *John Young & Co v Bankier Distillery Co* [1893] AC 691 (HL), 698 (Lord Macnaghten).

[60] Ibid. This is not true of percolating groundwater. See *Acton v Blundell* (1843) 12 M & W 324, 353–54; 152 ER 1223, 1235 (Tindal CJ); *Chasemore v Richards* [1859] 7 HLC 349, 374–76; 11 ER 140 (HL), 150–51 (Lord Chelmsford). See also *The Mayor, Aldermen and Burgesses of the Borough of Bradford v Pickles* [1895] AC 587 (HL).

[61] Richard A Epstein, 'How Spontaneous? How Regulated?: The Evolution of Property Rights Systems' (2015) 100 *Iowa Law Review* 2341, 2350.

One can also conceive of cases in which apparently complementary resource attributes are not bundled together in a legal thing. Despite the fact that one purchases a beach umbrella for the shade it provides, the resource attributes that together constitute a umbrella in the eyes of the law are the base, pole and canopy, but not the shadow that it casts on the sand on a hot summer's day.[62] Nevertheless, in the vast majority of cases, the question of what particular attributes together constitute a 'thing' is a simple one.[63] Thing definition is an area in which the law generally economises on information costs by sensibly piggybacking on the customary answers to such questions.

C. Acquiring Rights to Legal Things

In the vast majority of cases, we do not create original property rights, but acquire extant rights from someone else. Unlike the rules that define the things of property, the rules that determine how person A can transfer a property right in object B to person C are often technical.

If A wishes to make a gift of an ordinary chattel to C, then the basic rule is that A must deliver it to C. A declaration of one's present intention to make a gift, no matter how clear, is not sufficient to pass title to a donee.[64] This basic rule is, however, subject to exceptions. For instance, in the fifteenth century, English law recognised an exception whereby title to chattels could pass by the execution and delivery of a deed.[65] If the chattel in question is a 'good'[66] and C is not a donee but a purchaser who offers money consideration,[67] then title can also pass by virtue of the execution of a contract of sale.[68] As between a buyer and seller, the law does not always insist on actual delivery. 'Constructive delivery' of goods can be effected by the delivery of documents of title, attornment and so on.[69] If B is not a chattel but a parcel of land, then other rules apply. If the land is subject to a system of 'title by registration', C will become owner when an instrument in the correct form is lodged with the appropriate executive agency and the details contained within it are recorded in a centralised register. Because it is the administrative act

[62] This example was inspired by the discussion in Christopher Essert, 'Property in Licences and the Law of Things' (2014) 59 *McGill Law Journal* 559, 585, fn 81. This is probably an example in which there is a divergence between the relevant legal rule and customary norm.

[63] For similar observations see Smith, 'The Elements of Possession' (n 6) 71; Pollock (n 40) 318.

[64] *Cochrane v Moore* (1890) 25 QBD 57 (CA), 72–73 (Fry LJ).

[65] Ibid, 64.

[66] The definition encompasses all chattels except money. The definition also expressly excludes choses in action. See, eg, *Sale of Goods Act 1923* (NSW) s 5; *Sale of Goods Act 1979* (UK) s 61.

[67] *Sale of Goods Act 1923* (NSW) s 6(1); *Sale of Goods Act 1979* (UK) s 2(1). The *Sale of Goods Act* thus does not apply to contracts of barter.

[68] *Sale of Goods Act 1923* (NSW) s 23; *Sale of Goods Act 1979* (UK) s 18. These provisions are statutory recognition of ancient mercantile practice long since recognised by courts of common law. See JH Baker, *An Introduction to English Legal History*, 4th edn (Oxford, Oxford University Press, 2003) 384.

[69] See generally Royston Miles Goode and Ewan McKendrick, *Goode on Commercial Law*, 4th edn (London, Penguin, 2010) 289–93.

of registration that vests title in the registered owner,[70] transfers of land under such systems abandon the logic of *nemo dat*.[71] As a consequence, whilst a rare occurrence, it is possible for a purchaser to become the registered owner without the knowledge or concurrence of the vendor.[72]

This book is not, however, concerned with derivative but original rights to things.[73] For present purposes, the relevant question is, how are property rights created in the first place? Whilst the law on the acquisition of extant titles is large and complex, there are relatively few ways of creating an original property right in a tangible thing.[74] As discussed above, the effect of doctrines such as fixtures, accession and specification is not to create new rights in coats and ships, but to destroy extant rights in thread and planks of wood by holding that they no longer constitute legal things. The doctrine of mixtures occupies somewhat of a halfway house in which the law responds to an evidentiary problem by destroying individual rights in the several contributions and replacing them with co-ownership rights in the mass.

In contrast to affixation, accession and specification, original property rights are created by 'natural increase'. The law on natural increase is simple and intuitive. Rights to progeny or other 'fruits' belong to the owner of the object from which they spring.[75] The owner of a cow will automatically own her calves and the owner of an orchard will own its apples.[76] Although 'natural increase' is often discussed under the rubric of accession,[77] this classification obscures the fact that unlike accession, which is concerned with the merger of one thing into another, natural increase concerns the severance of one thing from another. Unlike adding a brick to a wall, the birth of a calf is an example of the creation, and not the extinction, of an object of property.

[70] *Breskvar v Wall* [1971] HCA 70; (1971) 126 CLR 376, 385 (Barwick CJ).

[71] Megarry et al (n 44) 147 [7-1001]; Kelvin FK Low, 'The Nature of Torrens Indefeasibility: Understanding the Limits of Personal Equities' (2009) 33 *Melbourne University Law Review* 205, 206. Indeed, the term 'transfer' is something of a misnomer in the circumstances.

[72] For example, the registration of an instrument forged by a third party will confer indefeasible title on the party to be registered even though the instrument is void at common law. See *Frazer v Walker* [1967] 1 AC 569 (PC), 584 (Lord Wilberforce). It should be noted that not all systems of 'title by registration' adopt the same absolutist view towards the 'immediate indefeasibility' of the registered party. For a comparison between the English and Australian regimes see generally Elise Bant, 'Registration as a Defence to Claims in Unjust Enrichment: Australia and England Compared' (2011) *Conveyancer & Property Lawyer* 309.

[73] McFarlane describes this as the difference between 'independent' and 'dependent' acquisition. See (n 10) 154.

[74] Discussion of land grants by the Crown is omitted from this analysis. The ability of the Crown to make grants to its subjects is a matter of public law and is thus not relevant to the subject matter of this book.

[75] William Blackstone, *The Oxford Edition of Blackstone's Commentaries on the Laws of England: Book II: Of the Rights of Things* (Oxford, Oxford University Press, 2016) 274.

[76] The obvious analogy here is the relationship of income to capital. See, eg, AM Honoré, 'Ownership' in AG Guest (ed), *Oxford Essays in Jurisprudence* (Oxford, Oxford University Press, 1961) 107, 117; Thomas W Merrill, 'Accession and Original Ownership' (2009) 1 *Journal of Legal Analysis* 459, 468.

[77] See, eg, Merrill, 'Accession and Original Ownership' (n 76) 464–65.

As with the doctrines discussed above, the legal significance of natural increase is not that it provides a uniquely legal definition of a 'thing'. When an apple falls from a tree or a cow gives birth to a calf, the observable cessation of contiguity leads us to regard the cow and the calf as two distinct things. Once again, the law's definition of a thing piggybacks on what Smith has described as the 'everyday ontology'[78] of things. The significance of the legal doctrine of natural increase is instead that it specifies the proprietary consequences of the event by providing that the newborn calf is not *res nullius* but is automatically owned by whomever owned the cow that gave birth to it.[79] Whilst one might regard the doctrine as an example of Pollock's general dictum that the common law 'abhors a vacuum of property',[80] its more immediate explanation is that a rule under which calves are *res nullius* would require primary producers to invest in costly precautions to guard against opportunists who would otherwise free-ride on their efforts.

The most significant and ubiquitous way of creating an original property right is to take possession of an object of property.[81] At common law, an act of possession functions, to borrow Pollock's famous description, as a 'root of title'.[82] The rule that possession creates an original property right in the object possessed is referred to throughout this book as the 'possession rule'. Although the possession rule is often discussed in the context of acts of 'first possession' over whales, foxes and other things that are *res nullius*, its significance is not limited to claims over unowned things. As is discussed in the succeeding chapters, the possession rule remains relevant in a world in which so little is unowned. This is not only because it underpins formal doctrines such as adverse possession and plays a prominent conceptual role in resolving disputes over lost chattels but, most importantly, because it remains the basic means by which people broadcast the claim that 'this thing is mine'. The respect afforded to the possession rule is so great that acts of possession create perfectly valid property rights in objects that are already owned; a phenomenon that finds formal expression in the common law doctrine of relative title, discussed in Chapter 2.

III. The Content of a Property Right

A. The 'Bundle of Rights' vs the 'Exclusion' Model

Whilst there are numerous events that lead to the destruction of a property right, there are not, on closer inspection, many events that actually create original

[78] Smith, 'The Elements of Possession' (n 6) 71.
[79] See McFarlane (n 10) 163.
[80] Pollock (n 40) 320.
[81] McFarlane (n 10) 154.
[82] Frederick Pollock and Robert Samuel Wright, *An Essay on Possession in the Common Law* (Oxford, Clarendon Press, 1888) 22.

rights to things.[83] Of these events, possession is the most significant. Having discussed the events that create property rights, the next question is, what is the content of the right created by an act of possession? In order to answer this question, it is useful to contrast two competing theories of property.

The central thrust of the influential 'bundle of rights' theory of property is, as Smith explains, to replace property as 'thing ownership' with property as a pure abstraction that has no fixed content and describes one of any number of combinations of rights, privileges, powers, etc., bundled together in order to serve a particular policy objective.[84] This view of property, untethered to the traditional understanding of property as rights to things, has represented the academic orthodoxy for much of the twentieth century.[85] Merrill and Smith write that:

> [i]t is a commonplace of academic discourse that property is simply a 'bundle of rights' and that any distribution of rights and privileges among persons with respect to things can be dignified with the (almost meaningless) label 'property.' By and large, this view has become conventional wisdom among legal scholars: Property is a composite of legal relations that holds between persons and only secondarily or incidentally involves a 'thing.' Someone who believes that property is a right to a thing is assumed to suffer from a childlike lack of sophistication – or worse.[86]

However, the bundle of rights' status as the default, sophisticated explanation of the institution of property has come under sustained attack from those who reject the notion that a property right has no fixed content and can be used to describe any possible combination of juridical concepts, whether they pertain to a thing or otherwise.[87]

Unlike the bundle of rights theory, the alternative 'exclusion model' does not appeal to metaphor in order to explain the nature of property. The exclusion model posits that the object of a property right is a thing and that the content of that right correlates to an *in rem* duty that forbids anyone and everyone from crossing the boundaries of its object. Unlike the bundle theory, this understanding of property shares much with Blackstone's seminal conception of property as that 'sole and despotic dominion which man claims and exercises over the external things of the world, in total exclusion of the right of any other individual in the universe.'[88]

[83] McFarlane takes a particularly strident view. He argues that mixing and natural increase are the only exceptions to the rule that original property rights can only be acquired by possession. See McFarlane (n 10) 163.

[84] Henry E Smith, 'The Language of Property: Form, Context, and Audience' (2003) 55 *Stanford Law Review* 1105, 1106.

[85] Thomas C Grey, 'The Disintegration of Property' in J Roland Pennock and John W Chapman (eds), *Property* (New York, New York University Press, 1980) 69.

[86] Thomas W Merrill and Henry E Smith, 'What Happened to Property in Law and Economics?' (2001) 111 *Yale Law Journal* 357, 357–58.

[87] Simon Douglas and Ben McFarlane, 'Defining Property Rights' in James E Penner and Henry E Smith (eds), *Philosophical Foundations of Property Law* (Oxford, Oxford University Press, 2013) 219, 219. See also Hanoch Dagan, *Property: Values and Institutions* (Oxford, Oxford University Press, 2011) 37, 38–39. For a concise history of the trends in contemporary property theory see James Penner and Henry E Smith, 'Introduction' in James E Penner and Henry E Smith (eds), *Philosophical Foundations of Property Law*, (Oxford, Oxford University Press, 2013) xv.

[88] Blackstone (n 75) 1.

B. The Use and Abuse of Hohfeld

The 'bundle of rights' picture of property is typically explained as a loose amalgam of Honoré's standard incidents of ownership and Hohfeld's jural concepts.[89] However, contrary to the standard explanation, the 'bundle of rights' is not a concept that can be attributed either to Honoré, who explicitly rejected the metaphor in his famous essay on ownership,[90] or to Hohfeld. Given the extensive use of Hohfeld's work by the American Legal Realists, this may come as a surprise.[91] What is crucial to appreciate is that Hohfeld's central lesson, the importance of distinguishing 'rights' from other sorts of advantage conferred by law, cannot provide the framework for a conception that so conspicuously conflates these discrete concepts. As Douglas and McFarlane have demonstrated,[92] Hohfeld's conceptual discipline demonstrates why the bundle of rights picture is analytically misconceived. In order to understand why this is so, it is necessary to give a brief description of his scheme of jural correlatives and opposites.

Hohfeld's most enduring contribution to jurisprudence was his insistence that the use of the term 'right' in most legal discourse is insufficiently discriminating. On his account, it is not enough to describe some advantage conferred by law as a 'right' because that generic appellation fails to distinguish between four distinct sorts of advantage: 'rights', 'liberties', 'powers', and 'immunities'.[93] For present purposes, the relevant distinction is that between a 'right', often referred to as a 'claim-right'[94] and a 'liberty'.

A true Hohfeldian right signifies that some other legal person is under a correlative legal duty to do or abstain from doing some particular act.[95] In Hohfeldian terms, 'right' and 'duty' are 'jural correlatives'; one is the jural mirror image of the other.[96] To say that I have a contractual right to the delivery of a dozen eggs is to say that some other legal person is under a legal duty to deliver a dozen eggs to me. To borrow Singer's pithy phrase, Hohfeldian rights 'are nothing but duties placed on others to act in a certain manner'.[97] The slightly perverse point to grasp about

[89] Penner, 'The 'Bundle of Rights' Picture of Property' (n 34) 711–14; Heller, 'The Tragedy of the Anticommons' (n 53) 662 and fn 183.

[90] Honoré (n 76) 134.

[91] Douglas and McFarlane (n 16) 220.

[92] Ibid.

[93] Wesley Newcomb Hohfeld, *Fundamental Legal Conceptions as Applied in Judicial Reasoning, and Other Legal Essays* (New Haven, Yale University Press, 1923) 35–36.

[94] Hohfeld said that a 'claim' is synonymous with a 'right': ibid, 38. However, he never used the compound noun 'claim-right'. This was coined by commentators who subsequently discussed his work. Throughout this book, the term 'right' should be understood as a Hohfeldian claim-right.

[95] This is the most generally accepted element of his scheme. See *Minister for Immigration and Multicultural and Indigenous Affairs v Al Khafaji* [2004] HCA 38; (2004) 219 CLR 664, 672 (Gummow J).

[96] Hohfeld (n 93) 35–38.

[97] Joseph William Singer, 'The Legal Rights Debate in Analytical Jurisprudence from Bentham to Hohfeld' (1982) 1982 *Wisconsin Law Review* 975, 987.

a Hohfeldian right is that, because it is always directed towards the conduct of the duty-ower, it never empowers the right-holder to do anything.[98]

A 'right' is conceptually distinct from a 'liberty'. In Hohfeld's scheme, whether some legal person may do or not do some particular act is not a matter of 'rights' but of 'liberties'. I have a 'liberty' to engage in certain conduct, not because someone owes me a correlative duty to allow me to do so, but instead because that conduct does not infringe any duty that I owe to anybody else.[99] In Hohfeld's words, 'a [liberty] is one's freedom from the right or claim of another'.[100] The clearest judicial exposition of the concept of a 'liberty' is Cave J's musing that:

> it was said that a man has a perfect right to fire off a gun, when all that was meant, apparently, was that a man has a freedom or liberty to fire off a gun so long as he does not violate or infringe any one's rights in doing so, which is a very different thing from a right the violation or disturbance of which can be remedied or prevented by legal process.[101]

The important practical distinction between a right and a liberty is that I cannot go to court and complain of conduct that prevents me from exercising a particular liberty unless that conduct also infringes some duty owed to me.[102]

IV. The Exclusion Model of Property Rights

A. 'Exclusive Liberties'

Hohfeld's scheme of jural relations demonstrates that, contrary to the bundle of rights picture, the architecture of a property right is simple, though asymmetrical. A property right correlates to a duty of non-interference in respect of some object of property, the imposition of which obliquely protects uses that the right-holder may exercise as a matter of legal liberty. The reason why a freeholder can make use of his land is not because any particular use is directly protected by a legal duty. Instead, it is because most uses, from cooking in the kitchen to planting a tree in the backyard, do not breach any duty he owes to others. Unlike the varieties

[98] Finnis explained that, '[a] Hohfeldian claim-right can never be to do or omit something: it always is a claim that somebody else do or omit something: A's claim-right is always to B's action or omission, never to A's'. John M Finnis, 'Some Professorial Fallacies about Rights' (1972) 4 *Adelaide Law Review* 377, 380.

[99] In Hohfeldian terms, a 'liberty' correlates to a 'no-right'. See Hohfeld (n 93) 38–39.

[100] Ibid, 60. Liberties and rights are thus 'jural opposites': at 38.

[101] *Allen v Flood* [1898] AC 1 (HL), 29.

[102] In Williams' words, whether someone can sue 'depends on his rights, not upon his liberties'. Glanville Williams, 'The Concept of Legal Liberty' (1956) 56 *Columbia Law Review* 1129, 1146.

of property rights recognised at law, there is no closed list or *numerus clausus* of permissible uses. Any use is permitted as long as it does not infringe a duty owed to anyone else. The set of these liberties is, to use Harris's phrase, 'open-ended'.[103]

One objection to the concept of a Hohfeldian liberty is that it does not describe a jural conception. Penner, for example, has written that, 'the liberty–no-right correlation is simply a false description of legal relations. The liberty–no-right correlation is a description of the absence of any legal norm, not of the institution of one'.[104] Likewise, Harris has asked:

> what is the point of insisting that every act which the law does not prohibit me from performing correlates with someone's 'no–right'? The law permits me to blow my nose. Why describe this situation in terms of multital privileges with every other citizen's 'no–right' that I should not do so?[105]

If a particular act can be performed by anyone, there seems little point in describing it as a legal 'liberty'. For instance, my ability to gaze at the night sky is not a particularly meaningful example of the 'liberty–no-right' jural correlate in action. However, not all liberties are like this. Some are 'exclusive' in the sense that they can only be exercised by people who hold a particular right. An 'exclusive liberty' describes one which, if exercised by anyone but the right-holder, would constitute a breach of duty.

Importantly, the duty of non-interference creates a whole range of use liberties that are exclusive to the right-holder. Unlike the ability to gaze at the night sky, which is a 'non-exclusive liberty' and perhaps of no jural significance at all, cooking in the kitchen and planting a tree in the backyard are activities that can only be undertaken by the right-holder if they are not to constitute a trespass.

This emphasis on exclusion has been described as 'extraordinarily negative and potentially misleading'[106] and disparaged as describing a 'hermit's property right'.[107] However, this criticism fails to appreciate the distinction between means and ends in property law. As Penner has explained, '[n]o one has any interest in merely excluding others from things, for any reason or no reason at all. The interest that underpins the right to property is the interest we have in purposefully dealing with things'.[108] Likewise, Smith has written that, '[t]here is no interest in exclusion per se. Instead, exclusion strategies, including the right to exclude, serve the interest in use; by enjoying the right to exclude through torts like trespass, an owner can pursue her interest in a wide range of uses that usually need not be legally specified'.[109] Property law is, in other words, right light and liberty heavy.

[103] Harris (n 2) 29.

[104] JE Penner, 'Hohfeldian Use-Rights in Property' in JW Harris (ed), *Property Problems: From Genes to Pension Funds* (London, Kluwer Law International, 1997) 164, 169.

[105] JW Harris, *Legal Philosophies*, 2nd edn (Oxford, Oxford University Press, 2004) 88.

[106] Alison Clarke, 'Use, Time, and Entitlement' (2004) 57 *Current Legal Problems* 239, 241.

[107] Lior Jacob Strahilevitz, 'Information Asymmetries and the Rights to Exclude' (2005) 104 *Michigan Law Review* 1835, 1841.

[108] JE Penner, *The Idea of Property in Law* (Oxford, Clarendon Press, 1997) 70–71.

[109] Smith, 'Property as the Law of Things' (n 40) 1693.

Given that duties of exclusion are justified by an interest in use, it is tempting to dispense with the cumbrous term 'exclusive liberty' in favour of 'right'. However, to insist on the use of this term in the present context is not pedantry. Unlike the appellation 'right', 'exclusive liberty' makes clear that we are dealing with a species of legal advantage that is incapable of being breached.[110] The term thus draws attention to an essential design feature of the law. Though a freeholder has an exclusive liberty to enjoy the view from her bedroom window, because this use does not correlate to a duty, her neighbour commits no legal wrong if, absent a restrictive covenant or easement, he obscures her view by adding a second storey to his house.[111]

B. Exclusion as a Solution to Complexity

If the aim of private property is to confer on some person the exclusive ability to make decisions about the use of a thing,[112] why has the law pursued this end via the circuitous route of exclusion? Why rely on a proxy in preference to a system of true use rights?

Smith has provided an answer to the question: 'Why does property law look the way it does?'[113] On his account, '[t]he architecture of property emerges from the process of solving the problem of how to serve use interests in a roughly cost-effective way'.[114] In a world of trade-offs, a proxy must be used where the 'first best solution' is, for some reason, too costly to pursue.[115] The sort of costs that fundamentally shape property are the information costs of determining who has what rights to which things.

To begin with, a system that did not use a proxy to create an open-ended set of use liberties, but instead created true use-rights, would face the problem of compiling an exhaustive list of duties that would correlate to every conceivable use of any given object of property. As Smith has written, '[a]t the hypothetical extreme, the law would implement a list of use rights holding between all potential pairwise combinations of persons with respect to any … conceivable activity that has any impact on anyone'.[116] Because neither a legislature nor any pair of

[110] See also Simon Douglas, 'The Content of a Freehold: A 'Right to Use' Land?' in Nicholas Hopkins (ed), *Modern Studies in Property Law: Volume 7* (Oxford, Hart Publishing, 2013) 359, 366.

[111] For a concise list of the relevant authorities see *Robson v Leischke* [2008] NSWLEC 152; (2008) 72 NSWLR 98, 118 [86] (Preston CJ).

[112] Penner, *The Idea of Property in Law* (n 108) 49.

[113] As Smith observes, if it appears that a system could be designed in a different way but, as a matter of fact, never is, '*that* is a fact worth explaining': Smith, 'Property as the Law of Things' (n 40) 1699.

[114] Ibid, 1704.

[115] A 'proxy' is thus a close relation of a 'heuristic', a simple question, the answer to which is substituted for a more difficult question. See generally Daniel Kahneman, *Thinking, Fast and Slow* (London, Penguin Books, 2011) 97–99.

[116] Henry E Smith, 'Exclusion and Property Rules in the Law of Nuisance' (2004) 90 *Virginia Law Review* 965, 972; Smith, 'Property as the Law of Things' (n 40) 1704.

contracting parties either could or would bear the costs of compiling such a list, the use of a proxy becomes essential.[117]

Just as importantly, where rights are *in rem*, that the contracting parties may be able to agree upon a limited set of use-rights at reasonable cost does not solve the information cost problem. The problem that remains is not one that affects the parties themselves. Although they must incur the usual bargaining costs, the contracting parties, as Fairfield has neatly observed, 'need no property system to apprise them of the terms of their own deal'.[118] Instead, it is a problem that affects third parties who become subject to duties that were created by agreements to which they were not a party. The relevant issue here is not the intractable philosophical question of why any given individual ought to be bound by a duty to which she did not consent, discussed in Chapter 5. Rather, it is that obtaining information about who has what rights to which things is costly when one is not privy to the transaction that created them. This problem becomes acute if parties are permitted to limitlessly tailor the content of such rights. As Lord Brougham LC observed:

> great detriment would arise, and much confusion of right, if parties were allowed to invent new modes of holding and enjoying real property, and to impress upon their lands and tenements a peculiar character, which should follow them into all hands, however remote. Every close, every messuage, might thus be held in a several fashion; and it would hardly be possible to know what rights the acquisition of any parcel conferred, or what obligations it imposed.[119]

The law limits the informational demands that *in rem* rights place on duty-owers by employing the rough proxy of exclusion as a central design feature. Exclusion allows an owner to choose between an enormous number of potential uses without also imposing an impossible tangle of duties on everyone else. All that any given duty-ower need do to avoid liability is to refrain from interfering with things that do not belong to him.[120] A system of property that clusters complementary attributes into 'things' and makes them objects of a duty of exclusion represents,

[117] This is a familiar idea in law and economics. For instance, the duty of loyalty in fiduciary law is often explained as a proxy that is used when the conferral of a broad discretion on an agent makes complete contracting impossible. See, eg, Frank H Easterbrook and Daniel R Fischel, 'Contract and Fiduciary Duty' (1993) 36 *Journal of Law & Economics* 425, 426.

[118] Joshua AT Fairfield, 'BitProperty' (2015) 88 *Southern California Law Review* 805, 855.

[119] *Keppel v Bailey* [1834] 47 ER 106, 114; Coop T Brough 298, 317. Hence Merrill and Smith's argument that the *numerus clausus*, or closed list, of property rights represents a compromise between the desirability of being able to tailor property rights and the information costs that such flexibility imposes on others. Thomas W Merrill and Henry E Smith, 'Optimal Standardization in the Law of Property: The Numerus Clausus Principle' (2000) 110 *Yale Law Journal* 1. For a different view see Henry Hansmann and Reinier Kraakman, 'Property, Contract, and Verification: The Numerus Clausus Problem and the Divisibility of Rights' (2002) 31 *Journal of Legal Studies* S373.

[120] Penner, *The Idea of Property in Law* (n 108) 75. Waldron makes a similar observation about the necessity of ownership as an 'organizing idea', in the absence of which there 'would be no other way of ensuring, in ordinary life, that one abided by the rules except to find out what they were and learn them by heart': Jeremy Waldron, *The Right to Private Property* (Oxford, Oxford University Press, 1991) 43.

in Smith's words, 'a shortcut over the 'complete' property system that would, in limitlessly tailored fashion, specify all the rights, duties, privileges and so forth, holding between persons with respect to the most fine-grained uses of the most articulated attributes of resources'.[121]

In the case of some particularly valuable resources, it may be desirable to shift from an exclusion-based regime to one that, at some cost to the transacting parties, specifies rules for proper use.[122] Importantly, while the law allows this as a matter of freedom of contract, it limits the informational burden that such fine-grained rules would otherwise impose on third parties by providing that, unless such rules fall within a recognised class of covenants or easements, they take effect as *in personam* rights that do not bind strangers to their creation.[123]

V. The Exclusion Model and Tort

A. Rights, Duties and Torts

The exclusion theory of property is appealing for several reasons. Unlike the 'bundle of rights' alternative, its conceptual parsimony appeals to our sense that a good theory is one that does 'more with less'. Its basic concern with entitlements to 'things' also means that it coheres with people's intuitive sense of property as an institution that forms a part of everyday life. To borrow Ackerman's phrase, the exclusion model conforms to 'ordinary property talk'.[124] Quite apart from these virtues, what is most important about the exclusion model is that, as the law of torts demonstrates, it is faithful to the detail of the regime that it purports to explain.

The claim that the law of torts confirms the truth of the exclusion model might, at first blush, appear unlikely. In common law systems, tort law and property law are generally viewed as distinct taxonomical categories. Douglas, for example, has written that, '[t]he Common Law protects property rights relating to chattels through the law of torts, not the law of property'.[125] The explanation for this strange taxonomical division is said to be that, unlike the *vindicatio* in

[121] Smith, 'Property as the Law of Things' (n 40) 1693.

[122] Natural flows, such as rivers, are obvious examples of resources that are ill-suited to a simple exclusion strategy. Smith describes property rules as existing on a continuum that stretches from 'exclusion' at one end to 'governance' on the other. See Henry E Smith, 'Exclusion versus Governance: Two Strategies for Delineating Property Rights' (2002) 31 *Journal of Legal Studies* S453, S454–55.

[123] Thomas W Merrill and Henry E Smith, 'The Property/Contract Interface' (2001) 101 *Columbia Law Review* 773, 797–99.

[124] Bruce A Ackerman, *Private Property and the Constitution* (New Haven, Yale University Press, 1978) 97.

[125] Simon Douglas, *Liability for Wrongful Interferences with Chattels* (Oxford, Hart Publishing, 2011) 4.

Roman law, English law knows no direct assertion of ownership[126] and can only protect property rights indirectly through the law of wrongs.[127]

If there is indeed a genuine taxonomical division between tort and property, then one would think that the former would reveal little about the content of the latter. However, this distinction is illusory. As Hohfeld demonstrated, a right is nothing more than the correlative of a duty that obliges someone to do, or refrain from doing, a particular act. If the content of the right is defined by the requirements of the duty, then its substantive content must be found in the body of law that is concerned with breaches of duties; namely, the law of tort.[128] Determining the content of one's *rights* requires one to start at the law of *wrongs* and work backwards. It is thus a curious feature of the common law that if I want to know how rights of property are created, transferred or encumbered, I will look for a book entitled 'Property'. However, if I want to know the content of that right, I will have to look on another shelf for a different book entitled 'Tort'.

B. The Gist of Liability in Tort

What, then, does the law of tort reveal about the content of, for instance, an ownership interest in goods? Is there some golden thread that runs through the torts of trespass, conversion, detinue and negligence that supports the central claim of the exclusion model? The traditional view has been that the gist of liability in the property torts, particularly conversion, was extremely difficult to discern. Lord Nicholls was moved to observe that, '[c]onversion of goods can occur in so many different circumstances that framing a precise definition of universal application is well-nigh impossible'.[129]

Douglas has challenged this conventional wisdom, persuasively arguing that the central criterion for tortious liability in respect of moveables is that of 'interference' and, by interference, the law means, with few exceptions, physical interferences of the most literal kind.[130] If his account is correct, it is thus possible to combine the strict liability torts of conversion, trespass and detinue

[126] For example, *OBG* (n 18) 87 [308] (Baroness Hale).

[127] Peter Birks, *Unjust Enrichment*, 2nd edn (Oxford, Oxford University Press, 2005) 64; Douglas, *Liability* (n 125) 64. Too much is made of this distinction. The only distinction between the *vindicatio* and the common law tort of detinue is the requirement in the latter case that the owner utter the words 'give it back'. Thus, as Epstein notes, the difference between a claim in tort and a pure proprietary claim is essentially 'aesthetic, with little practical consequence': Richard A Epstein, 'Inducement of Breach of Contract as a Problem of Ostensible Ownership' (1987) 16 *Journal of Legal Studies* 1, 27.

[128] See also Simon Douglas, '*Kuwait Airways Corporation v Iraqi Airways Company* [2002]' in Simon Douglas, Robin Hickey and Emma Waring (eds), *Landmark Cases in Property Law* (Oxford, Hart Publishing Ltd, 2015) 205, 214.

[129] *Kuwait Airways Corporation v Iraqi Airways Co (No 6)* [2002] UKHL19; 2 AC 883, 1084 [39] ('*Kuwait Airways*').

[130] Douglas, *Liability* (n 125) 24, 65–67, 116–17.

into a single tort that need only be distinguished from the fault-based tort of negligence.[131]

The decision in *Club Cruise Entertainment and Travelling Services Europe BV v Department for Transport*[132] provides an illuminating example of Douglas's thesis. The case concerned an invalid statutory detention notice issued by the defendant to the owners of a cruise ship on which there had been an outbreak of the highly contagious norovirus. Whilst there was no doubt that, by issuing the notice, the defendants prevented the claimant from using its ship, the issue was whether the act of handing the claimant the notice constituted a conversion. Flaux J did not doubt that, had the defendant chained the ship to the quayside, it would have committed a trespass to goods.[133] However, after reviewing the leading authorities, his Honour concluded that service of the invalid notice did not amount to a conversion, holding that:

> even on the basis that the Detention Notice was invalid, nothing the MCA did here amounted to an assumption of ownership or of dominion over the ship. The intention of the Detention Notice was merely to prevent the Claimant from using the ship in a particular way … for a short period of time. That was not conversion.[134]

As Douglas has recently discussed,[135] the result in *Club Cruise* is perfectly consistent with Bramwell B's illustration of the boundaries of conversion:

> [a] man is going to fight a duel, and goes to a drawer to get one of his pistols. I say to him, "You shall not take that pistol of yours out of the drawer," and hinder his doing so. Is that a conversion of the pistol by me to my own use? Certainly not. Or, again, I meet a man on horseback going in a particular direction, and say to him, "You shall not go that way, you must turn back;" and make him comply. Who could say that I had been guilty of a conversion of the horse?[136]

To say that conversion almost always requires some form of physical interference is not to say that all acts of physical interference therefore amount to a conversion. As Alderson B remarked in *Fouldes v Willoughby*, '[s]cratching the panel of a carriage would be a trespass; but it would be a monstrous thing to say that it would be a ground for an action of trover'.[137] What *Club Cruise* neatly illustrates is, once again, the distinction between means and ends in property law. Whilst the objective is to confer upon the right-holder the exclusive ability to make decisions concerning use, that objective is achieved through the simple expedient of obliging the world-at-large to 'keep off'. Although, as the claimant in *Club Cruise* argued,[138] the use

[131] Ibid, 137–38.
[132] *Club Cruise Entertainment and Travelling Services Europe BV v Department for Transport* [2008] EWHC 2794 (Comm), [2009] All ER 955 ('*Club Cruise*').
[133] Ibid, [50].
[134] Ibid, [53].
[135] Simon Douglas, '*Kuwait Airways*' (n 128) 222–23.
[136] *England v Cowley* [1873] LR 8 Exch 126, 129.
[137] *Fouldes v Willoughby* (1841) 151 ER 1153, 1157; 8 M&W 540, 549.
[138] *Club Cruise* (n 132) [50].

of a proxy such as exclusion may, on occasion, create lacunae in legal protection, these gaps are the price that must be paid for the system's epistemic efficiency.

Douglas's argument about the primacy of physical interference also finds support in real property law, as illustrated by the famous decision in *Victoria Park Racing and Recreation Grounds v Taylor.*[139] The plaintiff, the owner of a race course, sought an injunction restraining the defendants from broadcasting the results of horse races that they could observe from a tower that had been erected on neighbouring land for that very purpose. The plaintiff argued that the defendants' particular use of the neighbouring property constituted an actionable nuisance. By a majority of three to two, the High Court refused the injunction. The majority position was captured by Latham CJ's statement that:

> [t]he court has not been referred to any authority in English law which supports the general contention that if a person chooses to organize an entertainment or to do anything else which other persons are able to see he has a right to obtain from a court an order that they shall not describe to anybody what they see.[140]

In his famous article, Gray has attempted to explain the outcome in *Victoria Park* on the ground that the spectacle of a horserace, like a beam of light from a lighthouse, cannot be 'propertised' because it is not an 'excludable' resource.[141] In his words, 'it is not feasible for a legal person to exercise regulatory control over the access of strangers to the various benefits inherent in the resource'.[142] Accordingly, 'for purely physical reasons it was simply unrealistic in *Victoria Park* to attempt a comprehensive exclusion of unauthorised strangers from the benefits of the spectacle provided on the plaintiff's land'.[143]

Gray's quasi-public goods explanation is not entirely convincing. As the existence of enclosed entertainment centres demonstrates, it is perfectly possibly to exercise complete 'regulatory control' over spectacles, from musical concerts to tennis matches. The question is not whether it is possible to exclude strangers, but whether the return generated from the spectacle justifies the cost of doing so. To take another example, as the ubiquitous practice of illegal downloading makes clear, pop songs and television programmes are not readily 'excludable' assets. Nevertheless, they remain 'works'[144] over which the author has enforceable rights under copyright law.[145] If, due to technological innovation, it is effectively impossible to eliminate free-riding entirely, the question for the right-holder is not whether she has a right over a particular resource, but whether the cost of effectively enforcing it is so high as to negate the benefit of 'propertising' the resource

[139] *Victoria Park Racing and Recreation Grounds v Taylor* [1937] HCA 45, (1937) 58 CLR 479 ('*Victoria Park*').

[140] Ibid 496. See also Dixon J at 507.

[141] Kevin Gray, 'Property in Thin Air' (1991) 50(2) *The Cambridge Law Journal* 252, 268.

[142] Ibid.

[143] Ibid, 269.

[144] *Copyright Act 1968* (Cth) s 32; *Copyright, Designs and Patents Act 1988* (UK) ss 1 and 2.

[145] *Copyright Act 1968* (Cth) s 31(1); *Copyright, Designs and Patents Act 1988* (UK) s 16.

in the first place. This is not a conceptual but an empirical question, the answer to which will differ from case to case.

Just as importantly, Gray's explanation does not capture the essentially descriptive nature of the exercise in which the Court was engaged. As Rich J noted in his dissenting judgment,[146] the boundaries of nuisance are not set in stone. The majority judges could have broken new ground by joining the minority in holding that the defendants' conduct amounted to an actionable tort.[147] Alternatively, following the decision of the US Supreme Court in *International News Service v Associate Press*,[148] they could have extended the 'quasi-property right' recognised in 'hot news' to other time-sensitive information, such as the results of local horse races. However, they did not.[149] The majority made clear that, despite the defendants' 'impudent'[150] use of the neighbouring land, the plaintiff failed on the simple ground that the law knows no duty that forbids people from reporting on spectacles taking place on other people's land.[151] The result in *Victoria Park* thus follows from a simple application of Lord Camden CJ's famous dictum that, 'the eye cannot by the law of England be guilty of a trespass'.[152] Whilst the ability of the owner of land to use it as a race track is a liberty that he alone may exercise, it is not an activity that is directly protected by a legal duty.

To briefly note some other examples, though a landlord's act of disconnecting the utilities may be a breach of contract that substantially reduces the amenity of his tenants, it does not amount to a trespass for want of any 'interference with any part of the demised premises'.[153] Although the construction of a tall building may diminish the ability of the neighbours to use or enjoy their own land, such construction does not, without more, constitute an actionable nuisance.[154] If A negligently damages a cable that provides electricity to B's factory, B can recover compensation for damage to the plant and equipment caused by the power outage but cannot recover the pure economic losses caused by his inability to use the factory during the outage.[155]

[146] *Victoria Park* (n 139) 501.
[147] Ibid, 504–5 (Rich J), 521–22 (Evatt J).
[148] *International News Service v Associated Press* 248 US 215, 219 (1918) (Pitney J).
[149] In *Victoria Park*, Dixon J specifically endorsed Brandeis J's dissenting view in *International News Service* that the grant of an injunction was not in support of a property right, but equity's jurisdiction to restrain breaches of confidence: *Victoria Park* (n 139) 509.
[150] Ibid, 526 (McTiernan J).
[151] Ibid, 494 (Latham CJ), 510 (Dixon J), 527 (McTiernan J).
[152] *Entick v Carrington* (1765) 95 ER 807; 19 St Tr 1030, 1066. See also *Tapling v Jones* (1865) 11 HL Cas 290; 11 ER 1344 (HL), 1350 (Lord Westbury LC), 1353 (Lord Cranworth), 1355 (Lord Chelmsford). Thus, it is not tortious to create an image of someone else's property or a spectacle taking place on it. See *Bathurst City Council v Saban* (1985) 2 NSWLR 704, 706 (Young J); *Hickman v Maisey* (1900) 1 QB 752 (CA), 756 (AL Smith LJ); *Sports and General Press Agency Ltd v 'Our Dogs' Publishing Company Ltd* [1916] 2 KB 880 (KB), 883–84 (Horridge J). There is, however, evidence that, contrary to the uncompromising line taken by the majority in *Victoria Park*, the tort of nuisance can be used to protect privacy interests. See, eg, *Fearn v Board of Trustees of the Tate Gallery* [2019] EWHC 246 (Ch), [169] (Mann J); [2019] 2 WLUK 152.
[153] *Perera v Vandiyar* (1953) 1 WLR 672 (CA), 676 (Romer J).
[154] *Hunter v Canary Wharf Ltd* [1997] AC 655 (HL), 685 (Lord Goff) ('*Hunter*').
[155] *Spartan Steel & Alloys Ltd v Martin & Co Ltd* [1973] QB 27 (CA), 39 (Lord Denning MR). See also Douglas, 'Kuwait Airways' (n 128) 223–24.

These examples neatly illustrate why lawyers must be vigilant in separating the ends the law seeks to achieve from the formal jural structures it employs in order to achieve them.[156] Any complex system must balance the value of the objective that it is seeking to achieve against the costs of achieving it. In property law, the strategy of imposing a duty of exclusion over a collection of attributes that together constitute a 'legal thing' is, like all compromises, necessarily imperfect.

In some cases, the exclusion strategy is 'overinclusive' in the sense that it arrogates excessive decision-making authority to the right-holder and imposes unduly burdensome externalities on others. Take, for instance, the *ad coleum* rule. As a clear rule rather than a mushy standard, it provides a low-cost way of translating some portion of the earth into an object of property. Nevertheless, a column nominally bounded by the earth's core and the upper reaches of the atmosphere captures resources attributes that are not required in order to grow crops, build a shopping mall or do anything other than to replicate the Tower of Babel. If applied literally, the *ad coelum* rule would also instantly halt commercial air travel because the cost of negotiating a licence with every landowner under a given flight path would make the cost of a ticket prohibitively expensive.[157] When applied to the subterranean strata, the rule creates problems when potentially lucrative geological features, such as caves, cross property boundaries.[158]

However, exclusion can also be underinclusive. As the outcome in *Victoria Park* demonstrates, a system that limits wrongful behaviour to physical incursions will, in some circumstances, permit blatant free-riding on the efforts of others. The absence of legal protection will, in turn, force the right-holder to either invest in countermeasures or, if they are too costly, to discontinue the activity entirely.

Whether the particular rules of property law represent an optimal compromise between the benefits of property rights and the costs they impose on others is, as economists say, 'an empirical question' and one of enormous complexity. Nevertheless, the need for a compromise explains why, in cases such as *Victoria Park* in which a blameless plaintiff sues a morally unappealing defendant, the law's response is, almost literally, to tell the plaintiff to 'stop complaining and build a higher fence'.[159]

[156] Henry E Smith, 'Mind the Gap: The Indirect Relation between Ends and Means in American Property Law' (2009) 94 *Cornell Law Review* 959, 963–65.

[157] For discussion of this point see Thomas W Merrill, 'Trespass, Nuisance and the Costs of Determining Property Rights' (1985) 14 *Journal of Legal Studies* 13, 35–36. Unsurprisingly, courts have restricted the right-holder's entitlement to, 'such height as is necessary for the ordinary use and enjoyment of his land': *Lord Bernstein of Leigh v Skyviews & General Ltd* [1978] QB 479 (QB), 488 (Griffiths J). See, generally, *Bocardo SA v Star Energy UK Onshore Ltd* [2010] UKSC 35; [2011] 1 AC 380, 395–96 [19]–[20] (Lord Hope). In many jurisdictions, the position with respect to aircraft has been put on a statutory footing. See, eg, *Civil Liability Act 2002* (NSW) s 72(1).

[158] As was amply demonstrated by the dispute in *Edwards v Lee's Administrator* 96 SW 2d 1028 (1936 CA Ken). For discussion see Richard A Epstein, 'Holdouts, Externalities, and the Single Owner: One More Salute to Ronald Coase' (1993) 36 *Journal of Law & Economics* 553, 564–67.

[159] Latham CJ remarked that, '[a]ny person is entitled to look over the plaintiff's fences and see what goes on. If the plaintiff desires to prevent this, the plaintiff can erect a higher fence … the law cannot by an injunction in effect erect fences which the plaintiff is not prepared to provide.' *Victoria Park* (n 139) 494.

VI. Property Limitation Rules

A. The Limits of Liberties

The exclusion model of property insists that the use to which a freeholder may put his land is a matter of selecting from an open-ended set of use liberties. Importantly, 'open-ended' does not mean 'unlimited'. In some circumstances, an owner's liberties will be circumscribed by duties owed to others. Harris describes the rules that impose these duties as 'property limitation rules', 'whereby *prima facie* normative claims founded on the prevailing ownership conception are overridden'.[160] The existence of such rules is hardly surprising. No system could allow an owner to do what she liked with her property. Indeed, as Rose has shown,[161] not even Blackstone took literally his talk of 'sole and despotic dominion'. Examples of property limitation rules include planning, zoning and environmental laws and, historically most significantly, the tort of nuisance.

True property limitation rules are to be contrasted with what Harris calls 'property-independent prohibitions'.[162] Unlike the former, the latter presuppose no ownership interest in the thing whose range of use the law restricts. For example, the sorts of civil and criminal prohibitions that prevent me from assaulting someone with a baseball bat are 'property-independent prohibitions' because they do not presuppose that I have any interest in the bat. The distinction between 'property limitation rules' and 'property-independent prohibitions' reflects the fact that, as Waldron notes, '[t]he concept of property does not cover all rules governing the use of material resources, only those concerned with their allocation. Otherwise the concept would include almost all rules of behaviour'.[163]

B. The Place of Nuisance in the Exclusion Model

The purpose of this discussion of property limitation rules is not simply to highlight the obvious truth that a right-holder's use-liberties are not without restriction. It aims to draw attention to an aspect of the tort of nuisance that appears to challenge the key claim of the exclusion model of property; namely, the normative primacy of boundary crossing.

In his classic article, Newark described nuisance as 'a tort directed against the plaintiff's enjoyment of rights over land'[164] and one that protects 'the interest of

[160] Harris (n 2) 34.

[161] Carol M Rose, 'Canons of Property Talk, or, Blackstone's Anxiety' (1998) 108 *Yale Law Journal* 601, 603–4.

[162] Harris (n 2) 32–33.

[163] Waldron (n 120) 32.

[164] FH Newark, 'The Boundaries of Nuisance' (1949) 65 *Law Quarterly Review* 480, 482.

liberty to exercise rights over land in the amplest manner'.[165] Nuisance is a tort that restricts unreasonable uses of land by A in order to ensure that B can select from amongst the widest possible range of liberties in respect of his own land. The principle of 'reasonable user' at the heart of nuisance is, as Lord Goff put it, a 'principle of give and take as between neighbouring occupiers of land'.[166]

Historically, the distinction between trespass and nuisance depended on whether the wrongful conduct occurred within or outside the borders of the plaintiff's land. In the former case, the appropriate action was trespass; in the latter, the plaintiff had to sue in nuisance.[167] As a consequence of its procedural origins, claims for nuisance most often arise in connexion with emanations from the defendant's land such as noise, dirt, dust, fumes and vibrations.[168] More fundamentally, the existence of nuisance reflects the fact that, on occasion, the proxy of exclusion fails to achieve an optimal compromise between epistemic simplicity, on the one hand, and the benefits of more fine-grained but informationally burdensome duties, on the other.[169] In other words, and without attempting to answer the vexed question of what exactly amounts to a nuisance, the tort applies where the protection offered by trespass is so 'underinclusive' as to justify the higher information costs that are imposed on third parties by moving beyond a simple duty to 'keep off'.

Attempts have been made to reconcile nuisance with the exclusion model by arguing that, like trespass, nuisance is concerned with gross acts of boundary crossing.[170] On this account, common sources of nuisance such as noise, noxious odours and vibrations are conceived of as waves and particles crossing a boundary. If true, the only difference between conventional trespasses and nuisance is that, in the latter case, the act of boundary-crossing cannot be readily perceived by the eye. Unsurprisingly, some have found this boundary-crossing explanation of nuisance unconvincing.[171] Certainly, it cannot account for every case. For example, whilst the sight of prostitutes leading their clients to rooms in a residential street may amount to an actionable nuisance, it is implausible to suggest that the prostitutes' conduct involved an act of boundary crossing in any meaningful sense.[172]

[165] Ibid, 489. This definition was quoted with approval by Lord Goff in *Hunter* (n 154) 687–88. See also *Lawrence v Fen Tigers Ltd* [2014] UKSC 13; AC 822, 830 [2] (Lord Neuburger).

[166] *Cambridge Water Co Ltd v Eastern Counties Leather Plc* [1994] 2 AC 264 (HL), 299.

[167] Newark (n 164) 481–82.

[168] *Hunter* (n 154) 685 (Lord Goff).

[169] See Smith, 'Property as the Law of Things' (n 40) 1714. See also Smith, 'Exclusion and Property Rules in the Law of Nuisance' (n 116).

[170] Douglas, 'Content of a Freehold' (n 110) 368–69; Richard A Epstein, 'Nuisance Law: Corrective Justice and Its Utilitarian Constraints' (1979) 8 *Journal of Legal Studies* 49, 56.

[171] Donal Nolan, '"A Tort Against Land": Private Nuisance as a Property Tort' in Donal Nolan and Andrew Robertson (eds), *Rights and Private Law* (Oxford, Hart Publishing Ltd, 2011) 459, 466–67; Christopher Essert, 'Nuisance and the Normative Boundaries of Ownership' (2016) 52 *Tulsa Law Review* 85, 96–97.

[172] See, famously, *Thompson-Schwab v Costaki* [1956] 1 WLR 335 (CA), 339 (Lord Evershed MR). It should be noted that *Thompson-Schwab* was only an appeal against the grant of an interlocutory injunction.

Nevertheless, whether boundary crossing is a convincing explanation of the tort does not matter for the purposes of the account developed here. Whatever the basis of liability, the tort of nuisance presupposes the existence of the plaintiff's property right. As Lord Goff stressed in *Hunter*, liability in nuisance is not predicated on an interference with the plaintiff's enjoyment of land but instead with his enjoyment of his *rights* over land.[173] Consequently, an action for private nuisance can only be brought by a plaintiff who can demonstrate some right in the land that is subject to the nuisance.[174]

As Merrill has notably written, '[g]ive someone the right to exclude others from a valued resource ... and you give them property. Deny someone the right and they do not have property'.[175] It is only once the law has conferred upon someone the right to exclude, instantiated by the tort of trespass, that it can begin to optimise the outer boundaries of the entitlement. A similar point is made by Smith, who writes that:

> refinements in high-stakes borderline cases will be necessary, and liability rules have their place there, as in the law of nuisance. But these refinements are just that, they rest on a basic exclusory system, backed up by property rules, that avoids the cost of use-by-use delineation in the majority of situations.[176]

As a tort against land, private nuisance is clearly a property tort. However, it presupposes the existence of the 'primary' tort of trespass that gives effect to the exclusion strategy and, in doing so, creates the basic modules of the property system. Nuisance is thus best conceived of as a 'secondary' tort that is consistent with, because it rests upon, the foundation created by the right to exclude.

VII. Uncoupling 'Property' and 'Possession'

A. Is there a 'Right' to 'Exclusive Possession'?

Acts of possession create original property rights. Property rights correlate to duties that forbid others from interfering with the object of the right. If this description is correct, the content of a property right can be adequately explained without recourse to the concept of possession. Many standard treatments do not, however, observe the conceptual distinction between the creation and the content of a right. For instance, Swadling has written that, '[t]o all intents and purposes, the fee simple absolute in possession gives its holder a *right to the exclusive possession*

[173] *Hunter* (n 154) 688.
[174] Ibid.
[175] Thomas W Merrill, 'Property and the Right to Exclude' (1998) 77 *Nebraska Law Review* 730, 730.
[176] Henry E Smith, 'Property and Property Rules' (2004) 79 *New York University Law Review* 1719, 1754.

of land forever'.[177] Likewise, he writes of rights to chattels that, '[t]he starting point … is that the interest which a person can have in respect of, say, a car or a coat is single and indivisible, a *right to exclusive possession forever*'.[178] This language is also pervasive in the case law. To take a prominent example, what distinguishes a lease, a form of property right, from a licence, a mere contractual right, is that the former confers on its holder a right to 'exclusive possession', but the latter does not.[179]

It is easy to appreciate why the content of a property right is described as a 'right to possession'. Because rights correlate to duties, the content of the right is revealed by asking what amounts to a breach of duty. Although, as Douglas has convincingly argued, liability in tort is overwhelmingly predicated on physical interference with the *res*, the property torts are very often described in terms of interferences with possession. Trespass, for example, is described as a 'wrong to possession'.[180] Likewise, it has been said that the tort of conversion is concerned with conduct that excludes an owner from 'use and possession of the goods'[181] and that the 'essence of conversion is dealing with a chattel in a manner repugnant to the immediate right to possession of the person who has the property or the special property in the chattel'.[182] A leading academic account of conversion states that, '[s]imply stated, conversion protects the current superior possessory interest in personal property'.[183]

B. Distinguishing Possession and Exclusion

If the exclusion model of property rights is correct, then these formulations are inaccurate. It is not true to say that a property right is best understood as a right to the exclusive possession of some thing. If property is concerned with the imposition of an *in rem* duty of non-interference, then possession, which, following others,[184] might be preliminarily described as effective control, is conceptually irrelevant.

Defining a property right as a right to 'exclusive possession' obscures an important truth about the basic architecture of property law. Conduct that merely prevents a right-holder from exercising effective control over some object is not necessarily wrongful. As *Club Cruise* demonstrates, conduct generally only amounts to a tort if it involves some form of physical interference with the object itself. If A were

[177] William Swadling. 'Property' (n 5) 184 [4.38]. Emphasis added.
[178] Ibid, 208 [4.131]. Emphasis added.
[179] *Radaich v Smith* [1959] HCA 45; (1959) 101 CLR 209, 222 (Windeyer J); *Street v Mountford* [1985] AC 809 (HL), 816 (Lord Templeman).
[180] *Penfolds Wine Pty Ltd v Elliott* [1946] HCA 46; (1946) 74 CLR 204, 225 (Dixon J) ('*Penfolds*').
[181] *Kuwait Airways* (n 129) 1084 (Lord Nicholls).
[182] *Penfolds* (n 180) 229 (Dixon J).
[183] Green and Randall (n 23) 46.
[184] See, eg, Honoré (n 76) 113.

to take B's mobile phone from her pocket, A will have committed a conversion, not because he has denied B possession of her phone, but instead because he has physically interfered with it. Conversely, if A prevented B from exercising control over her phone by physically restraining her, though he will have committed a tort against the person, he will not have breached her property right in the phone. As Douglas notes,[185] if B is kidnapped by A, B will be unable to use her land or chattels. However, whilst A has undoubtedly breached B's 'personality rights', he has not breached her property rights. To take Bramwell B's example as a final illustration, if I forcibly prevent someone from taking his pistol from a drawer, I may have committed an assault, but I will not have converted the pistol.[186]

It may well be that exclusion is such an efficient proxy that there will be relatively few circumstances in which A can prevent B from exercising effective physical control over some object without also physically interfering with it. Nevertheless, there is another reason why it is important to sharply distinguish between possession and exclusion. The converse of the abovementioned point is that conduct which involves some physical interference with the *res* will be tortious even if that conduct does not disturb the right-holder's physical control over it in any meaningful sense. As the cases on apparently harmless interferences with airspace demonstrate, a freeholder or leaseholder need not be 'dispossessed' or 'ousted' from her land to bring a claim in trespass.[187] Any act of boundary crossing, no matter how ephemeral, constitutes a breach of duty. As Camden CJ declared, '[b]y the laws of England every invasion of private property, be it ever so minute, is a trespass. No man can set his foot upon my ground without my licence, but he is liable to an action, though the damage be nothing'.[188]

VIII. Conclusion

Gray commenced his influential article by provocatively asserting that:

> Proudhon got it all wrong. Property is not theft – it is fraud. Few other legal notions operate such gross or systematic deception. Before long I will have sold you a piece of thin air and you will have called it property. But the ultimate fact about property is that it does not really exist: it is mere illusion. It is a vacant concept – oddly enough rather like thin air.[189]

[185] Douglas, 'Kuwait Airways' (n 128) 218–19.

[186] *England v Cowley* [1873] LR 8 Exch 126, 129.

[187] *LJP Investments Pty Ltd v Howard Chia Investments Pty Ltd* (1989) 24 NSWLR 490, 487 (Hodgson J); *Bendal Pty Ltd v Mirvac Project Pty Ltd* (1991) 23 NSWLR 464, 468–69 (Bryson J); *Anchor Brewhouse Developments Ltd v Berkley House (Dockland Developments) Ltd* (1987) 2 EGLR 173 (Ch), 176 (Scott J).

[188] *Entick v Carrington* (1765) 95 ER 807; 19 St Tr 1030, 1066.

[189] Gray (n 141) 252.

If, by this passage, Gray meant no more than that property rights are not a natural condition of mankind, then he was essentially restating Bentham's insistence that there is no property without law.[190] If, however, he was suggesting that the concept of property in law is so hopelessly amorphous as to border on intellectual fraud, then the exclusion model of property suggests that he is wrong. Whilst we may never agree on the boundaries of property, its core is clear. Property, and private property in particular,[191] describes a system at the apex of which sits an individual upon whom the law has conferred sole decision-making authority in respect of a resource that constitutes an object of property.[192] Property law allows such a person to have the first and final say about the use of some object of by the simple expedient of conferring on her the right to exclude others from it, for any reason, or no reason at all.

The purpose of this account of property rights is not only to introduce concepts that are central to the analysis that follows, but also to highlight two important truths about the particular role that possession plays in the basic structure of property law. The first is that possession does not describe the content of a property right. Contrary to standard accounts, a right-holder cannot complain about conduct that interferes with her 'possession'. Irrespective of whether it impairs her ability to exercise control over some object, conduct will only amount to a legal wrong if it involves some physical interference with that object. The second, and related, truth is that a duty-ower *will* infringe a property right simply by physically interfering with an object of property that does not belong to him. Whether or not it prevents the right-holder from exercising effective control over the object in question, any form of physical interference will constitute a legal wrong.

In his famous essay on ownership, Honoré described possession as, 'the foundation on which the whole superstructure of ownership rests'.[193] If the foregoing analysis is accurate, this widely held view about possession and its role in property law is incorrect. Though possession describes those acts that create property rights, it does not describe their content. The right to exclude, and not the right to possess, is the foundation on which the superstructure of ownership rests.

[190] Bentham (n 1) 113. Although Hume's theory of property, discussed in Chapter 4, suggests otherwise.

[191] For a discussion of the distinction between property generally and private property in particular see Waldron (n 120) 31, 38–39.

[192] Even those who place less stress on the right to exclude emphasise the 'agenda-setting authority' of the owner. See, eg, Larissa Katz, 'Exclusion and Exclusivity in Property Law' (2008) 58 *University of Toronto Law Journal* 275, 277–78.

[193] Honoré (n 76) 113.

2

Facts, Rights and Other Things

Laying the Conceptual Foundations

I. Introduction

The previous chapter advanced two main arguments. First, that property is, at its core, a system that solves problems of inconsistent use by conferring upon a person called 'the owner' the first and final say about how some 'thing' is to be used. It does so by the simple expedient of demanding that everyone but the owner 'keep off'. Secondly, contrary to standard formulations, the substance of a property right is not a right to 'possess' but to 'exclude'. Possession is significant because it describes an act that creates an original property right, not because it describes the content of the right created by such an act.

Because property law is centrally concerned with rights to exclude created by acts of possession, one might expect the concept of possession in the law to refer to the simple notion of physical control.[1] This is not, however, the case. On the contrary, explanations of possession have become so esoteric and riddled with technical distinctions that any attempt to explain possession must begin with an embarrassing admission of conceptual failure. As was noted in the Introduction, this usually takes the form of the mandatory recitation of Earl Jowitt's lament that, '[i]n truth, English law has never worked out a completely logical and exhaustive definition of possession'.[2]

The argument advanced in this chapter is that the confusion surrounding possession cannot be explained on the basis that the concept is intrinsically complex. Unlike the broader notion of 'property', possession is not an inherently contested concept and can be adequately defined. The ongoing disagreement about the meaning of possession is instead attributable to two errors. The first is the tendency to conflate rights with facts or, in Hohfeldian terms, to confuse jural and non-jural concepts. The second is the persistent misunderstanding of the significance of 'ownership' in a system of property in which titles are relative and not absolute. If we disentangle jural from non-jural concepts and appreciate the

[1] See, eg, AM Honoré, 'Ownership' in AG Guest (ed), *Oxford Essays in Jurisprudence* (Oxford, Oxford University Press, 1961) 107, 113.

[2] *United States of America v Dollfus Mieg et Compagnie SA* [1952] AC 582 (HL), 605.

limited formal significance of ownership in a system in which titles to property are relative, then we can explain much of property law with a minimum of concepts. Consistently with the conclusion of Chapter 1, the analysis below demonstrates that there is no need for possession to denote anything other than a relationship of fact that creates a right to exclude.

II. What is Possession? Some Views from the Academy

A. Fact or Right?

The essential problem plaguing the concept of possession was summarised by Pollock in the following terms: '[i]t has constantly been asked: Is possession a matter of fact or of right?'.[3] One of the vital questions that any account of possession must answer is whether possession is an observable, factual relationship between a person and a tangible thing that creates a property right or whether it instead describes a distinctive jural interest in an object of property.

This relatively simple question raises many others. For example, if possession is a fact, then what sort of fact does it describe? Is it limited to the familiar notion of physical control or does it have a peculiarly legal meaning that is concerned less with actual physical dominion and more with the intention of the possessor? If, however, possession is a species of right or other jural interest, what sort of right does it describe and how does the content of that right differ from that of the generic property right described in Chapter 1? These questions have elicited a range of answers from leading commentators.

B. A Simple Fact?

At one end of the spectrum, some argue that possession in the law describes nothing other than physical control over some tangible thing. McFarlane argues that, '[t]he concept of physical control is a simple one. The only difficulties it causes are factual ones, and arise only in unusual situations'.[4] According to McFarlane, this basic truth about possession has been obscured by the importation into the common law of arcane Roman law rules about intention.[5] Indeed, he has gone so

[3] Frederick Pollock and Robert Samuel Wright, *An Essay on Possession in the Common Law* (Oxford, Clarendon Press, 1888) 10. See also Oliver Wendell Holmes, *The Common Law* (Boston, Little, Brown and Company, 1948) 213; Simon Douglas, 'Is Possession Factual or Legal?' in Eric Descheemaeker (ed), *The Consequences of Possession* (Edinburgh, Edinburgh University Press, 2014) 53, 53.

[4] Ben McFarlane, *The Structure of Property Law* (Oxford, Hart Publishing, 2008) 155.

[5] Ibid. On this point see Oliver Radley-Gardner, 'Civilized Squatting' (2005) 25 *Oxford Journal of Legal Studies* 727, 738.

far as to argue that the term 'possession' has become so bedeviled by unnecessary technical refinements that it is best avoided altogether.[6]

For scholars such as Douglas and McFarlane, there is no such thing as a 'possessory right' or a 'possessory title'. The juridical significance of possession is limited to its role in creating original rights to tangible things. Douglas argues that, '[w]hilst there may be good justification for the existence of a limited 'possessory right', it is suggested that it does not exist. The better view is that possession is not a type of property right that one can have in a chattel, but simply a way of independently acquiring 'ownership' of a chattel.'[7] Consistently with the picture of property rights presented in Chapter 1, this explanation draws a sharp distinction between the basic, observable fact of possession and the abstract, non-factual right of exclusion that it creates.

C. A Complex Legal Concept?

Although everyone agrees that possession is juridically significant, not everyone agrees that its significance is limited to a simple fact about physical control. Gray and Gray, for example, argue that possession bears a 'heavily specialised meaning in English law'.[8] In particular, they stress that possession is not a matter of mere occupancy but is rather 'an inherently behavioural phenomenon which incorporates a particular mindset'.[9] In a similar vein, but in the context of personal rather than real property law, Gleeson writes that:

> [a]lthough title is in essence a legal issue to be determined as a matter of law, possession appears to be an issue of fact. However, it is not. The question of whether a man possesses a thing is a complex legal issue in its own right, and the rules for determining it are far more complex than a simple assessment of relative location.[10]

Likewise, the authors of a leading work on conversion argue that:

> [p]ossession means a different thing to lawyers than it does to everyone else. The essence of legal possession, also referred to as constructive possession or the right to immediate possession, lies in the element of control exercised over an asset. More specifically, it is the cognitive element of control which is of the greatest relevance to legal possession, as opposed to the manual control which characterises actual possession ... legal possession is rights-based, not facts-based.[11]

[6] McFarlane (n 4) 155.

[7] Simon Douglas, *Liability for Wrongful Interferences with Chattels* (Oxford, Hart Publishing, 2011) 31.

[8] Kevin Gray and Susan Francis Gray, *Elements of Land Law*, 5th edn (Oxford, Oxford University Press, 2009) 153 [2.1.6].

[9] Ibid, 153 [2.1.7].

[10] Simon Gleeson, *Personal Property Law* (London, FT Law and Tax, 1997) 24.

[11] Sarah Green and John Randall, *The Tort of Conversion* (Oxford, Hart Publishing, 2009) 86.

Others have adopted a hybrid position. Pollock, for example, used the term possession to describe both a fact capable of generating a property right *and* a distinctive legal interest in a thing.[12] He wrote that, '[p]ossession in law is most easily understood as associated with possession in fact',[13] but went on to argue that the '[l]aw takes this popular conception as a provisional groundwork, and builds upon it the notion of possession in a technical sense'.[14] In his view, legal possession ought to be regarded as 'a definite right or interest'[15] and that right 'exists and has legal incidents and advantages apart from the true owner's title'.[16]

Rather more recently, the authors of *The Law of Personal Property* have written that, '[n]ecessarily the starting-point is the common sense 'factual' notion of possession',[17] but go on to conclude that 'possession as an interest in goods is a legal right to possession, being any interest in goods inferior to ownership'.[18] Likewise, Worthington argues that:

> [t]he layman's definition of possession is based on the notion of intentional physical control of an asset. The law's definition is not quite the same. The law distinguishes between the right to possess a thing physically and the package of advantages or rights which the law gives to possessors. This package of rights defines the possessory interest in property.[19]

On this view, possession is not merely a fact about physical control, but a particular legal interest in a thing exigible against other legal persons.[20] How this right or 'package of advantages' differs in content from the property right discussed in Chapter 1 is not, however, clear.

D. The Candidates Categorised

From this survey, one can detect three basic, though not necessarily discrete, positions. The first is that possession is a 'no frills' fact about physical control. On this view, the significance of possession is limited to the creation of property rights of the type discussed in Chapter 1. The second position is that possession is a fact, but one defined by peculiarly legal rather than social rules. According to this view, the legal concept of possession is a legally elaborated version of the lay notion and

[12] Pollock and Wright (n 3) 22.
[13] Ibid, 17.
[14] Ibid, 2.
[15] Ibid, 17.
[16] Ibid, 19.
[17] Michael Bridge et al, *The Law of Personal Property* (London, Sweet & Maxwell, 2013) 55 [2–036].
[18] Ibid, 66 [2–060].
[19] Sarah Worthington, *Personal Property Law: Texts and Materials* (Oxford, Hart Publishing, 2000) 51.
[20] See also Michael Bridge, *Personal Property Law*, 4th edn (Oxford, Oxford University Press, 2015) 30; Thomas Merrill, 'Ownership and Possession' in Yun-chien Chang (ed), *Law and Economics of Possession* (Cambridge, Cambridge University Press, 2015) 9, 24–26.

is less concerned with the physical act of possession and more with the particular intention with which it is carried out. The third position is that possession is not a fact about physical control, but describes, in Worthington's words, 'a package of advantages' in respect of a thing, whatever those advantages may be.

Not all these positions are mutually exclusive. Although one cannot argue both for and against the proposition that possession is a distinct form of jural interest in a thing, it is possible to hold that possession is both a complex fact and a sort of right in a thing. Likewise, one can consistently argue that possession is a fact, the function of which is limited to the creation of property rights, whilst also maintaining that its significance lies more in the possessor's intention than his ability to effectively control some object.

III. Playing Word Games: The Language of Possession

A. More is Not Necessarily Better: A Summary of the Nomenclature

This inability to agree upon the nature of possession in the law has spawned a vast and, at times, baffling lexicon of synonyms, antonyms and hybrid terms.[21] Though coined in an attempt to distinguish discrete concepts and states of affairs, these terms do not so much resolve the confusion as serve as a constant reminder of the law's inability to determine what possession means and why it matters.

To take the simplest case, when the law wishes to describe the relatively simple fact of physical control over some tangible thing it uses terms including, but not limited to, 'de facto possession', 'occupation', 'actual possession', 'detention', 'custody', 'bare possession' and 'physical possession'.[22] Generally speaking, these terms describe an observable fact and are not terms of art. Because terms such as 'actual' or 'de facto possession' simply denote the existence of a state of affairs they do not, of themselves, imply that the possessor has also acquired a property right in the object possessed.[23]

Whilst 'de facto possession' describes a particular fact that exists quite apart from the law, it is apt to be conflated with a form of legal relation because, as Pollock wrote, it is 'almost inevitable, when once we are in the presence of an

[21] For other, similar, observations, see Duncan Sheehan, *The Principles of Personal Property Law*, 2nd edn (Oxford, Hart Publishing, 2017) 10–19; AES Tay, 'The Concept of Possession in the Common Law: Foundations for a New Approach' (1964) 4 *Melbourne University Law Review* 476, 476–77; Jonathan Hill, 'The Proprietary Character of Possession' in Elizabeth Cooke (ed), *Modern Studies in Property Law: Volume 1* (Oxford, Hart Publishing, 2001) 21, 24; Mark Wonnacott, *Possession of Land* (Cambridge, Cambridge University Press, 2006) 161.

[22] Pollock and Wright (n 3) 26–28, 118–19.

[23] To borrow Wonnacott's description, these terms are synonymous with possession in the 'vulgar' sense. Wonnacott (n 21) 6.

apparent de facto possessor, to ascribe to him possession in law so far and so long as nothing appears to the contrary'.[24] Consequently, when the law wishes to make clear that it is referring to a factual relationship of physical control that does *not* create a right, it uses a different set of terms, including 'custody', 'detention' or 'bare possession'.[25] The most striking example of this is the master-servant rule, which attributes 'custody' of some object to the servant and 'possession' to his master.[26]

Where the law wishes to indicate the existence of something more than a mere fact, it uses another set of terms. As a general rule, terms such as 'possession in law' or 'legal possession' are employed to indicate the existence of some legal interest.[27] Despite what the name might suggest, it is possible for someone to have 'legal possession' or 'possession in the law' despite not having, or ever having had, actual control over the object in question.[28] To borrow Pollock's example,[29] if A, the owner of a coat, is wearing it, he has both actual possession and legal possession. If A gives it to his servant, B, who takes it to the tailor for alterations, A loses actual possession but retains legal possession. Importantly, it should not be assumed that legal possession also means 'lawful possession'.[30] It is perfectly possible for a wrongdoer to acquire legal possession. To take a simple example, a squatter clearly acquires legal possession of a parcel of land even though the act by which he acquired that possession was, and continues to be, a trespass.[31]

The separation of actual from legal possession is often, though not invariably, indicated by another cluster of terms, including 'right to possession', 'immediate right to possession' and 'constructive possession'.[32] A freeholder has an immediate right to possession against a trespassing squatter who has acquired both actual and legal possession of the land. Likewise, the victim of a conversion, though she no longer has actual possession, has an immediate right to possession against the tortfeasor who, through his act of conversion, has acquired actual and legal possession of the chattel.[33]

These terms can also be applied to consensual arrangements such as gratuitous bailments.[34] Likewise, a purchaser of goods to whom title has passed but who has not yet taken delivery has an immediate right to possession of those goods.

[24] Pollock and Wright (n 3) 18.
[25] Ibid, 18, 27–28. This applies equally to real property law. See Gray and Gray (n 8) 153 [2.1.7].
[26] *Ward v Macauley* (1791) 100 ER 1135, 1135; 4 TR 489, 490 (Buller J).
[27] Pollock and Wright (n 3) 16.
[28] Ibid, 145.
[29] Ibid, 26–27.
[30] Ibid, 20.
[31] Joshua Williams, *The Seisin of the Freehold* (London, Sweet & Maxwell, 1878) 7–8. The relevant passage was cited with approval by Dixon J in *Wheeler v Baldwin* [1934] HCA 58; (1934) 52 CLR 632, 632.
[32] Pollock and Wright (n 3) 27.
[33] Ibid.
[34] *Lotan v Cross* (1810) 170 ER 1219, 1219; 2 Camp 464, 465 (Lord Ellenborough).

'Constructive possession' is perhaps most often associated with those situations in which the separation of fact and right occurred with the right-holder's consent. To take the archetypal example, whilst a bailee at will has actual possession, his bailor retains constructive possession of the goods.[35] Constructive possession is also used to describe the transfer of title to goods by way of the delivery of some documentary intangible, such as a bill of lading.[36]

'Possessory title' is another term that is employed in several different senses.[37] Most generally, it is used to describe a property right created by an act of possession.[38] More specifically, it is also used to distinguish the newer title of the possessor from the older title of the 'paper owner'.[39] A squatter who is on her way to obtaining a clear title by adverse possession is frequently described as having a 'possessory' title.[40] The qualification 'possessory' is also applied to the title acquired by the finder of a lost chattel.[41] When applied to squatters and other wrongdoers, the adjective 'possessory' can also indicate that a title is fragile because it is subject to a superior title held by someone else. In *Buckley v Gross*, for example, Cockburn CJ sought to emphasise the limited right of the plaintiff, who had purchased melted tallow from someone who had no right to sell it, by holding that he 'had nothing but bare naked possession'.[42]

'Possessory title' is not confined to circumstances in which the loss of possession was involuntary or the act by which possession was obtained was wrongful. It can also denote the right of someone who came into possession with the consent of the owner. A bailee, for example, has a possessory title in the bailed goods. Thus, it has been said that:

> [i]nterests in a chattel can be shared and it is this fact that has given rise to the distinction between proprietary and possessory title. Thus, where an earlier possessor (the bailor) grants possession to a subsequent possessor (the bailee) on terms that reserve to the bailor a reversionary interest in the chattel, the bailor can be said to enjoy a 'proprietary title' and the bailee a 'possessory' title in the chattel.[43]

[35] *Ancona v Rogers* [1876] 1 Ex D 285 (CA), 292 (Mellish LJ). See also Royston Miles Good and Ewan McKendrick, *Goode on Commercial Law* 4th edn (London, Penguin, 2010) 47.

[36] Bridge, *Personal Property Law* (n 20) 35.

[37] For a recent, though different, analysis of the shortcomings of 'possessory title' see Luke Rostill, 'Terminology and Title to Chattels: A Case Against 'Possessory Title'' (2018) 134 *Law Quarterly Review* 407.

[38] *Russell v Wilson* [1923] HCA 60; (1923) 33 CLR 538, 546 (Isaacs and Rich JJ).

[39] Robert Chambers, *An Introduction to Property Law in Australia*, 3rd edn (Pyrmont, Thomson Reuters Australia, 2013) 58 [6.40].

[40] *Tower Hamlets LBC v Barrett* [2005] EWCA Civ 923; (2006) 1 P & CR 9, 137 [18] (Neuburger LJ). See also Robert Megarry et al, *The Law of Real Property*, 7th edn (London, Sweet & Maxwell, 2008) 86–87 [4-003]–[4-004].

[41] *Parker v British Airways Board* [1982] QB 1004 (CA), 1019 (Eveleigh LJ) ('*Parker*').

[42] *Buckley v Gross* (1863) 122 ER 213, 215; 3 B & S 566, 572 (Cockburn CJ).

[43] *Government of the Islamic Republic of Iran v The Barakat Galleries Ltd* [2007] EWCA Civ 1374; [2009] QB 22, 32 [16] (Lord Phillips CJ).

In this sense, possessory title is synonymous with constructive possession or 'special property', a term that is contrasted with 'general property' and which describes possession that is 'subject to the claims of other persons'.[44]

Quite differently again, possessory title can refer to the entitlement of someone who, though not an 'owner', can nevertheless recover substantial damages for the loss or destruction of goods. In *The Aliakmon* Lord Brandon held that:

> in order to enable a person to claim in negligence for loss caused to him by reason of loss of or damage to property, he must have had either the legal ownership of or a possessory title to the property concerned at the time when the loss or damage occurred, and it is not enough for him to have only had contractual rights in relation to such property which have been adversely affected by the loss of or damage to it.[45]

The most striking example of this is the right of a bailee, such as a carrier of goods, to sue and recover the full value of the bailed goods despite not being liable to his bailor for their value.[46]

IV. Jural and Non-Jural Concepts

A. Facts and Rights

The foregoing summary demonstrated two things. First, that Earl Jowitt's lament is justified and, secondly, that the common law will never solve the possession puzzle by creating an ever-more complex lexicon of technical terms. Take Latham CJ's attempt to explain the anomalous position of the servant or agent at common law. His Honour wrote that, '[t]he *possession* of a servant or agent is the *possession* of the master or principal … who therefore is regarded as having *actual possession* and not only a *right to possession*'.[47] Although this statement is not 'wrong' in a doctrinal sense, it reveals a body of law that is riddled with confusing fictions and conceptual elision. Any successful account of possession must begin by untangling these conceptual knots.

Much of the confusion evident in the foregoing summary arises from the failure to distinguish between facts, which are non-jural concepts, and rights, which are purely jural concepts. The distinction between a right and a fact can be stated succinctly. For present purposes, to describe something as a 'fact' is to say that it is a state of affairs that exists in the world independently of any particular legal system. Though a fact may have legal significance, its existence is not dependent on, nor is its content defined by, the constituent rules of that particular legal system.[48]

[44] *Webb v Fox* (1797) 101 ER 1037, 1041; 7 TR 391, 398 (Lawrence J).

[45] *Leigh & Sillivan Shipping Ltd v Aliakmon Shipping Co Ltd* [1986] AC 785 (HL), 809.

[46] *The Winkfield* [1902] P 42 (CA), 54 (Collins MR).

[47] *Penfolds Wine Pty Ltd v Elliott* [1946] HCA 46; (1946) 74 CLR 204, 216 ('*Penfolds*'). Emphasis added.

[48] This is the basis of the distinction between questions of fact and questions of law, on which see JD Heydon, *Cross on Evidence*, 10th edn (Chatswood, LexisNexis Butterworths, 2014) 371–72 [11005].

Hohfeld drew a distinction between two different sorts of fact, which he described as 'operative' and 'evidential', respectively.[49] An operative fact has a particular significance in a legal system because, whether by itself or in particular combinations with other such facts, it gives rise to jural relations.[50] That two people are *sui juris* and that one has made an 'offer' that the other has 'accepted' are the operative facts that together create a contract.[51]

An evidential fact, by contrast, is one that constitutes the evidence from which we can infer the existence of an operative fact, but which does not itself create jural relations.[52] The existence of some written instrument is an evidential fact because it is evidence from which we can infer the existence of an offer by the promisor and its acceptance by the promisee. To use another example, the various iterations of the Statute of Frauds require that declarations of trust over land be in writing and signed by the declarant.[53] The writing, whether a brief note on the back of a napkin or an exhaustively drafted deed, is an evidential fact from which we can infer the existence of the operative fact; the declaration that actually gives rise to the trust.

What, then, is a 'right'? Rights, or to use the Hohfeldian nomenclature, 'jural relations',[54] are abstract bilateral relations that obtain exclusively between those entities that are capable of enjoying legal rights and bearing legal duties. Unlike facts, rights are predicated on the existence of other legal persons and thus cannot exist independently of a legal system. Hohfeld summarised the distinction in the following terms:

> [a] man may indeed sustain close and beneficial *physical* relations to a given *physical thing* … But, obviously, such purely *physical* relations could as well exist quite apart from … the law of organized society: physical relations are wholly distinct from jural relations. The latter take their significance from the law; and since the purpose of the law is to regulate the conduct of human beings, all jural relations must…be predicated of such human beings.[55]

Although far more could be, and has been, said about the concept of a right, an appreciation of this basic distinction between non-jural and jural relations will suffice for present purposes.

For a slightly different account that distinguishes between 'legal' and 'ultimate' facts see Scott J Shapiro, *Legality* (Cambridge MA, Harvard University Press, 2011) 25–26.

[49] Wesley Newcomb Hohfeld, *Fundamental Legal Conceptions as Applied in Judicial Reasoning, and Other Legal Essays* (New Haven, Yale University Press, 1923) 32–35. See also Arthur L Corbin, 'Legal Analysis and Terminology' (1919) 29 *Yale Law Journal* 163, 164.

[50] 'Operative facts' thus describe what evidence lawyers describe as 'facts in issue'. See Colin Tapper and Rupert Cross, *Cross and Tapper on Evidence*, 12th edn (Oxford, Oxford University Press, 2010) 29.

[51] Hohfeld (n 49) 32.

[52] Ibid, 34.

[53] See, eg, *Property Law Act 1958* (Vic) s 53(1)(b); *Conveyancing Act 1919* (NSW) s 23C(1)(b); *Law of Property Act 1925* (UK) s 53(1)(b).

[54] Hohfeld (n 49) 36.

[55] Ibid, 75. For a similar observation, see Hans Kelsen, *Pure Theory of Law* (Berkeley, University of California Press, 1967) 130. Hohfeld abjured the Latin tag 'in personam' because it gives the erroneous impression that there can be rights against entities other than natural or juridical people. Hohfeld (n 49) 75.

Whatever else it may be, possession is a fact. As Pollock himself wrote, '[p]ossession in fact – the effective and exclusive control of a thing – is prior to ownership and indeed to every legal rule and idea. The facts which we will call actual or physical possession would still exist in a society where there was no recognition of individual property'.[56] Concepts such as 'legal possession' are confusing because, contrary to Pollock's simple definition, they allow that someone can 'possess' something in the absence of any form of physical control. If I create a gratuitous bailment by lending you my car for the weekend, the law continues to credit me with possession even after I hand you the keys.

If, following Pollock, we take as our starting point the notion that possession is a fact about effective and exclusive control, then it is clear that many uses of the term possession are, to a greater or lesser degree, fictions. Epstein has written of this issue that:

> all legal systems for obvious reasons of convenience (i.e. efficiency) have adopted the convention of continuous possession: possession once obtained is retained until it is lost by the actions of some other person or natural event. Thus the initial occupant who has marked the borders of his land does not return that land to the state of nature when he leaves it to hunt or trade.[57]

Likewise, Harris has observed that:

> [o]nce the facts which justify the application of the possessory rule arise in the first place, they need not necessarily continue to exist in the same form, degree or intensity. The court will continue to apply the word "possession" to the plaintiff's relationship with the object until the law recognizes that changed facts operate to divest the plaintiff of his possessory right.[58]

As an observation of what the law does, these statements are undoubtedly true. The more interesting question, however, is *why* the law has thought it necessary to persist with such a manifest fiction. Why do we need a 'convention of continuous possession' when we have the concept of a property right which, as a purely jural concept, need not depend upon an ongoing, factual relationship between a person and a thing?

One explanation is that this artificial concept of possession is a product of the law's failure to distinguish rights from facts; jural from non-jural relations. One of Hohfeld's more important, though less remarked upon, lessons was the need to 'emphasize the importance of differentiating the purely legal relations from the physical and mental facts that call such relations into being'.[59] Once we appreciate

[56] Frederick Pollock, *A First Book of Jurisprudence for Students of the Common Law*, 5th edn (London, Macmillan & Co, 1923) 181.

[57] Richard A Epstein, 'Possession' in Peter Newman (ed), *The New Palgrave Dictionary of Economics and the Law* (London, Palgrave Macmillan, 1998) vol III, 62, 63.

[58] DR Harris, 'The Concept of Possession in English Law' in AG Guest (ed), *Oxford Essays in Jurisprudence* (Oxford, Oxford University Press, 1961) 69, 73. See also *Bird v The Town of Fort Frances* [1949] 1 WLUK 28 (HC); 2 DLR 791, 799–800 (McRuer CJ).

[59] Hohfeld (n 49) 27.

that possession, as an operative fact, merely creates and does not define the amalgam of abstract jural relations that we call a property right, we can simply dispense with the fiction that owners invariably possess.

B. Distinguishing Ownership from Possession: A Medieval Legacy?

A more difficult question is why lawyers tend to elide the right of ownership with the operative fact of possession in the first place. The superficial answer is that liability in the property torts is expressly predicated on interferences with 'possession'. As Chapter 1 explained, this formulation is misleading in so far as it suggests that liability in the property torts turns on anything other than physical interference. If I leave my bicycle leaning, unchained, against my front fence whilst I am on an overseas holiday, there is no sense in which I exercise effective control over it. Nevertheless, if someone steals it in my absence, I can still sue the thief in conversion.

Given that my ownership right in my bicycle, which is purely jural, does not depend on a fact about my actual control over it, why are the property torts framed in terms of interferences with possession? One explanation is that this distinction between facts and rights was not always so obvious. Honoré remarked that, '[t]o have worked out the notion of 'having a right to' as distinct from merely 'having' … was a major intellectual achievement'.[60] According to Maitland, this inability to distinguish between 'things', which one can possess, and 'rights', which one cannot, was a characteristic feature of the medieval law of property. He described the failure to make this vital distinction as a sort of 'mental incapacity'[61] and remarked that a 'very large part of the history of Real Property Law seems to me the history of the process whereby Englishmen have thought themselves free of that materialism which is natural to us all'.[62]

In fairness to the medieval mind, this inability to distinguish facts from rights was not entirely due to a 'mental incapacity', but was also attributable to a deliberate policy, made in the interest of public order, of strictly forbidding disseisees from retaking control of their land through potentially violent acts of self-help.[63] This is strikingly demonstrated in the old learning on the assize of novel disseisin.

[60] Honoré (n 1) 115.

[61] FW Maitland, 'The Mystery of Seisin' (1886) 2 *Law Quarterly Review* 481, 489.

[62] Ibid, 490. Likewise, Pollock observed that, 'our ancestors simply couldn't understand owning anything one does not actually possess ("Give me the handle of the church door," says the grantee [of] an advowson)'. See Mark DeWolfe Howe (ed), *Holmes-Pollock Letters: The Correspondence of Mr. Justice Holmes and Sir Frederick Pollock, 1874–1932* (Cambridge MA, Harvard University Press, 1941) vol II, 186.

[63] Frederick Pollock and Frederic William Maitland, *The History of English Law Before the Time of Edward I*, 2nd edn (Indianapolis, Liberty Fund, 2010) vol II, 55.

If A were wrongly disseised by B, A had four days in which to retake possession by making a physical re-entry. After four days had passed, B would acquire seisin and could thus bring the assize against anyone, including A, who disseised him. The striking feature of the assize during the early to mid-thirteenth century was not merely that it put B, a vicious disseisor, back into possession of land, but that it did not allow A to set up his title as a defence to B's action.[64] It was only later that the law came to place less emphasis on the fact of possession, however obtained, and greater emphasis on title, whether accompanied by possession or not.[65]

For present purposes, what is important is that any system that restricts the ambit of its protection to those in actual possession does not create property rights as we understand them. This is because, as Austin has remarked, the hallmark of property is, in a very literal sense, the ability to put something down and pick it up again later.[66] Penner has written that:

> [a] system in which ownership depended on continuing factual possession might reasonably be characterized as having a deficient concept of ownership. Title derived in that way would restrict the right to the use of a thing to those uses which counted as possessory. In other words, 'ownership' would merely be a right not to be interfered with so long as one maintained a certain, positive, engagement with a thing.[67]

One could argue that such a system would not merely have a 'deficient' concept of ownership, but no concept of ownership at all. To require a right-holder to maintain possession as a condition of trespassory protection is simply to replicate the torts that prevent interferences with the person. As Lord Denman CJ observed long ago, rights of action that arise from interference with the right-holder's actual possession are simply 'an extension of that protection which the law throws around the person'.[68] Trespass, as opposed to trover, or conversion as it is now called, always required a direct interference with the plaintiff's possession. Hence, the rule that 'possession', as opposed to a 'right to possession', is necessary to maintain an action for trespass to goods.[69]

[64] See FW Maitland, 'Beatitude of Seisin: Part I' (1888) 4 *Law Quarterly Review* 24, 33–36; FW Maitland, 'Beatitude of Seisin: Part II' (1888) 4 *Law Quarterly Review* 286, 286–87.

[65] Maitland, 'Beatitude of Seisin: Part II' (n 64) 298. Holmes was thus wrong when he wrote that English law, 'always had the good sense to allow title to be set up in defence to a possessory action': Holmes (n 3) 210.

[66] Lisa M Austin, 'Possession and the Distractions of Philosophy' in James Penner and Henry E Smith (eds), *Philosophical Foundations of Property Law*, (Oxford, Oxford University Press, 2014) 182, 189.

[67] JE Penner, *The Idea of Property in Law* (Oxford, Clarendon Press, 1997) 147.

[68] *Rogers v Spence* (1844) 153 ER 239, 241; 13 M & W 571, 581. See also *Penfolds* (n 47) 241 (Williams J). According to Holdsworth, Lord Denman's famous dictum was not an anomaly but was 'merely putting explicitly what had been implicit in the judgments and dicta of his predecessors from the earliest days of the common law'. See Sir William Holdsworth, *A History of English Law* (London, Meuthen & Co, 1966) vol VII, 467.

[69] *Penfolds* (n 47) 226–27 (Dixon J); *Hampton v BHP Billiton Minerals Pty Ltd (No 2)* [2012] WASC 285, [299], [304]–[306] (Edelman J) ('*Hampton*'). Wright observed that, 'it is difficult to see how there can be a forcible and immediate injury *vi et armis* to a mere legal right; and there are some parts of the law of trespass and theft which are inexplicable on such a view': Pollock and Wright (n 3) 145

Fortunately, the tort of trespass is but one weapon in an owner's armoury. Because our law has long since taken the intellectual leap of faith necessary to break the bonds of 'materialism', an owner can sue for conversion of his goods whether or not he possesses them. The conceptual difference between the torts of trespass and conversion was famously described by Lord Kenyon in the following terms: '[t]he distinction between the actions of trespass and trover is well settled: the former is founded on possession: the latter on property'.[70]

C. Fictional Uses of Possession

Although Lord Kenyon was able to confidently assert this proposition in 1791, the common law has been unwilling to fully dispense with the notion that owners must also possess. Instead of embracing what might be described as the 'completed disaggregation' of the operative fact of possession from the right of ownership, it has instead settled on an awkward, and unnecessary, compromise in which owners are *deemed* to possess. The consequence of this unsatisfactory halfway house is a proliferation of obfuscating fictions.

In *Wilson v Lombank Ltd*,[71] the plaintiff left his car at a garage for repairs. After the repairs had been completed, the car was parked on the forecourt of the garage to be collected. A representative of the defendant, operating under the mistaken belief that the car belonged to the defendant company, took it away. In holding that the defendants were liable to the plaintiff in trespass, Hinchcliffe J remarked that, 'in my judgment the plaintiff was in possession of the car; not only did he have the right to immediate possession, but I do not think in the circumstances of the case he ever lost possession of the car'.[72] The notion that the plaintiff retained possession of the car throughout was an obvious fiction, but one that allowed the plaintiff to plead his case as one of trespass to goods rather than conversion. Contrary to Hinchcliffe J's position, if I drop my car off at a garage and hand the mechanic the key, it is quite clear that, though I remain its owner, I have relinquished possession.

Similarly, take the following statement from Mellish LJ:

> [i]t seems to us that goods which have been delivered to a bailee to keep for the bailor, such as a gentleman's plate delivered to his banker, or furniture warehoused at the Pantechnicon, would, in a popular sense, as well as in a legal sense, be said to be still

This passage was cited with approval by Dixon J in *Penfolds* (n 47) 227. It was not until the 1350s that English law abandoned the requirement that writs of trespass allege that the wrong was committed with 'force and arms'. See JH Baker, *An Introduction to English Legal History*, 4th edn (Oxford, Oxford University Press, 2007) 60–61.

[70] *Ward v Macauley* (1791) 100 ER 1135, 1135; 4 TR 489, 490. See further *Hampton* (n 69) [305] (Edelman J).

[71] *Wilson v Lombank Ltd* (1963) 1 WLR 1294.

[72] Ibid, 1297–8. The plaintiff's ability to sue was based on Hinchcliffe J's finding that the garage owner did not have a common law lien over the car. For a case in which a vendor's lien did prevent a purchaser for suing in conversion see *Lord v Price* [1874] LR 9 Exch 54, 55–56 (Bramwell B).

> in his possession, and we see no valid ground for holding that they are not still in his possession within the meaning of the Bills of Sale Act.[73]

This is also an obvious fiction. If I deliver plate or jewellery to be stored in a bank vault, it is perfectly clear that the bank takes possession of those items. After all, the bank's ability to exercise almost complete control over objects within its vault is the very reason why I chose to deposit valuable items with it in the first place. That I may resume control of my plate or jewellery upon request does not demonstrate that I have retained possession. On the contrary, it demonstrates that my right to do so does not depend on my ongoing possession of them.

One can appreciate the pragmatic impulse that leads courts to adopt such a strained definition of possession. Epstein has written that, '[i]f an owner entrusts his car to a parking attendant from whom it is taken by a thief, it is far better that the legal remedy be given to the party with the permanent interest in the property than to one who has at most momentary custody over the object'.[74] However, once we appreciate that the purely jural concept of ownership, whilst created by an act of possession, does not depend upon an ongoing relationship of control, we can achieve the same sensible remedial outcomes without persisting with the fiction that owners also invariably possess.

V. Ownership and Relative Title

A. Relative Title

The authors of *The Law of Personal Property* describe 'possession' as a legal interest in a chattel that embraces 'all proprietary interests in goods short of outright ownership'.[75] This statement is misleading in so far as it implies that there are two distinct forms of proprietary interests in goods; a greater right called 'ownership' and a lesser right called 'possession'. The erroneous notion that there are two distinct sorts of property rights is attributable to a failure to distinguish between the content and the exigibility of a property right.

English law allows that a potentially infinite number of people can hold valid and enforceable property rights in the same thing at the same time.[76] It achieves this by recognising that property rights at common law are not absolute but are relatively weaker or stronger as they are more or less recently created.

[73] *Ancona v Rogers* (1876) 1 Ex D 285 (CA), 292.
[74] Epstein (n 57) 67.
[75] Bridge et al (n 17) 56 [2–038].
[76] For a recent challenge to the orthodox view see Luke Rostill, 'Relative Title and Deemed Ownership in English Personal Property Law' (2015) 35 *Oxford Journal of Legal Studies* 31.

This principle, often captured by phrases such as 'first in time, better in right' or 'first in time prevails',[77] is generally regarded as an important and unique feature of property rights at common law.[78]

Importantly, the principle of relative title concerns the *exigibility* of a property right and not its *content*.[79] The holder of a newer, and thus weaker, right has precisely the same *sort* of right as the holder of an older and thus stronger right. In each case, the right correlates to an *in rem* duty of non-interference. The only difference between the two rights is simply that the holder of the newer right can enforce it against anyone *except* a person with an older right; her right is '*in rem* minus one'. The practical importance of relativity of title is that, in resolving a property dispute, courts are only ever required to determine which of the two parties to the action has the best right inter se.[80] As Lord Diplock explained in relation to disputes over real property:

> the court is only concerned with the relative strengths of title proved by the rival claimants. If party A can prove a better title than party B he is entitled to succeed notwithstanding that C may have a better title than A, if C is neither a party to the action nor a person by whose authority B is in possession or occupation of the land.[81]

The principle of relativity of title applies equally to personal property[82] and does so whether possession has been acquired by finding,[83] consensually under a bailment,[84] or through conduct that constitutes a tort.[85]

The corollary of the concept of relative title is, as Lord Diplock suggested, that a defendant cannot deny liability by demonstrating that some party, not before the court, has a property right that is older and therefore better than that of the plaintiff. If B steals A's bicycle, and C then steals the bicycle from B, C cannot resist B's claim on the ground that the bike, in fact, belongs to A. In formal terms, C cannot raise the *jus tertii* as a defence to an action in trespass or conversion.[86]

[77] Andrew P Bell, *Modern Law of Personal Property in England and Ireland* (London, Butterworths, 1989) 516.

[78] Rostill (n 76) 32.

[79] Douglas (n 7) 26.

[80] *Asher v Whitlock* [1865] LR 1 QB 1, 5 (Cockburn CJ).

[81] *Ocean Estates Ltd v Pinder* (1969) 2 AC 19 (PC), 25.

[82] Although this view is not universally shared. See David Fox, 'Relativity of Title in Law and in Equity' (2006) 65 *The Cambridge Law Journal* 330, 344.

[83] *Armory v Delamirie* (1721) 93 ER 664; (1722) 1 Str 505; *Parker* (n 41).

[84] *The Winkfield* [1902] P 42 (CA), 54–55 (Collins MR); *Alfred McAlpine Construction Ltd v Panatown Ltd (No 1)* (2001) 1 AC 518 (HL), 581 (Lord Millett).

[85] *Jeffries v Great Western Railway Co* (1856) 119 ER 680, 681; 5 El & Bl 802, 805 (Lord Campbell CJ) ('*Jeffries*'); *Sutton v Buck* (1810) 2 Taunt 302; 127 ER 1094, 1096 (Mansfield CJ), 1096 (Lawrence J), 1097 (Chambre J). See also *Russell v Wilson* [1923] HCA 60; (1923) 33 CLR 538, 546–47 (Isaacs and Rich JJ).

[86] *Jeffries* (n 85) 805 (Lord Campbell CJ). However, a statutory version of the *jus tertii* exists in the United Kingdom. See *Torts (Interference with Goods) Act 1977* (UK) s 8(1).

B. Does the Law Recognise 'Ownership'?

As was noted in the Introduction, it is, for pragmatic and conceptual reasons, extremely difficult to discuss property rights at common law without invoking the concept of 'ownership'. Despite this, some scholars insist that ownership has no place in a system in which property rights are relative and not absolute. Swadling, for example, insists that:

> [d]espite what the layman might think, there is no concept of ownership in English law. The proof of that proposition lies in the fact that English law provides no form of protection to anyone we might describe as the 'owner' of goods greater than that provided to someone who simply finds them in the street … all who sue in respect of interferences with goods have to bring their claims within the ambit of certain torts, and the only thing which those torts protect is the right to possession.[87]

If the concept of ownership is inherently exclusive in the sense that it demands that, at any given time, there can only be one such person, then it is true to say that the common law, unlike the classical Roman law,[88] has no concept of *dominium*, but only of superior and inferior rights to things.[89]

One way of rescuing 'ownership' in a system of relative titles is, as McFarlane argues, simply to substitute the concept of *an* owner for *the* owner.[90] However, not everyone is convinced by this simple solution. Katz has argued that this non-exclusive notion of ownership is so thin as to amount to little more than a restatement, though in different terms, of the received wisdom that the common law only recognises possessors and not owners.[91] She argues that, '[b]y placing everyone on an equal footing to make decisions, it gives up on a core structural feature of ownership: the exclusivity of the position that owners occupy'.[92]

Importantly, while the common law does not recognise a *dominus*, such a person does, in effect, exist in English law. The textbook example of someone who is, for all intents and purposes, an owner at common law is a person who takes possession of a wild animal, or anything else that is *res nullius*. However, we need not confine ourselves to ownerless things in order to make this point. Whilst several people may concurrently hold rights of an identical content to the same object, someone will always hold the oldest right and that person is, for

[87] William Swadling, 'Unjust Delivery' in Andrew Burrows and Alan Rodger of Earlsferry (eds), *Mapping the Law: Essays in Memory of Peter Birks* (Oxford, Oxford University Press, 2006) 278, 281. For similar observations see ELG Tyler and Norman Palmer, *Crossley Vaines' Personal Property*, 5th edn (London, Butterworths, 1973) 281; Green and Randall (n 11) 80.

[88] Fox (n 82) 335.

[89] This idea is most often invoked in land law. See, eg, *Hunter v Canary Wharf Ltd* [1997] AC 655 (HL), 703 (Lord Hoffmann).

[90] McFarlane (n 4) 145.

[91] Larissa M Katz, 'The Concept of Ownership and the Relativity of Title' (2011) 2 *Jurisprudence* 191, 199.

[92] Ibid.

all practical purposes, its *owner*.[93] Contrary to Katz's suggestion, these several right-holders, though they have rights with an identical content, are not 'on an equal footing to make decisions'. One's decision-making authority can be definitive without also being exclusive. Although the person with the oldest right does not have the exclusive ability to make decisions about the use of some resource, her decisions are nevertheless definitive because, unlike those with more recently created rights, they bind *everyone*.

Just as importantly, the common law contains numerous rules that have the effect of transforming mere right-holders into owners, in the limited sense used above. As is discussed in Chapter 7, every 'good faith purchase' exception to the *nemo dat* principle ensures that vendors are owners as far as good faith purchasers are concerned. The law of adverse possession clears away titles that pre-date the limitation period, thus transforming someone with a weak title into an owner by operation of statute.[94] The doctrine of accession, discussed in Chapter 1, overcomes a potential 'anticommons' problem by extinguishing pre-existing rights to the sub-components of an object of property. That these common law doctrines are effective in limiting an otherwise troublesome sprawl of property rights is demonstrated by the fact that, in daily life, there is seldom any dispute about the identity of the owner of some thing in this limited, though extremely important, sense.

None of this is to challenge the substance of Swadling's position, which remains doctrinally correct and important to appreciate. Although, in the vast majority of cases, it will be perfectly possible to identify a person with the best right to some thing and to regard that person as its 'owner', it remains the case that, in a system of property in which titles are relative, it is simply unnecessary to do so. As between competing claimants, the only relevant question is, 'whose right is best?', and no one gets additional points for demonstrating that his is the best possible right.[95]

C. Does the Law Recognise a 'Possessory Right'?

The foregoing discussion was necessary in order to make the following simple, yet important, point. If the term 'possessory title' does no more than to indicate that the right in question is not the oldest right, then it does not describe a distinct sort of interest in an object of property. The content of a right is determined by what the correlative duty demands of those who owe it. If a 'possessory right' is to qualify as a distinct sort of *in rem* right, then it must be because it correlates to a

[93] To borrow Fox's terminology, whilst it may not be possible to have an 'absolute' title, it is still possible to have the 'best' title. Fox (n 82) 335–36.

[94] *Limitation of Actions Act 1958* (Vic) s 18; *Limitation Act 1969* (NSW) s 65; *Limitation Act 1980* (UK) s 17.

[95] This is why the common law is perfectly happy for an admitted squatter to maintain a claim for trespass. See *London Borough of Harrow v Qazi* [2003] UKHL 43; [2004] 1 AC 983, 1015 (Lord Millett).

duty that demands something other than non-interference. As security rights and servitudes demonstrate, the property right described in Chapter 1 is not the only sort of *in rem* right that one may have in respect of a tangible thing. Nevertheless, there is no distinct form of entitlement known as a 'possessory right' within the *numerus clausus* of property rights at common law.[96]

To describe possession as a form of legal interest in a chattel that embraces 'all proprietary interests in goods short of outright ownership'[97] is not to describe a distinct sort of property right, but is to recognise, de facto, that property rights in common law systems are relative. Though it might be argued that, when applied to squatters, finders or bailees,[98] the term 'possessory right' usefully indicates the lurking presence of a better title, its tendency to suggest that the right of a finder or a squatter is substantively different from that of an owner or 'paper title holder' means that it should nevertheless be avoided.

VI. Conclusion

The persistent confusion that surrounds possession is not attributable to any complexity inherent in the concept. Instead, it is the result of two basic errors. The first is the failure to heed Hohfeld's warning about the need to distinguish the jural concept of a right from the non-jural concept of a fact. The second is the tendency to draw a false distinction between 'ownership' and other, 'lesser', forms of property right. In a system in which property rights are relative and not absolute, priority of creation, though important in a dispute between any two right-holders, does not alter the content of the correlative duty.

As far as the formal architecture of property law is concerned, there is simply no need for possession to denote anything other than a fact that creates the sort of property right described in Chapter 1. To posit the existence of a 'possessory right' is to add more clutter to the conceptual landscape without adding to our picture of an owner as a gate-keeper.[99] On the contrary, the existence of such a right detracts from this picture in so far as it suggests that the existence of her right to determine who can come in is dependent upon her occupying the gatehouse at all times. The consequence of insisting on the existence of a possessory right is to tether the

[96] See also Douglas (n 7) 30–31.

[97] Bridge et al (n 17) 56 [2-038].

[98] While there is an unresolved debate about whether particular sorts of bailment have proprietary or merely contractual consequences, it is clear that, in so far as a bailee has a property right, it correlates to a simple duty of non-interference, enforceable through the normal property torts. On this debate compare, for example, Bridge (n 20) 41–43 with William Swadling, 'The Proprietary Effect of a Hire of Goods' in Norman Palmer and Ewan McKendrick (eds), *Interests in Goods*, 2nd edn (London, Lloyd's of London Press, 1998) 491.

[99] The 'gate' metaphor is common in property theory. See, eg, Penner (n 67) 74.

modern law to a period, long since passed, in which people could not conceive of owning something that they did not also possess.

The argument advanced thus far is that we can adequately explain the rudiments of property law without recourse to the notion of a 'possessory right'. Within property's formal architecture, the concept of possession need only describe an operative fact that creates original property rights. However, this does not put an end to the enquiry. If we conclude that possession is indeed a fact, we then need to consider the further question: what sort of factual relationships between people and things count as possession for the purposes of the law? An answer to this question is provided in the next chapter.

3

An Expressive Theory of Possession

I. Introduction

Chapters 1 and 2 provided a conceptually parsimonious description of the foundations of property. It was argued that possession in the law does not describe a distinctive sort of jural relation but an operative fact which, when proved by evidential facts, creates original property rights in things that are capable of being possessed. However, as was observed in the conclusion to the previous chapter, this tells us nothing about what sorts of relationships between people and things count as 'possession'.

The account offered thus far has proceeded on the preliminary basis that possession describes a fact about one's control over some thing. Building on theories developed by Hegel and Rose, the explanation offered below will depart from this commonly held view by emphasising possession's expressive function. It will be argued that if we are to understand the nature of possession then we must abandon the notion that its significance lies in the ability of the possessor to exercise physical mastery over the *res*. While it is undoubtedly true that physical control, or something approximating it, constitutes a core case of possession, the concept is best understood as referring to those acts that function as recognised and accepted signals about one's intention to stake a claim to some object of property.

II. What Counts as 'Possession'?

A. 'Social Facts'

Before expanding on the expressive theory, it is useful to note one final category in our taxonomy of facts. As was discussed in Chapter 2, Hohfeld drew an important distinction between facts that create jural relations and those that do not. He described the former as 'operative' and the latter as 'evidential'. His taxonomy thus concerns the *legal* significance of particular facts. Another important distinction, the significance of which is not confined to the role of facts in a legal system, is that between 'hard facts' and 'social facts'.

The difference between 'hard' and 'social' facts can be briefly stated. Hard facts are of the sort, 'water is composed of two hydrogen atoms bonded to one oxygen atom'. Social facts, by contrast, are of the sort, 'Sarah is dependable' or 'Robert is rude'. Social facts are not based on immutable laws or objective truths about the universe. Instead, they are constructs, albeit ones with important and generally accepted social meanings. To draw on Hart's analysis of legal concepts, social facts are, like conclusions of law, best understood as conclusions arrived at by the application of a particular body of rules to particular events.[1] That is, they are 'rule defined'.[2] The statement 'Robert is rude' is a conclusion based upon the application of generally accepted non-legal rules about the meaning of 'rudeness' to 'hard' or empirical facts about Robert's behaviour.

Though not peculiarly legal, many social facts play a significant role in legal systems. Certain criminal offences may, for example, require a court to determine whether the accused's conduct was 'insulting'.[3] Whether or not certain behaviour is 'insulting' is, as Endicott has observed, 'undoubtedly a fact. A *social* fact, no doubt, not a *juridical* fact. If "insulting" were used as a standard in a statute, we could decide whether [certain] behaviour was insulting without any reference to the law'.[4] The law is full of such questions of social fact. As noted in Chapter 2, the law of contract requires courts to determine whether an 'offer' has been made by the promisor and whether it has been 'accepted' by the promisee before it is satisfied that a contract has been created. Whether someone has possession of an object is also a question of social fact because it depends upon the application of particular social rules to hard and empirically verifiable facts about physical proximity, extent of contact, the nature of the object and so on.[5] Possession is, to adapt Hart's terminology, 'open-textured'[6] and will thus, on occasion, be subject to interpretive disagreement.

The inevitability of borderline cases does not, however, mean that possession is therefore a hopelessly vague or indeterminate concept. As Waldron has observed, 'we must not assume in advance that the imprecision or indeterminacy which frustrates the legal technician is fatal to the concept in every context in which it is deployed'.[7] For every marginal case, there are numerous cases in which the application of the concept is clear and decisive. That uncontroversial cases do not, for obvious reasons, make it into the pages of the law reports tends to obscure this basic truth.[8]

[1] Hart famously illustrated this concept by reference to a cricket umpire's statement 'He is out'. See HLA Hart, 'Definition and Theory in Jurisprudence' (1954) 70 *Law Quarterly Review* 37, 42, 53–54.

[2] AWB Simpson, 'The Analysis of Legal Concepts' (1964) 80 *Law Quarterly Review* 535, 543–44.

[3] *Brutus v Cozens* [1973] AC 854 (HL).

[4] Timothy AO Endicott, 'Questions of Law' (1998) 114 *Law Quarterly Review* 292, 311.

[5] For a similar observation see FH Lawson and Bernard Rudden, *The Law of Property*, 2nd edn (Oxford, Clarendon Press, 1982) 41.

[6] HLA Hart, *The Concept of Law*, 2nd edn (Oxford, Oxford University Press, 1994) 128.

[7] Jeremy Waldron, *The Right to Private Property* (Oxford, Oxford University Press, 1991) 31.

[8] See also Frederick F Schauer, *Thinking like a Lawyer: A New Introduction to Legal Reasoning* (Cambridge, Harvard University Press, 2009) 20–23.

B. Examples of Possession in the Law

With this in mind, it is useful to give a brief summary of the diverse sorts of factual relationships between people and things that have been held to amount to 'possession' for the purposes of the law.

Possession of real property does not require the exercise of complete physical control over every square metre of some parcel of land for the obvious reason that, particularly in the case of large tracts of land, this is impracticable if not impossible.[9] Instead, as Pollock wrote, '[a]cts of dominion over part of the thing in dispute may be evidence of de facto possession of the whole'.[10] This includes land's vertical dimension, recognised by the *ad coelum* rule.[11] As cases on adverse possession demonstrate, acts of enclosure such as fencing, though not always necessary,[12] are very often sufficient to establish possession of a parcel of land.[13]

Due to their size, location or the fact that they may be living creatures, many chattels are also difficult, if not impossible, to control. As McCarthy J noted in *Popov v Hayashi*, '[i]t is impossible to wrap one's arms around a whale, a fleeing fox or a sunken ship'.[14] Nevertheless, the law allows that it is possible to possess such things. A salvage team can be in possession of a ship wrecked in open water even though, because of its size and location, its members cannot exercise complete physical dominion over it.[15] To take another, and very famous, example, whilst a huntsman in hot pursuit of a fox will not be in possession of it, the law does not require actual bodily seizure. Possession is established by the infliction of a mortal wound.[16] Fish, on the other hand, are subject to a slightly different rule. They are not within the possession of a fisherman unless and until they are securely entrapped in his net. Thus, a fisherman cannot bring an action in trespass against a rival who deliberately startles a school of fish so that they take fright and escape his net.[17] In the case of whales, the question is more complex. As is discussed in greater detail below, the question of whether the captain of a whaling ship is in possession of, and thus has property in, a whale does not depend solely on determining which of the rival ships' harpoons first lodged in the whale. The question instead turns on the application of customary rules which differ from fishery to fishery.[18]

[9] *Powell v McFarlane* (1977) 38 P & CR 452 (Ch), 471 (Slade J) ('*Powell*').

[10] Frederick Pollock and Robert Samuel Wright, *An Essay on Possession in the Common Law* (Oxford, Clarendon Press, 1888) 31.

[11] *Bocardo SA v Star Energy UK Onshore Ltd* [2010] UKSC 35; [2011] 1 AC 380, 399 [31] (Lord Hope).

[12] *Wuta-Ofei v Danquah* (1961) 1 WLR 1238 (PC), 1243 (Lord Guest).

[13] *Buckinghamshire County Council v Moran* [1990] Ch 623 (CA), 641–42 (Slade LJ) ('*Buckinghamshire CC*'); *George Wimpey & Co v Sohn* [1967] Ch 487 (CA), 506–8 (Harman LJ), 511 (Russell LJ).

[14] *Popov v Hayashi* (2002) WL 31833731 (Ca Sup Ct), 5 ('*Popov*').

[15] *The Tubantia (No 2)* [1924] P 78, 90 (Sir Henry Duke).

[16] *Pierson v Post*, 3 Cai R 175 (NY Sup Ct, 1805), 177–78 (Tompkins J) ('*Pierson*'); *Churchward v Studdy* (1811) 104 ER 596, 597; 14 East 249, 251 (Lord Ellenborough CJ).

[17] *Young v Hichens* (1844) 115 ER 228, 230; 6 QB 606, 611 (Lord Denman CJ).

[18] See *Fennings v Lord Grenville* (1808) 127 ER 825, 827–28; 1 Taunt 241, 246–47 (Lord Mansfield CJ).

III. The Expressive Theory of Possession

A. Possession's Expressive Function

It is clear from the examples given above that the law does not actually demand that a possessor demonstrate complete control over the object in question in the sense that she is able to exclude third parties who might meddle with it. The orthodox conclusion drawn from this observation is that possession in the law means 'possession of that character of which the thing is capable'[19] and that this is, in turn, established by an 'appropriate degree of physical control'.[20] Sheehan has summarised the position in the following terms:

> [i]t is quite possible to be in actual possession of a thing without physically holding it in your hands. What is required is that there be factual control of it. When I come to work therefore I do not relinquish possession of my furniture at home. Nor do I have to physically hold my car in my hands; it's just too big. *The corpus possessionis therefore consists of the power to factually control to the exclusion of others. The degree of factual control required will depend on the nature of the asset in question.*[21]

The argument defended throughout this book is that the view expressed in the italicised portion of this statement, though widely held, fails to capture the nature of possession. While it is undoubtedly true that what counts as 'possession' does indeed depend upon the characteristics of the object in question, this has little to do with the demonstration of an 'appropriate degree of physical control' in the sense of the possessor's actual ability to exclude others. The significance of the physical element of possession lies instead in its expressive function. Certain acts qualify as 'possession' because, whether they amount to actual control, they send the recognised signal by which someone communicates his intention to claim a stake in some thing. Lest this point be misunderstood, this account does not argue that physical control is irrelevant. Rather, it argues that its relevance is confined to the clarity of the signal that such acts send to the relevant audience.

This distinction between possession as physical control and possession as an expressive act was articulated by Hegel, who argued that there are three ways of taking possession of some object. On his account, '[t]aking possession is partly the simple bodily grasp, partly the forming and partly the marking or designating of the object'.[22] The concept of 'bodily grasp' is the familiar notion of physical control, and was described by Hegel as 'corporeal possession'.[23] 'Forming', by contrast,

[19] *Lord Advocate v Young* [1887] 12 App Cas 544 (HL), 556 (Lord FitzGerald).

[20] *Powell* (n 9) 470 (Slade J) cited with approval in *JA Pye (Oxford) Ltd v Graham* [2002] UKHL 30; [2003] 1 AC 419, 436 (Lord Browne-Wilkinson) ('*Pye*').

[21] Duncan Sheehan, *The Principles of Personal Property Law*, 2nd edn (Oxford, Hart Publishing, 2017) 11. Emphasis added.

[22] GWF Hegel, *Philosophy of Right* (Kitchener, Batoche, 2001) 63 [54].

[23] Ibid, 64 [55].

is a reference to manufacture, discussed in Chapter 1. According to Hegel, '[t]he fashioning of a thing is the kind of active possession which is most adequate to the idea, because it unites the subjective and the objective'.[24]

Finally, and most significantly, Hegel described possession by 'marking'. Marking is '[t]he kind of possession, which is not literal but only representative of my will, is a mark or symbol, whose meaning is that it is I who have put my will into the object. Owing to the variety of objects used as signs, this kind of possession is very indefinite in its meaning'.[25] He explained that:

> [o]f all kinds of possession this by marking is the most complete, since the others have more or less the effect of a mark. When I seize or form an object, in each case the result is in the end a mark, indicating to others that I exclude them, and have set my will in the object. The conception of the mark is that the object stands not for what it is, but for what it signifies ... In that man acquires possession through the use of a sign, he exhibits his mastery over things.[26]

For present purposes, the significance of this passage is not that Hegel's 'marking' account provides a morally defensible justification for the acquisition of property rights. Instead, it is that it accurately describes the way in which possession works in the law. What is important about possession is not control per se, but the message that particular factual relationships between people and objects of property send to other members of a particular interpretive community.

The argument that possession is best understood as a signal or statement of intention has more recently been developed by Rose.[27] In her seminal paper, she made the important claim that:

> [p]ossession as the basis of property ownership ... seems to amount to something like yelling loudly enough to all who may be interested. The first to say, "This is mine," in a way that the public understands, gets the prize, and the law will help him keep it against someone else who says, "No, it is mine."'[28]

As Rose has emphasised in recent writings,[29] the alternative, and widely held, 'realist' definition of possession, according to which possession describes the actual ability of the possessor to exclude others, is premised on an unrealistic assumption about the power of, for instance, a homeowner to exclude others. Though a homeowner may erect fences and lock her doors, her actual ability to exclude trespassers ultimately depends on the proficiency of the local police force.

[24] Ibid, 65 [56].
[25] Ibid, 67 [58].
[26] Ibid.
[27] Carol M Rose, 'Possession as the Origin of Property' (1985) 52 *University of Chicago Law Review* 73, 77.
[28] Ibid, 81.
[29] Carol M Rose, 'The Law Is Nine-Tenths of Possession: An Adage Turned on Its Head' in Yun-chien Chang (ed), *Law and Economics of Possession* (Cambridge, Cambridge University Press, 2015) 40, 48.

Hegel's 'marking' account and Rose's signalling account not only provide a more plausible account of the reality of ownership, they also provide a better explanation of the law. As noted above, the law allows that individuals can possess things that are not susceptible to the slightest degree of physical control. Take, as an obvious example, the Kidman & Co cattle station in central Australia. At its largest, the station occupied an area of land in excess of 100,000 square kilometres, which made it very nearly the same size as England. If the legal concept of possession requires even a de minimis level of physical control, in the sense of an actual ability to exclude non-invitees, then, even allowing that possession is a 'social fact' with fuzzy boundaries, the Kidman & Co cattle station is not an object of property that is capable of being possessed. Though less starkly, the same argument can be made about whales and wrecked ships.

Yet, as far as the law is concerned, large tracts of land, whales and wrecked ships can be satisfactorily possessed. Contrary to the dominant understanding, this is not because the possessor has demonstrated an 'appropriate degree of physical control'. Control, in these circumstances, is an illusory concept. Rather, it is because, as Rose argues, certain factual relationships between people and things send the *appropriate sort of signal* to others. To put it another way, as far as property entitlements are concerned, the importance of a fence is not that it actually keeps people out, but that it sends a recognised signal about someone's claim to a piece of land and, in addition, communicates the territorial extent of that claim.[30] 'Even the most modest fence', as Rose writes, 'says pretty clearly, "This is *mine*"'.[31]

Significantly, this concept of possession implicitly rejects the commonly held view, discussed in Chapter 2, that there is a 'legal' and 'lay' conception of possession,[32] and that '[p]ossession means a different thing to lawyers than it does to everyone else'.[33] If, consistently with Rose's thesis, possession is a means of announcing to the relevant audience that 'this is mine', then that announcement would be of very limited utility if it were made in a language that only lawyers could comprehend. The significance of simple possessory acts such as enclosing a piece of land with a fence is that, whether it is effective in excluding would-be trespassers, the fence sends a signal that other people, whether legally trained or not, both comprehend and accept. If the argument defended throughout this book is correct, there is only one concept of possession and that concept describes factual relationships between persons and things that function as recognisable claims to them.[34]

[30] As Ellickson has noted, visual signals are, for this reason, preferable to non-visual cues. See Robert C Ellickson, 'The Inevitable Trend toward Universally Recognizable Signals of Property Claims: An Essay for Carol Rose' (2011) 19 *William & Mary Bill of Rights Journal* 1015, 1028–29.

[31] Carol M Rose, *Property and Persuasion: Essays on the History, Theory, and Rhetoric of Ownership* (Boulder, Westview Press, 1994) 1.

[32] See, eg, the remarks of Lord Reid in *Warner v Metropolitan Police Commissioner* [1969] 2 AC 256 (HL), 281.

[33] Sarah Green and John Randall, *The Tort of Conversion* (Oxford, Hart Publishing, 2009) 86.

[34] As Tay has noted, 'there is not a lay animal and a zoological animal, just as there is not a lay possession and a legal possession in the common law'. AES Tay, 'The Concept of Possession in the Common Law: Foundations for a New Approach' (1964) 4 *Melbourne University Law Review* 476, 492.

B. Possession's Mental Element

One of the most vexed issues in this area of the law concerns the role of intention in the concept of possession. As will be recalled from the summary of academic opinion given in Chapter 2, there is substantial disagreement on this question. On the one hand, McFarlane argues that:

> It is true to say that, to have physical control of a thing, B must be aware of its existence. Apart from that, however, such technical refinements of the core concept of physical control ... are misleading. In English law, the test is a simple one: B independently acquires a property right *if* and *only if* he takes physical control of a thing. There is no need for B to show he also had an intention, on his own behalf, to exclude others from that thing.[35]

On the other hand, Green and Randall argue that, 'it is the cognitive element of control which is of the greatest relevance to legal possession'.[36] Although always a feature of Roman law,[37] the question of whether the so-called *animus possidendi* of Roman law is indigenous to or was introduced into English law is a matter of academic debate.[38] Questions of provenance aside, it is clear that the modern common law requires that the physical element, or *corpus*, be accompanied by the relevant intention, or *animus*. Lord Browne-Wilkinson has authoritatively stated that:

> there are two elements necessary for legal possession: (1) a sufficient degree of physical custody and control ('factual possession'); (2) an intention to exercise such custody and control on one's own behalf and for one's own benefit ('intention to possess'). What is crucial is to understand that, without the requisite intention, in law there can be no possession.[39]

That the formal definition of possession should include a mental element is not surprising. As is discussed in Chapter 6, because possession describes a purposeful act, it would be absurd to suggest that one can possess an object in ignorance of its very existence. As Lord Parker CJ remarked, 'if something were slipped into your basket and you had not the vaguest notion it was there at all, you could not possibly be said to be in possession of it'.[40] Likewise, in *Merry v Green* it was held that there could be no transfer of possession of an object if its existence was unknown to both the vendor and purchaser.[41] The common law is not alone in holding this

[35] Ben McFarlane, *The Structure of Property Law* (Oxford, Hart Publishing, 2008) 155.

[36] Green and Randall (n 33) 86.

[37] Barry Nicholas, *An Introduction to Roman Law* (Oxford, Clarendon Press, 1976) 112–14.

[38] See Oliver Radley-Gardner, 'Civilized Squatting' (2005) 25 *Oxford Journal of Legal Studies* 727, 734–36, 747.

[39] *Pye* (n 20) at 435. See also *Parker v British Airways Board* [1982] QB 1004 (CA), 1019 (Eveleigh LJ) ('*Parker*'); Oliver Wendell Holmes, *The Common Law* (Boston, Little, Brown and Company, 1948) 216; Pollock and Wright (n 10) 13.

[40] *Lockyer v Gibb* [1967] 2 QB 243, 249. See also *Chairman, National Crime Authority v Flack* [1998] FCA 932; (1998) 86 FCR 16, 30 (Tamberlin J) ('*Flack*').

[41] *Merry v Green* (1841) 151 ER 916, 920; 7 M&W 623, 632 (Parke B). See also *Moffatt v Kazana* [1969] 2 QB 152, in which it was held that the purchaser of a house was not entitled to a biscuit tin containing almost £2,000 in cash that the vendor had stored in the chimney and subsequently forgotten about.

position. The Romans also recognised that possession of a vessel did not necessarily amount to possession of its contents.[42]

Importantly, the 'claim-staking' explanation defended in this book goes much further than this. On this account, intention is the *sine qua non* of possession because the very purpose of any act that amounts to possession is to send a recognised signal about one's *intention* to claim an object for oneself.

C. Distinguishing 'Possession' from 'Custody'

The discussion in Chapter 2 criticised the sprawling nomenclature that has become such an unfortunate feature of this area of the law. Although the expressive theory regards possession as a unitary concept, it does demand one semantic distinction; that between *possession* and *custody*. This distinction reflects the fact that not all observable relationships between people and things constitute possession because, however they may appear to third parties, not all are intended to send the sort of 'claim-staking' signal discussed above.

Imagine that A sees B admiring his particularly fine watch and asks if she would like to try it on. B accepts and places the watch over her wrist. In doing so, B has entered into a factual relationship with the watch that resembles, as near as possible, physical control. Nevertheless, B is not a *possessor* of the watch because she has no intention to claim it for herself. The distinction between acts of physical control that create rights and those that do not is familiar to the law. As was discussed in Chapter 2, acts of *corpus* that do not amount to possession are often described as 'mere possession', 'custody' or 'occupancy'. To reflect this important distinction, physical interactions between people and things undertaken without the requisite intention should be described as examples of 'custody'.

Although simple to appreciate, the distinction between possession and custody can be difficult to apply because it turns on the inference of a mental fact. To borrow Bowen LJ's famous quip, 'the state of a man's mind is as much a fact as the state of his digestion'.[43] However, unlike other sorts of fact, mental facts are difficult to prove because they can only ever be inferred 'second hand' from physical conduct.[44] As Lord Hope remarked, 'acts of the mind can be, and sometimes can only be, demonstrated by acts of the body'.[45] In the present context, that means inferring a fact about intention from a potentially equivocal relationship

[42] Theodor Mommsen, Paul Krueger and Alan Watson (eds), *The Digest of Justinian* (Philadelphia, University of Pennsylvania Press, 1985) vol IV, 41.2.30pr. See also JA Borkowski and Paul J du Plessis, *Borkowski's Textbook on Roman Law*, 3rd edn (Oxford, Oxford University Press, 2005) 164. At common law, it has been said that a person in possession of a receptacle is 'presumed' to be in possession of its contents. See *Grafstein v Holme* (1958) 12 DLR (2d) 722 (CA), 738 (LaBel JA).

[43] *Edgington v Fitzmaurice* (1885) 29 Ch D 459 (CA), 483.

[44] It is thus implausible for Green to suggest that '[t]he cognitive indicia of possession, are the easiest to demonstrate, regardless of the characteristics of the object in question': Sarah Green, 'To Have and to Hold? Conversion and Intangible Property' (2008) 71 *Modern Law Review* 114, 116.

[45] *Pye* (n 20) 446. See also *Tecbild v Chamberlain* (1969) 20 P & CR 633 (CA), 643 (Sachs LJ).

between a person and a thing. In some cases, general social knowledge will make it relatively easy for a third-party observer to distinguish between possession and custody. As Pollock observed of the master-servant rule:

> a servant's custody is often so manifestly exercised not on his own account but on his master's that it has no colour of apparent ownership. If we regard acts according to their apparent intent and effect, as measured by the common knowledge of mankind, we can hardly say that a groom exercising his master's horse is even in *de facto* possession of the horse. He is in appearance as much as in fact, in fact as much as in law, the master's instrument for exercising the master's power. There is no appearance of acting on his own behalf which could mislead a man of ordinary judgment.[46]

However, as the watch example demonstrates, this will not always be the case. It is undoubtedly true that if C, a third party, were apprised of the interaction between A and B, he would appreciate that B's legal interest in the watch is limited to a non-contractual licence. However, in the absence of this information, C may well draw a 'false positive' by wrongly concluding that, by her conduct, B is staking a claim to it.

That such false positives may occur is a reflection of both the inherent difficulty of proving mental states and the limitations of an allocative mechanism that relies on occasionally ambiguous physical acts. However, the presence of these errors is not, in itself, grounds to conclude that the possession rule is ineffective or inefficient. Although a system of registration, for instance, may eliminate these false positives, the question, as is discussed further in Chapter 7, is whether the costs of establishing, updating and checking a register are justified given the value of the asset in question, the frequency of transactions and the error rate generated by the possession rule. As others have also noted,[47] while possession may be a 'rough and ready' way of announcing an ownership claim, its corresponding advantage is that it is a cheap and quick means of verifying title in high-volume, low-value transactions. If C wishes to purchase the watch, the relevant question is whether its value warrants the costs of verifying the vendor's title. This is an empirical question that cannot be answered in the abstract.

D. Possession as a Vocabulary of Signals

The law frequently emphasises that whether some relationship between a person and a thing amounts to possession will depend upon the nature of the thing. The expressive theory is consistent with the notion that what constitutes possession may differ from object to object and population to population. However, what the

[46] Pollock and Wright (n 10) 18.

[47] Henry E Smith, 'The Elements of Possession' in Yun-chien Chang (ed), *Law and Economics of Possession* (Cambridge, Cambridge University Press, 2015) 65, 67–68; Thomas W Merrill, 'Property and the Right to Exclude II' (2014) 3 *Brigham-Kanner Property Rights Conference Journal* 1, 18.

expressive theory insists upon is that possession is not about exercising the greatest possible degree of control over some object but sending an intelligible signal. While in many cases it may be that the greater the control, the clearer the signal, this will not invariably be true. Possession is thus a sort of vocabulary and what constitutes possession in any given case is a question of social fact to be determined by the members of the relevant interpretive community.

Custom furnishes numerous instances of this. In his influential paper, 'Towards a Theory of Property Rights', Demsetz cites anthropological studies that describe the way in which native tribes in North America demarcated exclusive hunting zones by marking or 'blazing' their crests on particular trees.[48] Similarly, Sugden describes a custom in a Yorkshire fishing village which permitted the first person to arrive on the beach after a storm to gather as much driftwood as he wished without interference from subsequent arrivals. As long as the wood was gathered into piles and marked with two stones, that person was entitled to leave it in situ and return to collect it at a time of his choosing.[49] To take a more recent example, Rose and Epstein report on a wintertime parking custom in Chicago, according to which a resident who clears snow from a curb-side car park and then marks the space with a chair or other object is entitled to its exclusive use until the snow thaws.[50] One can think of other, analogous, customs. It is generally acknowledged, for example, that placing one's towel on the beach confers an entitlement to that area of sand for the duration of the day.[51] Likewise, the same sort of claim-staking custom applies to coats draped over the back of seats in cinemas or on busy trains.[52]

It goes without saying that these customs do not create a property right, of the sort discussed in Chapter 1, that is recognised by the positive law. By clearing the snow from the curb in front of her house, a resident does not acquire an estate in land that expires when the snow thaws. Someone who parks in a cleared space in defiance of the social convention will have reaped what he did not sow but will not have committed an actionable trespass. Likewise, the legal prohibition that prevents one cinema patron from evicting another from his seat is ultimately to be found in the law of wrongs against the person, not the law of property.[53] Nevertheless, these are clearly examples of the possession norm in action and, importantly, they demonstrate that physical control is not required in order to send a recognised and respected signal about a claim to some tangible thing. Purely symbolic acts,

[48] Harold Demsetz, 'Toward a Theory of Property Rights' (1967) 57 *The American Economic Review* 347, 352.

[49] Robert Sugden, 'Spontaneous Order' (1989) 3 *Journal of Economic Perspectives* 85, 85.

[50] Rose, 'Origin of Property' (n 27) 81; Richard A Epstein, 'The Allocation of the Commons: Parking on Public Roads' (2002) 31 *Journal of Legal Studies* S515, S528–33.

[51] This example also appears in Epstein ibid n 50, S527–28.

[52] See also Thomas Merrill, 'Ownership and Possession' in Yun-chien Chang (ed), *Law and Economics of Possession* (Cambridge, Cambridge University Press, 2015) 9, 13. As Harris notes, theatre seats are somewhat of a 'hallowed example', having been discussed by Cicero and Seneca: JW Harris, *Property and Justice* (Oxford, Clarendon Press, 1996) 214–15.

[53] See also Harris, ibid n 52, 214.

such as placing one's coat on the back of a cinema seat during a trip to the snack bar, can and do suffice. Possession is not a conceptual monolith but a set of signals that, being sensitive to subject matter and context, develop by a process of creative analogy from the core case of physical control.

Although the biological evidence, briefly discussed in Chapter 4, suggests that an appreciation of the significance of possession might, at least to some degree, be hard-wired, these examples demonstrate that what counts as 'staking a claim' to some thing is a form of cultural knowledge that is learned by exposure and imitation.[54] However the relevant knowledge is acquired, the important point is that questions of possession seldom turn on the sole criterion of physical control.

IV. Limiting the Vocabulary of Possession

A. Too Many Signals?

The benefit of uncoupling possession from the cruder and larger illusory concept of physical control is that it allows a theory of possession to explain how and why purely symbolic acts, such as placing a coat on a seat, constitute valid property claims. However, uncoupling 'possession' from 'control' does raise a potential problem. That is, if possession is not moored to an observable act of physical control, or its closest approximation, what ensures that possession remains a sort of universal language comprehensible to all? If what constitutes possession is to be determined on an audience-by-audience basis and there are a huge number of potential audiences, what prevents the *law* of property from fragmenting into a series of *laws* of property intelligible only to the particular in-group to which they apply? To answer this question, it is useful to examine the ways in which small groups or, in the language of this book, 'small audiences', tailor basic property rules to better suit their particular circumstances.

B. Rules for Small Groups

Ellickson has advanced the argument that 'close-knit' groups will, if left to their own devices, develop an efficient set of extra-legal property norms.[55] On his account, a rule or norm is welfare-maximising when it minimises the sum of deadweight losses and transaction costs.[56] Ellickson supports his thesis by reference to

[54] See also Merrill, 'Ownership and Possession' (n 52) 27–28.

[55] Robert C Ellickson, 'A Hypothesis of Wealth-Maximizing Norms: Evidence from the Whaling Industry' (1989) 5 *Journal of Law, Economics & Organization* 83; Robert C Ellickson, *Order without Law: How Neighbors Settle Disputes* (Cambridge MA, Harvard University Press, 1994) chs 10–11.

[56] Ellickson, 'A Hypothesis of Wealth-Maximizing Norms', ibid, 87.

rules developed by whalers operating in different fisheries during the eighteenth and nineteenth centuries.

What is significant about Ellickson's account is his description of the way in which the possession rule was modified by whalers in response to the peculiar characteristics of individual fisheries. British whalers operating in the Greenland fishery adopted the 'fast-fish, loose-fish' rule, which provided that property in a whale, whether dead or alive, was awarded to the first ship to harpoon it. However, the right only persisted for as long as the whale remained tethered to the ship that fired the harpoon. If the whale broke free then it, or its carcass, became *res nullius* and thus fair game for other ships.[57]

The 'fast-fish, loose-fish' rule has the virtue of simplicity in its application. However, because it allows rival ships to lay claim to a dead or wounded whale without participating in the most difficult and dangerous part of the hunt, it also has the potential to encourage free-riding. As Ellickson explains, the 'fast-fish, loose-fish' rule was, in fact, well adapted to the conditions of the Greenland fishery because the Right Whale, the species of whale primarily hunted within it, is relatively docile and unlikely to break free from the ship once harpooned. Consequently, the first ship to successfully land a harpoon was usually rewarded with the prize.[58] Because of the Right Whale's temperament, whalers within the Greenland fishery were able to employ a low-cost, 'bright-line' allocative rule without the risk of incurring the deadweight losses resulting from free-riding.

What about a fishery in which the principal whale species is aggressive and likely to break free of the boat that landed the first harpoon? According to Ellickson's theory, we would expect to see a bright-line rule replaced by one which, though more complicated to apply, obviates the risk of free-riding by removing the requirement that the whale remain tethered to the ship. According to Ellickson, this is precisely what happened. In fisheries where the faster and more aggressive Sperm Whale predominated, whalers employed the 'iron-holds-the-whale' rule, which provided that the first ship to lodge a harpoon in a whale acquired a property right which persisted even if the whale broke free. However, to place some limit on that entitlement, custom required that the ship from which the harpoon was launched remain in 'fresh pursuit'.[59] Although, due to the fresh pursuit requirement, the 'iron-holds-the-whale' rule was not as simple as the 'fast-fish, loose-fish' rule, it reduced the potential for free-riding while also providing sufficient incentive for others to pursue whales that had managed to escape the clutches of the original ship.[60]

Ellickson also discusses a third rule, the so-called 'waif holds the whale' rule that applied to Pacific fisheries. This permitted whalers to plant a flag, known as a 'waif', into the carcass of a dead or mortally wounded whale as a means publicising their claim.[61] By foregoing the tethering requirement, it allowed whalers to maximise

[57] Ibid, 89.
[58] Ibid, 89–90.
[59] Ibid, 90–91.
[60] Ibid, 92.
[61] Ibid, 91.

their catch, particularly of Sperm Whales, which typically swim in large schools.[62] Unlike the rules discussed above, the 'waif holds the whale' rule required neither physical control nor fresh pursuit. This rule was thus, in all material respects, identical to draping one's coat over a cinema seat.

One of the most significant features of Ellickson's account of bottom-up whaling rules is his discussion of the concept of possession. He writes that:

> [a]n easily administered rule would be one that made the possession of a whale carcass normatively decisive. According to this rule, if Ship *A* had a wounded or dead whale on a line, Ship *B* would be entitled to attach a stronger line and pull the whale away. A possession-decides rule of this sort would threaten severe deadweight losses, however, because it would encourage a ship to sit back like a vulture and freeload on others' efforts in the early stages of the hunt. Whalers never used this norm.[63]

Ellickson is here using possession in the realist sense of an actual ability to exclude others. For Ellickson, 'possession' appears to require something approximating 'carcass on the ship'. This usage is inconsistent with the account being advanced in this book. According to the expressive theory, planting a waif in the whale carcass, though a purely symbolic act, in fact constituted a sufficient act of possession in the fisheries in which that rule prevailed. Contrary to Ellickson's claim in the passage above, the possession rule was, in fact, 'normatively decisive' in all the cases that he describes. It is simply that what counted as possession was not uniform across all fisheries.[64]

The wealth-maximisation calculus that Ellickson describes requires individual communities to grapple with the tension between rules that are intelligible and simple to administer, and thus impose minimal costs, and those that are complex and difficult to administer, but ensure that any individual's share in the spoils is proportionate to her contribution to their creation.[65] The optimal compromise between these competing considerations will depend upon material features of the environment in which the rule is to apply. The argument made here is that this trade-off can be optimised, at least in part, by altering what acts count as possession.

In fisheries in which the 'iron-holds-the-whale' rule applied, possession was established by successfully lodging a harpoon in a whale. Where the 'waif-holds-the-whale' rule applied, possession was established by the act of planting a flag in the whale. The form of entitlement created by these acts of possession was not identical to the generic property right described in Chapter 1. Unlike that right, the duty that the other whalers owed to the right-holder was either dependent upon some ongoing act, such as fresh pursuit, or only survived for as long as was

[62] Ibid.

[63] Ibid, 87.

[64] For a similar observation see Merrill, 'Property and the Right to Exclude' (n 47) 18.

[65] Ellickson, 'A Hypothesis of Wealth-Maximizing Norms' (n 55) 87; Ellickson, *Order without Law* (n 55) 172–74.

reasonably required to collect the dead or wounded whale. Nevertheless, these two rules can be usefully contrasted with the 'fast-fish, loose-fish' rule, which provided that a right of non-interference only persisted as long as the whale was tethered to the ship from which the harpoon was successfully launched. This rule did not create a true property right because the right only persisted as long as the whaler maintained something approximating physical control over the whale. To use the nomenclature introduced in Chapter 2, such a right does not have the quality of 'disaggregation'. Instead, it more closely resembles one's right, protected by torts that prevent interferences with the person, that a stranger not physically wrest some chattel from my grasp.[66] As Ellickson noted, the relatively paltry protection offered by this rule is explained by the fact that it was unlikely that a Right Whale would escape once harpooned.

Ellickson's analysis of whaling industry norms is illuminating because it demonstrates that, although possession is a unitary concept, the acts that count as possession can and do change depending on the features of the environment in which the norm must operate and the knowledge of the audience to whom the claim-staking signal is sent. This, however, raises a further, and important, question: what prevents the possession rule from devolving into an ever-more specialised series of 'dialects' that are only intelligible to those who have been initiated into the norms of a particular group?

C. The Cost of Communication

Ellickson stresses that his welfare-maximising theory only applies to the sorts of small populations that he describes as 'close-knit' groups.[67] He is agnostic about its application to larger groups because the emergence of bottom-up cooperative norms is dependent upon the existence of a 'social network whose members have credible and reciprocal prospects for the application of power against one another and a good supply of information on past and present internal events'.[68]

This reasoning is based on the insights of game theorists who have demonstrated that a necessary precondition for the emergence of cooperation in situations that share the structure of the Prisoners' Dilemma is that participants must interact in

[66] Some commentators have described these sorts of rights as 'superstructural' or 'background' rights. See, for example Arianna Pretto-Sakmann, *Boundaries of Personal Property Law: Shares and Sub-Shares* (Oxford, Hart Publishing, 2005) 98–99; McFarlane (n 35) 133–34. One presumes that, where the 'fast fish, loose fish' rule applied, whalers did acquire a fully-fledged property right if they managed to return to port with their quarry secured to the ship.

[67] Ellickson, *Order without Law* (n 55) 177.

[68] Ibid, 181. The existence of relatively small, stable communities is often regarded as a prerequisite for the emergence of efficient endogenous norms governing resource use and allocation. See, for example, Elinor Ostrom, *Governing the Commons: The Evolution of Institutions for Collective Action* (Cambridge, Cambridge University Press, 1990) 176–77.

the knowledge that they will meet again in the future.[69] This knowledge gives each participant a reason to hope that cooperation will be met with cooperation and a fear that defection will be met with retaliation. This may well explain why only small groups can manipulate their basic property rules in this way. However, it does not, nor was it intended to, explain what prevents a sort of systemic balkanisation in which every in-group develops a possessory 'dialect' which, though suitable to its particular needs, is incomprehensible to non-members. The answer to this question lies in the costs of certain types of communication.

To understand why this is, it is useful to recapitulate an important element of the expressive theory of possession. The expressive theory does not deny that effective physical control, or something approximating it, constitutes a paradigm case of possession. Its claim is instead that possession, like all rule-defined 'social facts', has a clear core, based on something like effective control, which shades into an ever-more diffuse penumbra. The outer boundaries of the concept expand because, over time, non-core cases are drawn into the core by a process of analogy. So, for example, everyone would accept that erecting a razor-wire fence or digging a moat around a plot of land is a clear case of possession. Likewise, everyone would accept that erecting a simple chicken-wire fence also constitutes a clear case of possession despite the fact that, unlike razor wire or a moat, chicken wire does not actually prevent acts of trespass. Once we realise that erecting a chicken-wire fence is a largely symbolic act, it is only a small step to appreciate that purely symbolic markers, such as a winter coat left on a cinema seat, can constitute acts of possession. Importantly, however, although we can discern the existence of a golden thread that connects castle moats with winter coats, it should not be assumed that the move from the former to the latter is a costless exercise.

As will be recalled from Chapter 1, the formal architecture of property is, in large part, shaped by the need to minimise information costs. Smith, in particular, has stressed that there is an inevitable trade-off between the intensiveness of a message and its extensiveness.[70] One can communicate a complex message to a small audience. However, if one wants to reach a very broad audience, one's message must be simpler. Rights that correlate to *in rem* duties must deliver a simple message, which is, for the most part, to 'keep off'. This insight about the trade-off between intensiveness and extensiveness is not limited to the content of a property right. It applies equally to the sort of acts that constitute a property claim.

[69] The Prisoner's Dilemma is a two person, non-zero-sum game that famously highlights a paradox of human rationality. Although mutual 'cooperation' represents a better outcome than mutual 'defection', the payoff structure of the game is such that each player will nevertheless choose to defect. In game-theoretic terms, the choice to defect is 'strictly dominant'. However, in a famous study, Axelrod demonstrated that cooperation can emerge spontaneously between self-interested players in an indefinitely repeated game if each gives the other reason to believe that present cooperation will be rewarded with future cooperation. See Robert M Axelrod, *The Evolution of Cooperation* (New York, Basic Books, 1984).

[70] Henry E Smith, 'The Language of Property: Form, Context, and Audience' (2003) 55 *Stanford Law Review* 1105, 1125.

This is best illustrated by reference to what is perhaps the most famous possession case in any common law jurisdiction, *Pierson v Post*.[71]

Pierson concerned a dispute over a dead fox. Post, who was riding to hounds, was in pursuit of the fox. However, before he could capture it Pierson, an interloper intent on disrupting the hunt, killed it and carried it off.[72] The question for the court was whether Pierson had, by killing and removing the fox, breached a duty that he owed to Post. In order to answer this question, the Court was faced with the anterior question of whether Post, by virtue of being in hot pursuit, had acquired a property right in the fox. In the language of this book, was the act of pursuing the fox a recognised act of possession?

The enduring interest that legal scholars have shown in *Pierson* is not attributable to its outcome but to the divergence between the majority and dissenting opinions. The majority held that, although actual bodily seizure was not required, hot pursuit was insufficient. At a minimum, possession required mortal wounding. Tompkins J, delivering the opinion of the majority, wrote that:

> actual bodily seizure is not indispensable to acquire a right to, or possession of, wild beasts; but that, on the contrary, the mortal wounding of such beasts, by one not abandoning his pursuit, may, with the utmost propriety, be deemed possession of him; since thereby the pursuer manifests an unequivocal intention of appropriating the animal to his individual use, has deprived him of his natural liberty, and brought him within his certain control.[73]

The majority argued that the test of mortal wounding was necessary:

> for the sake of certainty, and preserving peace and order in society. If the first seeing, starting or pursuing such animals, without having so wounded, circumvented or ensnared them, so as to deprive them of their natural liberty, and subject them to the control of their pursuer, should afford the basis of actions against others for intercepting and killing them, it would prove a fertile source of quarrels and litigation.[74]

Livingston J, in dissent, argued that this 'knotty point'[75] ought not to have come before the Court, but should instead have been 'submitted to the arbitration of sportsmen'.[76] In other words, it should have been a matter determined by in-group norms peculiar to those who 'ride to hounds'. Because the dispute was not resolved by an appeal to local custom, it was left to the Court to determine what particular act constituted possession in the circumstances. Appropriately, in light of the

[71] *Pierson* (n 16).

[72] For an illuminating historical account of the case see Bethany R Berger, 'It's Not about the Fox: The Untold History of Pierson v Post' (2005) 55 *Duke Law Journal* 1089.

[73] *Pierson* (n 16) 178.

[74] Ibid, 179.

[75] Ibid, 180.

[76] Ibid. However, given that Pierson was a 'saucy intruder' whose aim was to disrupt the hunt, it is not clear why the dispute should have been determined by the 'in-house' rules of fox hunting. As Berger has demonstrated, neither party cared about the fox nor its pelt. The legal action was the culmination of a long-standing feud between two local families over the use of the commons. See Berger (n 72) 1126–33.

foregoing discussion of whaling rules, Livingston J was concerned that a requirement of actual seizure would encourage free riding and thus reduce the incentive to eradicate an animal that was considered vermin. In a memorably florid phrase, his Honour asked rhetorically:

> [b]ut who would keep a pack of hounds; or what gentleman, at the sound of the horn, and at peep of day, would mount his steed, and … pursue the windings of this wily quadruped, if, just as night came on, and his stratagems and strength were nearly exhausted, a saucy intruder, who had not shared in the honors or labors of the chase, were permitted to come in at the death, and bear away in triumph the object of pursuit?[77]

Livingston J thus held that it is possible to acquire a property right in a wild animal 'without bodily touch … provided the pursuer be within reach, or have a reasonable prospect … of taking what he has thus discovered'.[78] This test was satisfied on the uncontested facts of the case.

Rose has given an extremely influential account of *Pierson*. On her account, *Pierson* should be understood as a case in which the majority and minority held differing opinions about which particular group constituted the relevant audience for the relevant claim-staking act. In contrast to the majority, who regarded the relevant audience as people generally, Livingston J believed that it was sufficient if the import of the act was understood by those hunt foxes on horseback.[79] As this audience was small, the act by which possession is established need not have been universally intelligible.[80] Rose's audience-based explanation of the dissenting judgment in *Pierson* thus complements Ellickson's analysis of whaling rules.

This does not, of course, tell us which approach is more desirable. According to Smith, the answer is that we should prefer the act whose meaning and import is comprehensible to the widest possible audience. He writes that:

> [t]he choice of whose symbols count implicates information intensiveness and the nature of the audience. One way to frame the question is to note that a rule that control is required for possession is appropriate for a wide audience and for a wide range of cases. It can apply to many resources without relying much on detailed information about those resources; and, because of its lack of detail, the rule is correspondingly easy to communicate to the world. These two reasons – lack of detail and ease of broadcasting – are related in the sense that having one general norm rather than many specific ones reduces what someone who interprets the acts of possession needs to know.[81]

In other words, moving from core to penumbral cases of possession requires that we assume more and more background knowledge on the part of the audience.

[77] *Pierson* (n 16) 180–81.

[78] Ibid, 182.

[79] Rose, 'Origin of Property' (n 27) 82, 85. According to Epstein, fox hunters in the region did, in fact, follow the 'hot pursuit' rule: Richard A Epstein, 'Possession as the Root of Title' (1979) 13 *Georgia Law Review* 1221, 1231.

[80] Rose, ibid at 85. See also Smith, 'The Language of Property' (n 70) 1117–18.

[81] Smith, ibid, 1118.

However, if, as is very often the case, we want to make a general claim to a large and diffuse audience, background knowledge is something that we cannot assume. Smith writes that:

> [p]ossession, however, relates to how we define objects for purposes of ownership, which involves the widest set of anonymous interactions among the most heterogeneous audience that the law addresses. What is needed is a determinate rule that will not lead to multiple interpretations, even by those without detailed background knowledge. The occupancy or certain-control test does achieve these goals, as long as the certain control is apparent to the relevant audience, which, in the case of possession, is prototypically the entire world.[82]

Smith's argument is not that property claims are limited to acts by which the putative right-holder demonstrates physical control over the *res*. It is instead that, because basic property claims are very often made to large and heterogeneous audiences, the acts or symbols that are used to communicate that claim cannot be specialised in the sense that they demand a high degree of background knowledge.[83]

It follows from this that we would expect to see the emergence of a standardised set of claim-staking acts or symbols that are universally intelligible. Indeed, this very claim has been made by Ellickson, who argues that 'humans have been developing, over the past several millennia, a *universal sign language* (i.e. a set of nonverbal visual clues) for asserting claims to tangible property',[84] and that this tendency towards convergence is only being accelerated by the forces of globalisation.[85] For present purposes, the importance of Smith's and Ellickson's arguments is that, while there is no need to confine the concept of possession to acts of obvious physical control, the imperative that one's claim-staking signal be comprehended by a large and potentially heterogeneous audience will naturally limit the size of the 'vocabulary' of possession.

D. A Dialogue, Not a Monologue

The essence of the expressive theory is that acts of 'possession' are those acts, or symbols, which have the effect of signalling one's intention to stake a claim to some tangible thing. A necessary condition for any symbol or act to count as 'possession' is thus that it be understood by the relevant audience. As Rose has recently written, 'property begins in a social context. A manifestation to inform the world means that there is, in fact, an audience out there and the audience has to "get it"'.[86]

[82] Ibid, 1119.

[83] See also Henry E Smith, 'Community and Custom in Property' (2009) 10 *Theoretical Inquiries in Law* 5, 24–25.

[84] Ellickson, 'The Inevitable Trend' (n 30) 1025.

[85] Ibid, 1030–33.

[86] Carol M Rose, 'Introduction: Property and Language, or, the Ghost of the Fifth Panel' (2006) 18 *Yale Journal of Law and the Humanities* 1, 6.

A second question, but one that receives less attention in the literature, is whether the audience's comprehension of the claim is not only a necessary but also a sufficient condition. The argument made here is that it is not. Consider, once again, the decision in *Pierson*. Rose summarised the import of the case in the following terms:

> the court's majority, citing much venerable authority, decided that the fox went to the shooter. Why? Because by shooting the fox (or mortally wounding it) the shooter "manifests an unequivocal intention" to take the animal and remove it from its wild and free former life. Mere pursuit was not enough; it did not give a clear enough "manifestation" to the world and would lead to "quarrels and litigation" among claimants.[87]

As a summary of the majority's reasoning, this is doubtless correct. As noted above, Tompkins J held that, unlike mere pursuit, someone who mortally wounds an animal 'manifests an unequivocal intention of appropriating the animal to his individual use, has deprived him of his natural liberty, and brought him within his certain control'.[88] However, as a description of the actual dispute, it is inadequate. *Pierson* was not a case in which conflict over a resource was caused by one party's failure to comprehend the significance of the other party's act. As the head note to the case makes clear, Pierson knew that Post was in pursuit of the fox. This is why he was described as a 'saucy intruder'.[89] Rather, *Pierson* was fundamentally a case about one party's failure to accept the legitimacy of the other's claim-staking act. Irrespective of the prevailing custom amongst those who hunted foxes, Pierson simply did not accept that Post's unilateral act of pursuing the fox placed him under a non-consensual duty not to interfere with it.

Pierson thus demonstrates that possession is a bilateral rather than a unilateral phenomenon. It is not sufficient that the audience merely understands that, through his conduct, some individual is announcing his claim to some thing. For that property claim to be accepted, those audience members must also agree that he is announcing his claim in the prescribed manner. Rose's argument that possession 'seems to amount to something like yelling loudly enough to all who may be interested',[90] highlights this very point. As a matter of common experience, it is clear that expressing, however loudly and unambiguously, one's intention to claim an object is, without more, seldom determinative. As anyone who has observed the frenzied behaviour of shoppers at the annual sales will appreciate, if one wishes to claim a particular item, mere communication of that intention, however clear, is insufficient. One only secures one's claim by what Smith might describe as the 'clear act' of getting there first.

While this observation does not purport to explain why it is that, irrespective of their clarity, some acts are regarded as amounting to possession and others are

[87] Ibid, 5.

[88] *Pierson* (n 16) 178.

[89] Ibid, 181 (Livingston J). Once again, this underlines the fact that *Pierson* was not a dispute *between* fox hunters.

[90] Rose, 'Origin of Property' (n 27) 81.

not, the important point is that the particular act must be both comprehended *and* accepted by the relevant audience as a legitimate way in which to stake a claim to a particular thing. Whether some gesture or earmark counts as possession ultimately depends on the empirically verifiable fact of whether others respect the claim it purports to make.

V. Do Courts Apply the Expressive Theory?

A. Deficiencies in the Orthodox Conception

Canonical statements about the nature of possession in the law, such as that made by Lord Browne-Wilkinson in *Pye*, emphasise that possession is a composite concept consisting of a fact about a sufficient degree of physical control, called 'factual possession' and a second fact about the putative possessor's intention, described as an 'intention to possess'.[91] The argument made here is not that such formulations are hopelessly wrong, but instead that they fail to capture the true significance of those relations between people and objects of property that count as possession.

According to the expressive theory, the significance of those acts that we call 'possession' is that they send a claim-staking signal that is both recognised and accepted. This has several important implications. First, contrary to formulations that stress the need for a sufficient or 'appropriate degree of physical control',[92] the significance of the physical act does not depend on control per se. While it may be that, following Smith's analysis of the costs of communication, a higher degree of control sends a clearer signal to more people, it remains the case that the significance of particular physical acts is not that they confer actual control, but that they manifest the possessor's intention in the recognised way.

This leads to a second significant implication concerning the relationship between the elements of 'factual possession' and 'intention to possess'. Although courts acknowledge that, '[i]n general, intent has to be inferred from the acts themselves',[93] leading accounts of possession invariably present these two concepts as discrete elements. To once again borrow from *Pye*, Lord Browne-Wilkinson stated that:

> there has always, both in Roman law and common law, been a requirement to show an intention to possess in addition to objective acts of physical possession. Such intention

[91] This definition of possession was not intended to be specific to claims of adverse possession. According to Lord Browne-Wilkinson, the relevant question to be answered was, 'what … constitutes "possession" in the ordinary sense of the word?': *Pye* (n 20) 435 [39].

[92] *Powell* (n 9) 470 (Slade J); *Buckinghamshire CC* (n 13) 641 (Slade LJ); *Pye* (n 20) 436 [41] (Lord Browne-Wilkinson).

[93] *Tecbild Ltd v Chamberlain* (1969) 20 P & CR 633, 643 (Sachs LJ).

> may be, and frequently is, deduced from the physical acts themselves. But there is no doubt in my judgment that there are two separate elements in legal possession.[94]

Contrary to such orthodox formulations, the expressive theory insists that there is no sharp divide between 'factual possession' and 'intention' to possess. Rather, the former represents the particular, accepted, way in which the latter is made manifest to the relevant audience. In other words, the physical conduct is the *only* evidence from which we can infer the existence of the relevant intention.[95] Courts should not ask one question about the physical act and a second, discrete, question about the actor's intention. The question is, instead, whether the requisite intention is manifested through acts that are, within the relevant community, accepted ways of claiming a right to some object of property.

B. The Expressive Theory in Action?

The expressive theory described in this chapter thus departs from the formal definitions of possession set down in the case law. However, this does not mean that courts fail to appreciate that acts amounting to possession are expressive in nature. Take the decision in *Pye* itself. Pye was the 'paper title' owner of valuable undeveloped land in Berkshire. While waiting for planning permission, Pye granted Graham, the owner of an adjoining farm, a grazing licence over the vacant land. After it expired, Graham sought a renewal of the licence, but Pye refused. Despite this, Graham continued to use and maintain the land as if it were part of his farm.[96] Pye subsequently sought an order for possession of the land but Graham resisted the application, arguing that, as he had been in adverse possession for 12 years, Pye's title had been extinguished by operation of statute. The House of Lords unanimously agreed.

Lord Browne-Wilkinson, who delivered the leading speech, highlighted that the land was enclosed and that the Grahams held the key to the gate that gave access to the public highway.[97] This led his Lordship to conclude that, '[t]he Grahams were in occupation of the land which was within their exclusive physical control. The paper owner, Pye, was physically excluded from the land by the hedges and the lack of any key to the road gate'.[98] At first blush, Lord Brown-Wilkinson's speech appears to affirm what Rose described as the 'realist' understanding of possession that stresses physical control.

However, this observation is subject to two important qualifications. First, his Lordship did not actually believe that the hedges and locked gate did anything

[94] *Pye* (n 20) 435–36 [40].

[95] One may wonder how else one might infer the existence of this mental fact, particularly given that, as Slade J noted, subsequent statements about one's subjective intention will almost certainly be self-serving and thus of no probative value: *Powell* (n 9), 476.

[96] *Pye* (n 20) 443 [58].

[97] Ibid, 427 [8].

[98] Ibid, 436 [41].

other than block vehicular access. As he noted on several occasions, the disputed land remained accessible by foot from the public highway.[99] Secondly, and more importantly, it is clear that what was most significant in the circumstances was not the Grahams' possession of the key, but their extensive use of the disputed land. After the expiration of the grazing agreement:

> the Grahams did not vacate the disputed land … They spread dung on the land, harrowed it and rolled it. They overwintered dry cattle and yearlings in a shed on the land … the Grahams repeatedly did things on the disputed land which they would have had no right to do under the old grazing agreement even if it had still been in force. The objective facts demonstrated that the Grahams made such use of the disputed land as they wished irrespective of whether it fell within the terms of any hypothetical grazing agreement.[100]

Lord Browne-Wilkinson concluded that, '[f]or all practical purposes the Grahams used the land as their own';[101] they were behaving *as if they were owners*.

It is true that, prior to the expiration of the limitation period, the Grahams were prepared to pay for a grazing licence and, in its absence, took the risk that, had Pye sought an order for possession, their investment in the land would have been lost.[102] Nevertheless, the sum total of their behaviour over the course of several years sent unmistakable claim-staking signals to all who cared to see. That it had the desired effect is proved by the evidence that many people simply believed that the Grahams owned the disputed land.[103] That they could not, in fact, effectively 'control' access to the land was of no importance. What was important was that, as confirmed by the evidence of the neighbours, they had staked their claim in a way that others both understood and respected.

The decision of the Victorian Court of Appeal in *Whittlesea City Council v Abbatangelo*[104] is equally illuminating. In *Abbatangelo*, the plaintiff successfully claimed title by adverse possession over vacant land owned by the defendant council. As with all modern adverse possession cases, the Victorian Court of Appeal commenced its judgment by reciting the principles enunciated in the classic decision of Slade J in *Powell v McFarlane*. In particular, the Court stated that possession in the law requires both 'factual possession' and an 'intention to possess' and that the former 'requires a sufficient degree of physical custody and control'.[105]

Though much of both the trial and appeal was consumed by addressing conflicting submissions about who was responsible for the construction and maintenance

[99] Ibid, 428 [10], 444 at [61].
[100] Ibid, 443 [58] (Lord Browne-Wilkinson).
[101] Ibid, 444 [61].
[102] Ibid, 429 [17] (Lord Browne-Wilkinson). Importantly, a willingness to pay does not negate the relevant intention to possess: 438 at [46] (Lord Browne-Wilkinson).
[103] Ibid, 429–30 [19]. To this might be added the testimony of an experience land surveyor, who gave evidence that he could not think of anything that an owner-occupier might have done to or with the land that the Grahams had not done.
[104] *Whittlesea City Council v Abbatangelo* [2009] VSCA 188; (2009) 259 ALR 56 ('*Abbatangelo*').
[105] Ibid, 60 [6] (the Court).

of the fences,[106] it was significant that, as in *Pye*, much of the enquiry focused on the claimant's extensive use of the disputed land.[107] Not only did the family allow their livestock onto the disputed land, they also maintained it and used it for recreational activities and social gatherings, such as barbeques and childrens' birthday parties. As was the case with the Grahams in *Pye*, the claimant and her family simply behaved as if the land was theirs.[108] Indeed, as the uncontested evidence of five neighbours demonstrated, the belief that the land in fact belonged to the claimant and her family was widely held in the local community.[109]

While most of the submissions regarding fencing were of little relevance to the question in issue, the judicial discussion of the nature of fencing proved very significant in light of the argument made above. At trial, Pagone J remarked that:

> [t]he fencing on the southern, that is the street, boundary of the disputed land over the years did, in my view, amount to an act of possession and exclusion. The fact that it might, from time to time, or indeed even always, have been different from the fences on either side of the disputed land does not detract *from the nature of a fence as a sign to all who see it not to enter. That it might be easy to climb through that particular fence, or that kind of fence (as it was also easy to climb through the other and different fences on the Abbatangelo property), does not detract from the signal which the existence of the fence would ordinarily convey, namely, that the land behind it had been enclosed by someone and from everyone else.*[110]

In affirming Pagone J's decision, the Court of Appeal held that:

> his Honour did not err in finding that ease of access through the fence on the southern boundary of the land did not detract from the nature of a fence as a sign to all who saw it not to enter. As we have said already, the fact that a person, including an employee of the council, could have physically entered the land on foot by stepping through the wire strands was neither determinative nor necessarily of central importance. *The question was not whether the respondent had not done her best to exclude the appellant – because, for example, a different type of fence would have been more effective for this purpose – but whether it could be inferred from all of her acts that she intended to exercise custody and control of the land on her own behalf and for her own benefit.*[111]

The italicised portions of these passages demonstrate that, despite the ritually incanted formula that stresses the need for control, courts do, in fact, appreciate that possession is expressive in nature. This is not to say that this account of possession explains the entirety of the case law. As the discussion on the 'finders' cases' in Chapter 6 demonstrates, it plainly does not. The more modest claim being defended is that judges appreciate that, in a society in which property rights are routinely respected, the significance of a fence is not to be found in its ability to

[106] Ibid, 64 [27]–[29], 69–72 [55]–[62] (the Court).
[107] Ibid, 60 [48] (the Court).
[108] Ibid, 71–72 [61] (the Court).
[109] Ibid, 66 [43], 77 [82] (the Court).
[110] *Abbatangelo v Whittlesea City Council* [2007] VSC 529, [20]. Emphasis added.
[111] Ibid, 79 [95] (the Court). Emphasis added.

keep anyone out but in the unambiguous message it sends to others. Fences that guarantee effective control by actually excluding others are only required if the members of the relevant population do not accept the legitimacy of the *in rem* duty that fencing and the other symbolic acts that we call 'possession' purport to impose upon them. Unless we live in a fortified castle with a moat and portcullis, our actual ability to exclude intruders is in reality, as Rose has noted, dependent on our ability to call the police.[112]

C. The Role of Extra-Legal Knowledge in the Law

According to the orthodox account, disputes about possession are resolved by the application of an undisputed legal test that stresses the need for physical control. By contrast, the account offered here argues that this test cannot, if applied on its own terms, explain the outcomes in disputes about, for instance, the adverse possession of land. This alternative account stresses that judges actually resolve disputes about possession by drawing on a body of extra-legal knowledge about what sorts of acts constitute a legitimate property claim in the interpretive community in which they live. The truth of this argument is neatly demonstrated by the decision in *Popov*.[113]

Popov concerned a dispute over the ownership of the baseball that, when struck into the crowd by Barry Bonds, set a new record for home runs hit in a single season. According to custom, home run balls become abandoned property.[114] As a consequence, and as was not disputed in the case, the first person to take possession of the Bonds ball would become its new owner. Unsurprisingly, in light of its value, the scramble for the ball quickly degenerated into an unseemly and dangerous melee that required intervention from security.[115] The question for the Court was whether, in McCarthy J's words, the plaintiff, 'did enough to reduce the ball to his exclusive dominion and control. Were his acts sufficient to create a legally cognizable interest in the ball?'[116]

The evidence, such as it was, suggested that the ball landed in the webbing of the plaintiff's mitt. Unfortunately for the plaintiff, though his mitt 'stopped the trajectory of the ball',[117] it subsequently rolled out from underneath the tangle of bodies and was gathered up by the defendant. What could not be determined on the available evidence was whether the plaintiff's loss of control was attributable to a fumble on his part or to the gross physical interference of the other fans.

Given the exiguous evidence, McCarthy J resolved the case by the novel means of declaring that the plaintiff had a 'pre-possessory interest' in the ball which arises

[112] Rose, 'Nine-Tenths' (n 29) 48.
[113] *Popov* (n 14).
[114] Ibid, 3.
[115] Ibid, 2.
[116] Ibid, 4.
[117] Ibid, 1.

'[w]here an actor undertakes significant but incomplete steps to achieve possession of a piece of abandoned personal property and the effort is interrupted by the unlawful acts of others'.[118] Because, on this basis, both the plaintiff and the defendant had a proprietary interest in the ball, it was ordered that the ball be sold and the proceeds divided equally between them.

Though undoubtedly novel, the manner in which McCarthy J resolved the dispute is not what is of interest in this case. Quite apart from the question of equal division, it is clear that, as Chambers has also noted,[119] a 'pre-possessory interest' is a jural oddity that is exclusive to the common law of California. For present purposes, what is significant is the nature of the question that the Court was being asked to resolve. Although it was presented as a complex question of law that required the judge to refer to the opinions of no fewer than four eminent law professors,[120] it was clear that, in order to establish 'possession', the plaintiff simply had to prove that he had 'caught' the ball, in the normal sense of that word. As McCarthy J noted, '[t]he custom and practice of the stands creates a reasonable expectation that a person will achieve full control of a ball before claiming possession'.[121] While his Honour wrote in terms of the need to, 'retain control of the ball after incidental contact with people and things',[122] it is clear that, despite this complex phrasing, the question presented to the Court amounted to no more than the following: did the plaintiff catch the ball, or did he drop it?

Although the paucity of evidence made it impossible for the Court to answer that question, it should be obvious that there is nothing peculiarly legal about it. Whether or not someone 'caught' or 'fumbled' a ball is a question of social fact that has no uniquely legal dimension. The only controversy, which was purely evidential, was whether the plaintiff in fact did so. Although *Popov* is a particularly striking illustration, the argument defended in this book is that, despite the legal window dressing, all questions of possessions are, in the final analysis, questions of social fact that are resolved by the application of customary, rather than uniquely legal, knowledge.

VI. Conclusion

Building on accounts first offered by Hegel and Rose, the argument made in this chapter is that possession as a source of entitlement to tangible things has little to do with the possessor's ability to exclude other people. Instead, the significance of

[118] Ibid, 6.

[119] Robert Chambers, *An Introduction to Property Law in Australia*, 3rd edn (Pyrmont, Thomson Reuters Australia, 2013) 52 [6.14]. At the very least, its existence would seem to fall foul of the *numerus clausus* principle.

[120] *Popov* (n 14) 4–6.

[121] Ibid, 5.

[122] Ibid, 6.

particular factual relationships with particular things is that, within a particular population, they constitute the accepted way of staking a claim to an object of property.

The expressive theory of possession developed above does not deny that acts of actual physical control, such as placing a valuable item in a safe, constitute core and unmistakable cases of possession. Nor does it insist that, despite the misleading formulations in cases such as *Pye*, the judicial decisions are wrong. Instead, it emphasises that, in a society that habitually respects property rights, the relevance of certain physical acts is not to be determined by an indicium of control, but by the clarity of the signal that they send to others. As long as the signal is clear and accepted, it does not matter that the 'possessor' exerts no actual control over the *res*. If it were otherwise, then acts such as attaching a 'keep out' sign to a wooden stake or placing a coat over a seat in a cinema would have no effect.

In some respects, the insights of the expressive theory should be obvious. In many cases, land being perhaps the most prominent example, the notion that one can exercise effective control is largely, if not entirely, illusory. Moreover, and perhaps more importantly, if the law actually required the possessor to exercise effective control, then what additional benefit would a state-enforced property right confer on its holder? Despite this, our understanding of possession continues to be obscured by the law's insistence that possession is a concept that consists of one fact about physical control combined with a second, discrete, fact about an intention to possess. The expressive theory rejects this two-part understanding and instead insists that particular relations with things, whether or not they amount to actual control, are best understood as the accepted acts by which a property claim is communicated to the relevant audience.

In his seminal article, Epstein remarked that investigations into possession require one to ask a 'little' and a 'large' question.[123] The little question is what particular acts count as possession; the large question is why acts of possession create property rights at all. The account of possession offered in this chapter addressed the 'little' question. In Chapter 4, it is argued that this expressive theory of possession also plays an important role in addressing the 'large' question. Possession's function as a signalling device forms a core component of explanations advanced by theorists of spontaneous order who seek to explain why possession has the effect of creating original property rights.

[123] Epstein, 'Root of Title' (n 79) 1225.

4

The Possession Convention

I. Introduction

Waldron has written that a system of private property is one in which 'a rule is laid down that, in the case of each object, the individual person whose name is attached to that object is to determine how the object shall be used and by whom. His decision is to be upheld by society as final'.[1] The argument made in Chapter 3 was that the concept of possession is best understood as describing those acts that are recognised within a particular community as fulfilling the allocative function of determining whose name is attached to which objects.

Whilst the account offered in Chapter 3 may have answered the '*What?*' question, it does not answer the '*Why?*' question. That is, it does not address the deeper mystery of why possession, as opposed to some other mechanism, fulfils this most basic role. If it is reasonable to assume that sophisticated legal orders are concerned with the consequences of creating private entitlements to scarce resources, then why should the creation of those entitlements depend upon a mechanism as apparently crude as possession? To take a different sort of objection, if possession is a signalling device that is functionally equivalent to 'yelling loudly enough to all who may be interested'[2] about one's claim to some thing, then why, if I have made my claim sufficiently clear, does the law insist that I also enter into a particular physical relationship with it? In short, what is so special about possession and why does it justify the creation of non-consensual duties that bind, at least nominally, the whole world?

Numerous jurists and philosophers have sought to answer this most difficult of questions. Startling as it may seem, the argument advanced in this chapter is not only that all have failed but that all were doomed to fail. Although such theories may provide an independent *justification* for the 'possession rule', they cannot *explain* why it, as opposed to some other allocative mechanism, such as flipping a coin, has come to fulfil the role of allocating 'names to things'. All attempts to explain the mystery of the possession rule by reference to some rationale peculiar to it erroneously assume that it was, at some level, consciously selected as the basic rule for reducing objects of property to private ownership. Building on the work

[1] Jeremy Waldron, *The Right to Private Property* (Oxford, Oxford University Press, 1991) 39.

[2] Carol M Rose, 'Possession as the Origin of Property' (1985) 52 *University of Chicago Law Review* 73, 81.

of Hume, Hayek and, more recently, Sugden, it will be argued that the possession rule is not a product of conscious design but is an example of a convention that has arisen spontaneously and unconsciously through the repeated interaction of self-interested individuals.

Once we appreciate that the possession convention, and the formal legal rule into which it has evolved, was never consciously selected, then we can dispense with the notion that its origin can be traced to some elusive rationale, whatever that may be. Possession triumphed as the mechanism for resolving the most elementary questions of mine and thine, not because it is especially efficient or morally desirable but because, for largely inscrutable reasons of human psychology, it is salient to those who are confronted with the coordination problem created by the ineradicable condition of scarcity.

II. Explanations of the Possession Rule

A. Instrumental Explanations

Jurists from Savigny to Holmes to Merrill have puzzled over why possession, independently of its lawfulness, is a source of rights.[3] Finding an answer to this question famously preoccupied several nineteenth-century German jurists.[4]

Savigny's influential answer was that the protection afforded to the non-owning possessor is required in order to prevent potentially violent acts of dispossession and consequent disruptions to public order.[5] He argued that when possession is interfered with:

> an independent right is not … violated with the person, but some change is effected in the condition of the person to his prejudice; and if the injury, which consists in the violence against the person, is to be wholly effaced in all its consequences, this can only be effected by the restoration or protection of the *status quo*, to which the violence extended itself.[6]

Gordley and Mattei note that Savigny:

> suggests two rather different explanations for the protection of possession, each of which had its champions among the German jurists. According to the first, the law protects the peace and order of society against unlawfulness and force. According to the

[3] James Gordley and Ugo Mattei, 'Protecting Possession' (1996) 44 *American Journal of Comparative Law* 293, 295; Oliver Wendell Holmes, *The Common Law* (Boston, Little, Brown and Company, 1948) 206; Thomas Merrill, 'Ownership and Possession' in Yun-chien Chang (ed), *Law and Economics of Possession* (Cambridge, Cambridge University Press, 2015) 9, 9.

[4] Gordley and Mattei (n 3) 294.

[5] Frederick Pollock and Frederic William Maitland, *The History of English Law before the Time of Edward I*, 2nd edn (Indianapolis, Liberty Fund, 2010) vol II, 43–44.

[6] Friedrich Karl von Savigny and Sir Erskine Perry, *Von Savigny's Treatise on Possession, or, The Jus Possessionis of the Civil Law: Translated from the German*, 6th edn (London, S Sweet, 1848) 28.

> second, the law protects the victim himself. The victim has a legally protectable claim against unlawful interference even though he does not have a legally protectable claim to possession.[7]

Though which of the two explanations Savigny himself preferred is unclear, the first is most widely accepted.[8]

Ihering, Savigny's most famous critic, argued that Savigny was approaching the question from the wrong end.[9] Ihering denied that the law protected possession because it wished to protect the possessor from violent acts of dispossession and the broader society from the consequent disruptions to public order. According to his account, the rule has nothing to do with possessors per se. Instead, by allowing the fact of possession to constitute sufficient proof of title, the rule is best understood as an evidentiary concession for the benefit of owners.

Ihering's argument is thus predicated on the assumption that most possessors are also owners. Whether or not it is true, this assumption is widely held. Pollock argued that, 'for the very reason that possession in fact is the visible exercise of ownership, the fact of possession, unless otherwise explained, tends to show that the possessor is owner'.[10] Likewise, in *Allen v Roughley*, Kitto J opined that:

> [i]t is of fundamental importance to recognize that the presumption of title from the fact of possession does not rest upon an artificial rule arbitrarily adopted by the courts, and that the question before us is not whether such a rule is subject to an equally artificial qualification that the possession must have lasted for twenty years. The presumption is one of fact, and the reason for it is simply that 'men generally own the property they possess' … The law recognizes the probability which common experience suggests.[11]

Although the success of Ihering's explanation depends in large measure upon the truth of the assumption that most possessors are also owners, the existence of non-owning possessors is not fatal to his theory. Instead, these 'false positives' are, as with any heuristic, the inevitable price that must be paid when an easier question, about possession, is substituted for a harder one, about ownership.[12]

Gordley and Mattei remark of the continental debate that, '[r]arely if ever have more brilliant legal minds argued. Yet they found no convincing answer. Whenever one German jurist suggested a solution, another was able to explain why it would

[7] Gordley and Mattei (n 3) 296.

[8] Ibid.

[9] This summary follows that given in John M Lightwood, 'Possession in the Roman Law' (1887) 3 *Law Quarterly Review* 32. See also RWM Dias, *Jurisprudence*, 5th edn (London, Butterworths, 1985) 276–77.

[10] Frederick Pollock and Robert Samuel Wright, *An Essay on Possession in the Common Law* (Oxford, Clarendon Press, 1888) 25.

[11] *Allen v Roughley* [1955] HCA 62; (1955) 94 CLR 98, 138. Citations omitted.

[12] In Pollock and Maitland's words, '[i]n order that right may be triumphant, the possessory action must be open to the evil and the good, it must draw no distinction between the just and the unjust possessor': Pollock and Maitland (n 5) 44. See also Henry Bond, 'Possession in the Roman Law' (1890) 6 *Law Quarterly Review* 259, 263.

not work'.[13] Gordley and Mattei pessimistically conclude that '[s]tudying the debate should convince us that [that] question is unanswerable'.[14]

In studying Savigny and Ihering, it should be borne in mind that neither was proposing a purely normative account of possession. Each was also attempting to explain the doctrines of the Roman law. Their accounts were thus constrained by the requirement that they 'fit' the legal materials that they were seeking to explain.[15] That qualification aside, each account has shortcomings when viewed in light of the broader question.

The basic flaw in Savigny's explanation is that his central concern has little to do with the basic function of the law of property. As was argued in Chapter 2, the hallmark of property is the concept of 'disaggregation'; the notion that the existence of the right does not depend upon some ongoing, physical connection with its subject matter. If one is concerned with the bodily integrity of the possessor and public order more generally, then one should not look to the concept of property, but to assault and other wrongs concerned with the physical integrity of the person.[16] Savigny's explanation justifies no more than allowing possessors to sue for trespass, a tort which, as was explained in Chapter 2, requires interferences with 'actual possession'.

Ihering's account is open to a different objection. He argued that possession is protected because it is a simple means by which an owner can prove her title. That possession will yield the wrong answer in those cases in which a possessor is not also an owner is the inevitable price that must be paid for its convenience. However, even if we give Ihering the benefit of the doubt and assume that these false positives will be relatively rare, his theory does not explain why the law protects possession in cases where it can be proved that a possessor is not also an owner. To presage an issue that will be discussed in Chapter 7, it does not explain why we should protect the possession of those who are proven to be thieves or why, as was discussed in Chapter 2, legal systems sometimes refuse to allow owners to raise their title as a defence to an action against a wrongful possessor.[17]

Importantly, there is also a more fundamental shortcoming that is common to both explanations, namely their insistence on drawing a sharp distinction between 'possessors' and 'owners'. If a non-owner is defined as one who does not have the right to possess, it becomes impossible to explain why the law protects the possession of someone who is not an owner.[18] In other words, neither Ihering nor Savigny could explain why a possessor should not simply be considered an

[13] Gordley and Mattei (n 3) 295.

[14] Ibid.

[15] Although Dias remarked of Savigny's account that, '[a]s an explanation of Roman law this theory is demonstrably wrong': Dias (n 9) 275.

[16] See also Holmes (n 3) 207; Gordley and Mattei (n 3) 296–97.

[17] See also Gordley and Mattei (n 3) 299.

[18] Gordley and Mattei describe this problem as a 'theoretical box canyon' from which the continental jurists never emerged: ibid 293. See also James Gordley, *Foundations of Private Law: Property, Tort, Contract, Unjust Enrichment* (Oxford, Oxford University Press, 2006) 53.

owner. The basic error committed by both Savigny and Ihering is that of regarding 'possession' as a form of legal interest that is distinct from 'ownership'. This error is not confined to nineteenth-century continental writers. Merrill, for instance, recently observed that, '[o]ne of the enduring mysteries about property is why the law protects both ownership and possession'.[19] However, there is no mystery here. As Chapters 1 and 2 explained, the law does not protect possession; it protects ownership. The *fact* of possession is simply the way in which the *right* of ownership is created. The real mystery, and one which neither of these famous accounts addresses, is why the act of possession creates property rights *in the first place.*

B. Non-instrumental Explanations

Although their arguments have often failed to find favour with lawyers,[20] moral philosophers have attempted to resolve this deeper mystery by developing accounts that purport to explain why the act of possession justifies the creation of rights *in rem*. To take a prominent example, Hegel argued that:

> [t]o have something in my power, even though it be externally, is possession. The special fact that I make something my own through natural want, impulse or caprice, is the special interest of possession. But, when I as a free will am in possession of something, I get a tangible existence, and in this way first became an actual will. This is the true and legal nature of property, and constitutes its distinctive behaviour.[21]

Hegel stressed that possession and, by extension property, is not merely of instrumental value. Rather, because it is a way of manifesting free will, the act of possession is a valuable end in itself: '[s]ince our wants are looked upon as primary, the possession of property appears at first to be a means to their satisfaction; but it is really the first embodiment of freedom and an independent end'.[22]

Locke approached the matter rather differently. Whereas Hegel was concerned with external things in so far as they were a means of manifesting the human will, Locke proposed a labour-based theory that was ultimately founded upon an axiom of self-ownership.[23] According to his famous account:

> [t]hough the earth and all inferior creatures be common to all men, yet every man has property in his own person; this nobody has any right to but himself. The labour of his body and the work of his hands, we may say, are properly his. Whatseover then he removes out of the state that nature hath provided and left it in, he hath mixed his labour with, and joined to it something that is his own, and thereby makes it his property.

[19] Merrill (n 3) 9.

[20] See, eg, Holmes (n 3) 206–7; Bond (n 12) 264–65.

[21] GWF Hegel, *Philosophy of Right* (Kitchener, Batoche, 2001) 58 [45].

[22] Ibid.

[23] Alexander and Peñalver write that, unlike Hegel, Locke was concerned with 'placing an aspect of herself into the object'. Gregory S Alexander and Eduardo M Peñalver, *An Introduction to Property Theory* (Cambridge, Cambridge University Press, 2012) 63.

> It being by him removed from the common state nature placed it in, it hath by this labour something annexed to it that excludes the common right of other men. For this labour being the unquestionable property of the labourer, no man but he can have a right to what that is once joined to, at least where there is enough and as good left in common for others.[24]

Although Hegel and Locke were concerned with possession for different reasons, both accounts can be used to provide an a priori, moral justification for the rule that acts of possession create a property right that binds others without their consent.[25]

Empirical studies have demonstrated that people do indeed believe that something like the Lockean labour theory creates a moral entitlement to a resource.[26] However, that people *feel* they are entitled to some resource does not, of course, mean that they are.[27] There are numerous, often well-rehearsed, objections to the sorts of arguments advanced by Locke and Hegel. As Nozick noted, Locke's argument does not demonstrate why the labourer gains a resource instead of losing his labour.[28] And even if 'mixing one's labour' does create an entitlement to the resource, it does not follow that the labourer should therefore secure an entitlement to the entire resource, rather than to the increase in its value attributable to his labour.[29] Moreover, because Locke's theory is ultimately based on an axiom of self-ownership, it is also vulnerable to the 'spectacular *non sequitur*' noted by

[24] John Locke, *Two Treatises of Government and A Letter Concerning Toleration* (New Haven, Yale University Press, 2003) §27, 111–12.

[25] Although, as Waldron notes, Locke's own examples do not make it clear whether his theory is ultimately based on entitlement through labour or first possession. See Waldron, above n 1, 173.

[26] See, eg, Elizabeth Hoffman and Matthew L Spitzer, 'Entitlements, Rights, and Fairness: An Experimental Examination of Subjects' Concepts of Distributive Justice' (1985) 14 *Journal of Legal Studies* 259, 280–3. Hoffman and Spitzer found that the participants' attitudes to patterns of distributive justice were more 'Lockean' and less 'egalitarian' when initial allocations turned on the outcome of a game requiring moderate skill rather than on the outcome of a coin flip.

[27] Amartya Sen, 'The Moral Standing of the Market' (1985) 2 *Social Philosophy and Policy* 1, 17. In one version of Hoffman and Spitzer's bargaining game, initial entitlement, in the form of being designated the 'controller' of the bargaining process, was determined by the prior outcome of a game requiring moderate skill. Though less obviously arbitrary than a coin flip, it is not at all clear why, despite what the participants thought, the outcome of that game should confer such an entitlement on the winner. It is also notable that the game of skill used to select the 'controller' could always be won, as in 'noughts and crosses', by the player selected to make the first move. Thus, in the limit, one's ability to control the bargaining process depended on the fluke of this prior selection process. Importantly, this is not a criticism of the study, which simply did not consider whether the participants' beliefs were actually justified. See Hoffman and Spitzer (n 26) 273–74.

[28] Nozick famously illustrated this deficiency by asking whether, if one poured a can of tomato juice into the ocean, one would come to own the ocean or lose one's right to the tomato juice. Robert Nozick, *Anarchy, State, and Utopia* (New York, Basic Books, 2013) 174–75. The deeper mystery here is why Nozick, or anyone else, would have a can of tomato juice.

[29] Richard A Epstein, 'Possession as the Root of Title' (1979) 13 *Georgia Law Review* 1221, 1226. In this connexion, it is revealing that English law gives mistaken improvers no claim, either personal or proprietary, over the improved land. See *Falcke v Scottish Imperial Insurance Co* (1886) 34 Ch D 234 (CA), 248 (Bowen LJ). Even when an improver does have a claim in, for instance, unjust enrichment, the quantum of the claim is the value of improver's services and not the increase in the value of the property attributable to her services. See, eg, *Cobbe v Yeoman's Row Management Ltd* [2008] UKHL 55; 1 WLR 1752, 1773 [41] (Lord Scott).

Harris;[30] namely, that the truth of the proposition that nobody owns me does not entail the conclusion that I therefore own myself.

Objections can also be made to Hegel's theory. For instance, even if it is granted that one has the right to 'put his will' into an external object, it does not follow that he should therefore obtain a property right in that object of infinite duration.[31] A more general objection to will theories is that they can neither explain why the will to commit a wrong, such as theft, should be respected, nor whose will ought to prevail in the event that there is more than one possessor of some object.[32]

Importantly, the shortcomings of these theories are not of paramount importance to the account offered below because each is subject to the same 'meta-objection'; namely that, to the extent that each provides some non-consequentialist justification of the possession rule, each is predicated on the false assumption that the mystery of the possession rule can be explained by some underlying moral rationale that is peculiar to, or immanent within, the act of possession itself.[33] The argument advanced below is that any resemblance is purely accidental. The possession rule was never 'chosen' for its moral qualities. Rather, it is a convention that has evolved unconsciously through the repeated interaction of self-interested individuals.

While moral arguments can be deployed as a means of assessing the moral desirability of the possession rule, they cannot explain why possession, as opposed to some other potential allocative mechanism, came to answer the most basic questions of mine and thine. To attribute the existence of the possession rule to some unique, underlying rationale, whether moral or otherwise, is to fail to appreciate that there is no such rationale.

III. David Hume's Theory of Property

A. The Idea of Spontaneous Order

Apart from their other flaws, the German jurists' insistence on drawing a distinction between owners and non-owners prevented them from addressing the essential, anterior question: why does the act of possession create original property rights in the first place? Although philosophers such as Hegel and Locke attempted to give a rights-based answer to this question, they laboured under the misapprehension that it was possible to *explain* the origin of the rule. This does not mean that

[30] JW Harris, *Property and Justice* (Oxford, Clarendon Press, 1996) 196.

[31] Lawrence C Becker, *Property Rights: Philosophic Foundations* (London: Routledge and K Paul, 1977) 29–30.

[32] For discussion of these points see Gordley and Mattei (n 3) 298.

[33] It might be objected that Locke's theory was one of 'labour' and not 'possession'. However, as Epstein has observed, Locke's own examples show that possession, rather than labour, is sufficient for the purposes of his theory. See Richard A Epstein, 'From Natural Law to Social Welfare: Theoretical Principles and Practical Applications' (2015) 100 *Iowa Law Review* 1743, 1756.

their accounts are without merit. However, it does mean that what appear to be ex ante explanations can, in fact, only ever be ex post justifications for the rule. The explanation offered in this chapter diverges substantially from these established accounts because it argues that it is not possible to give such a rational, ex ante explanation of the possession rule because the possession rule, both in custom and in the law, is an example of 'spontaneous order'.

Spontaneous order is the idea that complex and stable systems can emerge from anarchy without conscious planning and independently of the positive law or any other form of state decree. Writing in 1767, Ferguson explained that, '[e]very step and every movement of the multitude, even in what are termed enlightened ages, are made with equal blindness to the future; and nations stumble upon establishments, *which are indeed the result of human action, but not the execution of any human design*'.[34] The most famous modern proponent of spontaneous order was Freidrich Hayek, who offered the following explanation:

> [i]t would be no exaggeration to say that social theory begins with – and has an object only because of – the discovery that there exist orderly structures which are the product of the action of many men but are not the result of human design. In some fields this is now universally accepted. Although there was a time when men believed that even language and morals had been 'invented' by some genius of the past, everybody recognizes now that they are the outcome of a process of evolution whose results nobody foresaw or designed.[35]

Hayek's basic position, and one which he shared with Hume,[36] was the rejection of 'constructivism'; the fallacy that the order that we observe in the world is attributable to some rational, designing mind.[37] According to Hayek, spontaneous orders are not consciously designed but instead evolve.[38] Building on the work of Hume and, more recently, Sugden, it will be argued that the possession rule in the law is best understood in this way.

B. Hume and Property Rights

Waldron has made the claim that scarcity is 'a presupposition of all sensible talk about property'.[39] This basic assumption also underpins David Hume's famous account of the origin of property rights. Hume's starting point was that:

> [o]f all the animals, with which this globe is peopl'd, there is none towards whom nature seems, at first sight, to have exercis'd more cruelty than towards man, in the numberless

[34] Adam Ferguson, *An Essay on the History of Civil Society* (Kitchener, Batoche, 2001) 143. Emphasis added.

[35] FA Hayek, *Law, Legislation, and Liberty: A New Statement of the Liberal Principles of Justice and Political Economy* (London, Routledge and Kegan Paul, 1973) Vol 1, Rules and Order, 37.

[36] John Gray, *Hayek on Liberty*, 3rd edn (London, Routledge, 2013) 30.

[37] Ibid, 29.

[38] Ibid, 30.

[39] Waldron (n 1) 31.

> wants and necessities, with which she has loaded him, and in the slender means, which she affords to the relieving these necessities.[40]

Hume argued that resources are not scarce because, as in a famine caused by a severe drought, there is simply insufficient quantities of some resource to satisfy people's basic needs. Instead, resources are scarce because, even in times of plenty, humans are insatiably acquisitive. Hume wrote that:

> [t]his avidity alone, of acquiring goods and possessions for ourselves and our nearest friends, is insatiable, perpetual, universal and directly destructive of society. There is scarce any one, who is not actuated by it; and there is no one, who has not reason to fear from it, when it acts without any restraint, and gives way to its first and most natural movements. So that upon the whole, we are to esteem the difficulties in the establishment of society, to be greater or less, according to those we encounter in regulating and restraining this passion.[41]

Given this fact about human psychology, what ultimately limits our acquisitiveness is not a quasi-moral feeling that we have 'sufficient', but the diminishing marginal utility of each new acquisition. As we value each new asset less than the last, an equilibrium or 'natural distribution' of resources will emerge, not when we experience a feeling of psychic wellbeing at having acquired enough, but when the subjective benefit derived from the 'nth' unit of some resource is less than or equal to the cost of acquiring and defending it from predation.[42]

For Hume, our insatiable acquisitiveness poses a constant and existential threat to society.[43] Hume's explanation for the spontaneous emergence of property rights begins with the manifest advantages of stable societies when compared with the solitary misery of the state of nature:

> '[t]is by society alone [man] is able to supply his defects, and rise himself up to an equality with his fellow-creatures, and even acquire a superiority above them. By society all his infirmities are compensated; and tho' in that situation his wants multiply every moment upon him, yet his abilities are still more augmented, and leave him in every respect more satisfy'd and happy, than 'tis possible for him, in his savage and solitary condition, ever to become.[44]

This observation is not, however, sufficient to explain the emergence of property rights. As Hume himself remarked, '[b]ut in order to form society, 'tis requisite not only that it be advantageous, *but also that men be sensible of its advantages*'.[45]

[40] David Hume, *A Treatise of Human Nature* (Oxford, Oxford University Press, 2000) 311 [3.2.2.2].
[41] Ibid, 316 [3.2.2.12].
[42] For this argument see, eg, James M Buchanan, *The Limits of Liberty: Between Anarchy and Leviathan* (Chicago, University of Chicago Press, 1975) 24–25. As Buchanan has argued, this 'natural distribution' of resources, though relatively stable, is not what we would recognise as a structure of rights.
[43] Indeed, Hume went as far as to make the implausible suggestion that once property rights have been established, 'there remains little or nothing to be done towards setting a perfect harmony and concord'. Hume (n 40) 315–16 [3.2.2.12].
[44] Ibid, 312 [3.2.2.3].
[45] Ibid, 312 [3.2.2.4]. Emphasis added.

On Hume's account, we become sensible of the advantages of society because we are able to extrapolate from the beneficial governance arrangements that arise, by virtue of the natural bonds of affection between parent and child, within the nuclear family.[46]

On Hume's account, the spontaneous emergence of property rights can thus be explained exclusively by individual self-interest, albeit of an enlightened variety. He stressed that 'a regard to public interest, or a strong extensive benevolence, is not our first and original motive for the observation of the rules of justice; since 'tis allow'd, that if men were endow'd with such a benevolence, these rules would never have been dreamt of'.[47] Property rights arise because we appreciate that 'the principal disturbance in society arises from those goods, which we call external, and from their looseness and easy transition from one person to another'.[48] The only way to prevent such traumatic disturbances is:

> a convention enter'd into by all the members of society to bestow stability on the possession of all those external goods, and leave everyone in the peaceable enjoyment of what he may acquire by his fortune and industry … Instead of departing from our own interest, or from that of our nearest friends, by abstaining from the possessions of others, we cannot better consult both these interests, than by such a convention; because it is by that means we maintain society, which is so necessary to their well-being and subsistence, as well as to our own.[49]

Hume's state-of-nature story thus departs sharply from the more famous alternative given by Hobbes. According to Hobbes, the war of all against all could only be resolved by a mutual and explicit agreement to cede our rights to a sovereign invested with unlimited coercive powers: 'it is manifest, that during the time men live without a common Power to keep them all in awe, they are in a condition which is called Warre; and such a warre, as is of every man, against every man'.[50]

By contrast, Hume's explanation does not require the existence of a Leviathan who, by the imposition of severe sanctions, enables cooperation to emerge from conflict.[51] Because, on his account, order-creating norms serve both the individual and collective interest, they are self-enforcing.[52] The particular genius of Hume's explanation is his understanding that these norms are *conventions*. The essential

[46] Ibid.
[47] Ibid, 318 [3.2.2.19].
[48] Ibid, 314 [3.2.2.9].
[49] Ibid.
[50] Thomas Hobbes, *Leviathan* (London, Penguin Books, 1968) 185.
[51] As Hobbes wrote, '[c]ovenants without the Sword, are but Words, and of no strength to secure a man at all': ibid, 223. Hobbes's state of nature shares the structure of the Prisoners' Dilemma. The existence of the all-powerful sovereign with coercive powers allows those caught on the horns of the dilemma to escape by changing the payoffs: Edna Ullmann-Margalit, *The Emergence of Norms* (Oxford, Clarendon Press, 1977) 65–67.
[52] See also Peter Vanderschraaf, 'The Informal Game Theory in Hume's Account of Convention' (1998) 14 *Economics and Philosophy* 215, 231.

idea of property, according to Hume, consisted in a 'convention enter'd into by all the members of the society to bestow stability on the possession of those external goods'.[53]

In discussing the emergence of order from chaos in terms of spontaneously emergent conventions, Hume anticipated, by several hundred years, many of the advances that modern game theory has made to our understanding of social institutions.[54] But what, precisely, does it mean to describe something as a 'convention'?

IV. Conventions

A. Conventions as Solutions to Coordination Problems

Although complex at the margins, the essence of the philosophical concept of a convention is simple to appreciate. When driving down a road, one must either deviate to the right or the left when confronted with oncoming traffic. When arriving at a busy intersection, one must either yield or maintain speed. When separated from one's friends at a shopping centre, one must consider the most likely rendezvous point.

These are all mundane examples of 'coordination problems'. A coordination problem is one of interdependent decision making in which there are two or more choices and the objective of all participants is to settle upon some common choice. In such situations, as Ullmann-Margalit has explained, 'the best choice for each depends upon what he expects the others to do, knowing that each of the others is trying to guess what *he* is likely to do'.[55]

The problem is that, in the absence of prior agreement, it is very difficult to know what the other person *will do* in the circumstances. Take the question of which side of the road to drive on, often referred to as the 'driving game'. There are two 'solutions' to this game; 'everyone drives on the left' and 'everyone drives on the right'.[56] Either will answer to the needs of road users. Thus, for any given pair of drivers, called 'Player A' and 'Player B', there are four potential outcomes.

[53] Hume (n 40) 314 [3.2.2.9].

[54] KG Binmore, *Fun and Games: A Text on Game Theory* (Lexington, DC Heath, 1992) 21. This would doubtless have surprised Hume, whose work was often met with indifference or hostility by his contemporaries. Hume famously described the *Treatise* as having fallen 'dead-born from the press'. See Dennis C Rasmussen, *The Infidel and the Professor: David Hume, Adam Smith, and the Friendship That Shaped Modern Thought* (Princeton, Princeton University Press, 2017) 201–2.

[55] Ullmann-Margalit (n 51) 78.

[56] In fact, this game has three Nash equilibria. In addition to left-left and right-right, driving on either the left or the right with a probability of 50 per cent is also a Nash equilibrium. However, for reasons discussed later in this chapter, it is not one that we would expect to survive. The concept of a 'Nash equilibrium' is explained below.

The 'payoffs', the utility of any given choice in light of the other player's choice, for each outcome are shown in Figure 1, below.[57]

Figure 1

		Player A	
		Left	**Right**
Player B	**Left**	*10*, 10	*−10*, −10
	Right	*−10*, −10	*10*, 10

Of the four potential outcomes, 'left-left' and 'right-right' represent 'solutions' that will satisfy each player. The problem is that, while the players wish to coordinate their choices, there is no uniquely rational reason for selecting one over the other.[58] As a consequence, neither player's choice of strategy will turn on a priori reasoning or 'logic', but on his beliefs about what the other player will choose in the circumstances. What is required to solve this coordination problem is the existence of a notorious belief that people drive either on the left or the right. The philosophical concept of convention describes the existence of such a belief within a particular population. Postema has written that:

> conventions *solve* [coordination] problems because they represent established ways in which people caught up in such problems overcome the uncertainty in their situation by adopting a common rule that correlates their choices and actions in a way that enables them to achieve cooperatively their individual (or collective) aims. The convention 'anchors' free-floating, mutually conditional preferences or expectations to a single equilibrium.[59]

A convention does not refer to a mere regularity of behaviour or habit. For instance, people's tendency to incessantly play with their smart phones while on public transport is not a convention in this sense. The philosophical concept of a convention refers not merely to an observable regularity of behaviour but also, as McAdams notes, to the set of expectations that sustain it.[60] One follows a convention because of one's belief that others follow it too.[61] A convention is thus a sort

[57] In all "payoff matrices", the strategy of Player A can be found in the columns, and the strategy of Player B in the rows. Throughout this book, the payoffs of Player B will be indicated by italics. No significance should be attached to the cardinal value of the payoffs selected. All that matters is that their ordinal ranking reflects the preferences of the players.

[58] As Sugden notes, classical game theory cannot tell us which of these two equilibria the parties will select. See Robert Sugden, 'The Evolutionary Turn in Game Theory' (2001) 8 *Journal of Economic Methodology* 113, 115.

[59] Gerald J Postema, *Legal Philosophy in the Twentieth Century: The Common Law World* (Dordrecht, Springer, 2011) 490.

[60] Richard H McAdams, 'Conventions and Norms: Philosophical Aspects' in James D Wright (ed), *International Encyclopedia of the Social & Behavioral Sciences*, 2nd edn (Amsterdam, Elsevier, 2015) vol 4, 844, 846.

[61] Robert Sugden, 'Conventions' in Peter Newman (ed), *The New Palgrave Dictionary of Economics and the Law* (London, Palgrave Macmillan, 1998) vol I, 453, 454.

of self-fulfilling prophecy and, the more that people follow it, the more entrenched it becomes.

Hume, writing in 1738, well understood this. In a passage that has become a classic in the field, he argued that:

> I observe that it will be for my interest to leave another in the possession of his goods, *provided* he will act in the same manner with regard to me. He is sensible of a like interest in the regulation of his conduct. When this common sense of interest is mutually express'd, and is known to both, it produces a suitable resolution of behaviour. And this may properly enough be called a convention or agreement betwixt us, tho' without the interposition of a promise, since the actions of each have reference to those of the other, and are perform'd upon the supposition that something is to be performed on the other part. Two men who pull the oars of a boat do it by an agreement or convention, tho' they have never given promises to each other. Nor is the rule concerning the stability of possession the less deriv'd from human conventions, that it arises gradually, and acquires a force by a slow progression and by our repeated experiences of the inconveniences of transgressing it. On the contrary, this experience assures us still more that the sense of interest has become common to all our fellows, and gives us a confidence of the future regularity of their conduct; and 'tis only on the expectation of this that our moderation and abstinence are founded.[62]

In this passage, Hume identifies two vital aspects of a convention. First, conventions do not arise from explicit agreements. Secondly, conventions both create and rely upon expectations about how, absent agreement, people will behave in particular circumstances. 'Justice', in Hume's words, establishes itself because 'every single act is performed in expectation that others are to perform the like'.[63]

As Hume demonstrated, the emergence of order from chaos need not be attributed to either altruism or the presence of a sovereign wielding a big stick. Order arises because it is in people's best interest that it does so. As Sugden explains:

> the most important lesson to be learned from the study of conventions is that a society can be ordered without anyone ordering it. In many significant cases, the coordination of individuals' actions can be brought about by self-reinforcing expectations, which evolve spontaneously out of the repeated interaction of self-interested individuals.[64]

B. Pure and Impure Coordination Problems

A coordination problem is one in which two or more people with coinciding interests must fix upon the same choice, the classic example being deciding on which side of the road to drive. The 'driving game' is a particularly clear example of a coordination problem because, at least in the generic case, no driver has any

[62] Hume (n 40) 314–15 [3.2.2.10].
[63] Ibid, 320 [3.2.2.22].
[64] Sugden, 'Conventions' (n 61) 460.

particular preference for 'left' or 'right', or, if they do, this preference is dwarfed by the potentially catastrophic consequences of a head-on collision. In these situations, conformity is its own reward.[65]

The strong convergence of interests that characterises coordination problems of this type neatly demonstrate how order can emerge spontaneously and why conventions that solve such problems are self-enforcing. However, it is obvious that many, if not most, problems of human interaction are not like the driving game because people very often have a preference about which action they would like to take. As Schelling observed, games of pure coordination and games of pure conflict do not cover the field of human interaction.[66] Instead, they are best seen as limiting cases between which sit those many and varied interactions that involve differing degrees of both conflict and mutual dependence. Schelling called these sorts of interactions games of 'mixed-motive'.[67]

An important sub-set of mixed motive games are 'impure coordination games', a classic example of which is the 'intersection game', which models the simultaneous arrival of two cars at an intersection. Determining which car must brake is a coordination problem because we can assume that a collision is regarded by each driver as the least favourable outcome. As a consequence, the players must coordinate their choices. However, unlike the driving game, it is 'impure' because neither participant is indifferent as to their choice. Each would prefer that the other brake. The payoffs in the intersection game are represented in Figure 2, below.[68]

Figure 2

		Player A	
		Maintain speed	**Brake**
Player B	**Maintain speed**	−*10*, −10	*5*, 3
	Brake	*3*, 5	*0*, 0

The payoffs in this matrix reflect the fact that if Player A maintains speed, Player B's best course of action is to brake, and vice versa, because if both players maintain speed, the outcome will be a potentially catastrophic collision. Likewise, if both parties brake, then, while they will have avoided the worst possible outcome of a collision, they will also have failed to solve their original problem. The strategies 'maintain speed–maintain speed' and 'brake–brake' are thus 'miscoordination events'.

[65] See also Ullmann-Margalit (n 51) 85.
[66] Thomas C Schelling, *The Strategy of Conflict* (Cambridge MA, Harvard University Press, 1960) 84.
[67] Ibid, 89.
[68] This matrix is taken from Robert Sugden, *The Economics of Rights, Co-Operation, and Welfare* Oxford, B Blackwell, 1986) 38.

The strategies 'maintain speed-brake' and 'brake-maintain speed' are, by contrast, solutions to the problem. In game theory, these solutions are said to constitute 'Nash equilibria'.[69] The concept of a Nash equilibrium is essentially one of 'best reply'. While it may not represent the best outcome for one or, indeed, either player, a pair of strategies will be in Nash equilibrium if each represents the best reply to the other. Each is the best choice *given* the other player's choice. The concept is simple to illustrate. If I believe that the other car approaching the intersection will not yield, though I would prefer that it did, my best choice is to play the submissive strategy of braking. Playing 'brake' to 'maintain speed' is a Nash equilibrium because neither party can, by unilateral action, improve his position.

The concept of a Nash equilibrium is perhaps the most significant contribution that game theory has made to social inquiry because no solution to a problem of human interaction will succeed in the long term unless it represents a Nash equilibrium. As Binmore has observed, the rules that human societies create to regulate their affairs are 'rules for *sustaining an equilibrium* within the game of life'.[70]

C. Scarcity as an Impure Coordination Problem

Coordination problems are not limited to those situations in which there is little or no divergence of interests between those who must agree upon complementary choices. Despite a divergence of interest between the participants, any problem will be one that requires some element of coordination if it is one in which the decision of each participant to pursue her most desired outcome *irrespective* of the decision of the other will result in the worst outcome for both.[71]

The crucial question is whether this is also true of competition over scarce things. In other words, does the problem caused by the excess of 'wants over things' create a coordination problem or a game of pure conflict, of no particular strategic interest, in which the quantum of the loser's loss is equal to that of the winner's gain? The answer is that scarcity does create a coordination problem.

Imagine, to borrow an oft-used example, a stand-off between two people over a piece of firewood. If the only consequence of the competition were that one party acquired the firewood at the expense of the other, then this would be a purely

[69] Douglas G Baird, Robert H Gertner and Randal C Picker, *Game Theory and the Law* (Cambridge MA, Harvard University Press, 1998) 21–23, 310.

[70] Ken Binmore, *Game Theory and the Social Contract: Playing Fair* (London, MIT Press, 1994) 26. See also Brian Skyrms, *The Stag Hunt and the Evolution of Social Structure* (Cambridge, Cambridge University Press, 2004) 9.

[71] This is unlike the more famous 'Prisoner's Dilemma' in which the decision to 'defect' rather than 'cooperate' is the best choice, irrespective of the other participant's choice. In the non-iterative version of the Prisoner's Dilemma, the decision to defect is 'strictly dominant'. As McAdams has recently noted, the tendency of scholars to see every competitive interaction as a manifestation of the Prisoners' Dilemma has, unfortunately, obscured the fact that many of these interactions actually pose problems of coordination. See Richard H McAdams, 'Beyond the Prisoners' Dilemma: Coordination, Game Theory, and Law' (2008) 82 *Southern California Law Review* 209.

competitive, zero-sum game in which neither party has any incentive to defer to the other. In reality, however, being successful or unsuccessful in acquiring the firewood is not the only consequence to which the parties must attend. This is because one potential outcome of unrestrained competition is a violent conflict in which one or more of the disputants may be injured, or worse. If one makes the reasonable assumption that most people regard such conflicts as the least desirable outcome in the circumstances, then each party has an incentive to place limits on otherwise unconstrained competition. Thus, despite the strong divergence of interests between those making rival claims to the same resource, the fact of scarcity creates a coordination problem, albeit of a very impure variety.[72]

Game theorists and biologists have often used the 'Hawk-Dove' game as a model for the emergence of property rights.[73] Hawk-Dove shares the logic of 'Chicken', the test of nerve in which teenagers demonstrate their *bravura* by simulating the conditions of a head-on car crash, the winner being the party who is last to take evasive action or 'chicken out'.[74] Using the accepted game-theoretic nomenclature, 'Hawk' describes a belligerent strategy. Someone who adopts this strategy will invariably fight for mastery of a disputed resource. 'Dove', however, is a submissive strategy. Someone who adopts this strategy will test the waters but defer to his opponent at the first sign of conflict. Assuming more-or-less equal fighting ability, the payoffs for these various outcomes are represented in Figure 3, below.[75]

Figure 3

Player A

		Dove	**Hawk**
Player B	**Dove**	1, 1	0, 2
	Hawk	2, 0	−2,−2

The payoffs in Figure 3 reflect the following preference ranking, from least to most preferred, as viewed from the participant whose strategy choice is in bold: (1) **Hawk** plays Hawk; (2) **Dove** plays Hawk; (3) **Dove** plays Dove; (4) **Hawk** plays Dove.

When a Hawk meets another Hawk, both parties are assured of conflict and each runs the risk of sustaining a potentially devastating injury. When a Dove

[72] See also ibid, 223–24.

[73] For an overview of the literature see James E Krier, 'Evolutionary Theory and the Origin of Property Rights' (2009) 95 *Cornell Law Review* 139, 150–57.

[74] Apparently the 'game-like' quality of this test of nerve was first noticed by Bertrand Russel who, in 1959, likened the game to the nuclear standoff between the United States and the Soviet Union. See William Poundstone, *Prisoner's Dilemma* (New York City, Doubleday, 1992) 197–98.

[75] These payoffs are taken from Sugden, *Economics of Rights* (n 68) 60. In evolutionary game theory, these payoffs represent reproductive fitness, being the number of viable offspring.

plays a Hawk, the Dove avoids the risk of injury but, in doing so, forgoes the entire resource. Where a Dove plays another Dove, the parties avoid the risk of injury, but must be content to divide the resource equally between themselves. Finally, when a Hawk meets a Dove, the Hawk takes the entire resource without risk of injury. It should be clear from the payoffs in Figure 3 that the outcomes Hawk-Dove and Dove-Hawk are Nash equilibria and thus are potential solutions to this coordination problem. On the other hand, the outcomes Hawk-Hawk and, for reasons discussed below, Dove-Dove are not.

Determining who gets to play Hawk and who must be content with Dove in any given encounter over some object of property is precisely the role played by the basic allocative rule in any system of private property.

D. The Assumptions of the Hawk-Dove Model

Before proceeding, it is important to articulate the assumptions underlying Hawk-Dove as a model for the evolution of property rights.

The first relates to assumptions about the participants' rationality. Perhaps the most common criticism made of the application of game theory to problems of human interaction is that it is premised on the demonstrably false assumption that people behave rationally when interacting with each other.

This sort of criticism very often misunderstands what is meant by 'rational' in this context. For the purpose of what follows, rationality does not require that one's subjective preferences reflect one's best interests when viewed objectively. Nor does it demand that psychological biases be removed by 'nudges' so as to make 'choosers better off, *as judged by themselves*'.[76] Rather, '[w]hatever is preferred (whether it seems selfish or altruistic from certain points of view) is assigned the higher utility'.[77] If, for some perverse reason, I enjoy the thrill of being involved in a potentially fatal car accident, then the preference order that defines the 'intersection game' simply does not apply to me.[78]

What game theory instead requires is 'instrumental rationality', which simply demands that that participants in a 'game' have a complete and transitive set of preferences.[79] This concept can be illustrated using a simple example. Imagine that

[76] Richard H Thaler and Cass R Sunstein, *Nudge: Improving Decisions about Health, Wealth and Happiness* (New Haven, Yale University Press, 2008) 5.

[77] Anatol Rapoport, *Fights, Games, and Debates* (Ann Arbor, University of Michigan Press, 1960) 122.

[78] That is, utility functions are based on the theory of revealed preference. What people prefer is revealed by what they actually do. See generally Ken Binmore, *Rational Decisions* (Princeton, Princeton University Press, 2009) 27–29.

[79] See generally Shaun P Hargreaves Heap and Yanis Varoufakis, *Game Theory: A Critical Text*, 2nd edn (New York, Routledge, 2004) 7–8; Morton D Davis, *Game Theory: A Nontechnical Introduction* (Mineola, Dover Publications, 1997) 62–65.

I am offered the choice between an apple, a pear and a mango and that I prefer mangos to pears and pears to apples. Instrumental rationality requires that, if offered the choice between a mango and an apple, I choose the mango.

There are many situations in life in which people do not have a complete and transitive set of preferences. Finnis, who is sceptical about the utility of applying game-theoretic analyses to law, is surely right to argue that, 'in real life, alternatives do not present themselves for choice in fully bounded situations or in transitive rankings'.[80] However, while this is often true, it is not universally so. Whether a game, such as Hawk-Dove, can persuasively serve as a model for some form of social interaction depends on the accuracy of the assumptions it makes about the preferences of the nominal players. The assumptions made by the Hawk-Dove model are broadly that people are generally acquisitive and seek to avoid violent confrontations where possible. While these assumptions are not true of all people all of the time, they are true of a great many people much of the time, making it reasonable to assume that, when confronted with a dispute over a scarce object, people's choices will, more or less, conform to the preference order that defines this particular game.

This observation raises an important point. As Rose has noted of the payoffs in Figure 3, the average payoff for the pacific Dove-Dove strategy is equal to that of Hawk-Dove and Dove-Hawk.[81] Given this, why do rational parties not simply agree to share the resource equally and thereby avoid conflict? The superficial answer is that, on the payoff structure that defines the game, Dove-Dove is not a Nash equilibrium. If I know my opponent will adopt the submissive Dove strategy, I can always improve my payoff by switching to Hawk. The more fundamental answer, however, is that Dove-Dove cannot form the basis of a stable property regime because the Hawk-Dove model is founded on the Humean assumption that, with some notable exceptions, humans are insatiably acquisitive and will take some disputed resource in its entirety if there is no cost to be paid for doing so.

The final assumption underlying the Hawk-Dove model is that it assumes some level of abundance.[82] As resources become scarcer, their value to the players will rise. If this continues, there will ultimately come a point at which, due to the threat of starvation, their value to any given player will outweigh the cost of fighting for them. When this occurs, the payoff ranking that defines the Hawk-Dove game will no longer reflect most people's preferences and Hawk will become the dominant strategy. Whilst this is undoubtedly true, the one qualification that must be made is that as resources become scarcer, disputes over them will be more fiercely fought,

[80] John Finnis, *Philosophy of Law: Collected Essays Volume IV* (Oxford, Oxford University Press, 2011) 68.

[81] Carol M Rose, 'Psychologies of Property (and Why Property Is Not a Hawk-Dove Game)' in JE Penner and Henry E Smith (eds), *Philosophical Foundations of Property Law*, (Oxford, Oxford University Press, 2013) 272, 281.

[82] See also John Maynard Smith, *Evolution and the Theory of Games* (Cambridge, Cambridge University Press, 1982) 96; Krier (n 73) 156.

and the risk of injury will be correspondingly higher. Thus, we would not expect the Hawk strategy to become dominant until the relevant resource is approaching exhaustion.

V. The Role of Salience in Conventions

A. Symmetric Games and the Problem of 'Mixed Strategy Equilibria'

Maynard Smith has explained that a game such a Hawk-Dove will be 'symmetric' when:

> the two contestants start in identical situations: they have the same choice of strategies and the same prospective payoffs. There may be a difference in size and strength between them, which would influence the outcome of an escalated contest, but if so it is not known to the contestants and therefore cannot affect their choice of strategies.[83]

Symmetric games assume homogeneity amongst the players. The most glaring shortcoming of the 'symmetric' Hawk-Dove game is its failure to reflect the reality that, in many cases, there will be a substantial and appreciable disparity in size or fighting ability between the players. In such cases, the inability of the weaker party to harm the stronger party simply means that there is no coordination problem.

However, the success of Hawk-Dove as a model for the spontaneous emergence of property rights does not depend upon it applying to every dispute over a scarce thing. In any case, instances in which Hawk-Hawk confrontations will result in no harm to the winner must be rare. This is particularly true if the 'cost' of a Hawk-Hawk encounter includes the sense of embarrassment that one feels after, for example, conducting a screaming match in public.[84] These issues aside, the more fundamental problem is that, in a perfectly symmetric game, no convention can arise. In order to explain why this is so, it is necessary to briefly return to the concept of a Nash equilibrium.

A pair of strategies will be in Nash equilibrium where each is the best reply to the other. Hawk-Dove and Dove-Hawk are in Nash equilibrium because, even though the Dove player will not get exactly what she wants, she cannot improve her position *given* the other player's decision to play Hawk. Crucially, however, Hawk-Dove and Dove-Hawk are not the only two Nash equilibria in the game. In repeated play and, assuming the payoffs in Figure 3, the players will also have reached a stable equilibrium where each player plays the Dove strategy with the

[83] Maynard Smith, ibid, 22.

[84] See also Richard H McAdams and Janice Nadler, 'Testing the Focal Point Theory of Legal Compliance: The Effect of Third-Party Expression in an Experimental Hawk/Dove Game' (2005) 2 *Journal of Empirical Legal Studies* 87, 95.

probability of 2/3 and the Hawk strategy with the probability of 1/3.[85] This strategy is a Nash equilibrium because, once established, neither party can improve his position by departing from it and any deviations from it will be self-correcting.[86]

Unlike Hawk-Dove and Dove-Hawk, which are 'pure strategy equilibria', strategies that direct a player to play 'Strategy A' with probability x% and 'Strategy B' with probability 1-x% are called 'mixed strategies'.[87] As McAdams also notes, mixed strategies in equilibrium do not answer to the definition of a convention.[88] The expectations at the core of any convention depend upon a strong regularity of behaviour being exhibited by members of the relevant population. Any strategy that contains some randomising element will, by definition, not have this quality.

Just as importantly, these non-conventional, mixed strategies make poor solutions to coordination problems. This is demonstrated by the intersection game. Imagine that, instead of 'brake if on the left, maintain speed if on the right', or some such, people instead negotiated intersections by adhering to the rule 'maintain speed with probability x% and brake with probability 1–x%. Though it may be stable, such a convention will inevitably result in the miscoordination events of yield-yield and, more worryingly still, maintain speed-maintain speed, in a certain percentage of cases.

Returning to Hawk-Dove, assuming the payoffs in Figure 3, the mixed strategy of playing Dove with the probability 2/3 and Hawk with the probability 1/3 creates a world in which 56% of all disputes over property are of the Hawk-Hawk or Hawk-Dove varieties.[89] In other words, over half of all disputes over scarce natural resources are resolved by force or the threat of force. This, as Sugden observes, does not look like a peaceful world, but one which is languishing in Hobbes's state of nature.[90]

What is required is a convention which, just like 'give way to the right', enables any given person to determine, without the need for actual or threatened conflict, who is entitled to the disputed resource and who must defer. In other words, what is required is an allocative rule which determines who is to play Hawk and who must be content to be a Dove, in respect of any given object of property.

We have now isolated the fundamental problem with purely symmetric games. As noted above, Hawk-Dove has three Nash equilibria, two of which are pure, and thus constitute possible conventions, and one of which is mixed, and thus

[85] Sugden, *Economics of Rights* (n 68) 61. This does not require that every individual play Dove with probability 2/3. A population will be in equilibrium if 2/3 of the population play Dove as a pure strategy while the remaining 1/3 play Hawk as a pure strategy. See Richard H McAdams, 'Focal Point Theory of Expressive Law' (2000) 86 *Virginia Law Review* 1649, 1692.

[86] Sugden, ibid, 61; McAdams, ibid, 1692–3.

[87] Baird, Gertner and Picker (n 69) 37.

[88] McAdams, 'Focal Point Theory of Expressive Law' (n 85) 1695. McAdams thus defines a convention as 'the prevailing pure-strategy equilibrium and the expectations that support it': at 1694.

[89] Sugden, *Economics of Rights* (n 68) 61.

[90] Ibid. It also results in a lower average payoff than that which would be achieved under the pacific, hough unstable, Dove-Dove compromise.

does not. An important insight of evolutionary game theory is that, if the relevant population consists of perfectly homogenous players about whom all that is known is their preferences, as represented by their ordinal payoff rankings, the mixed-strategy equilibrium is, in fact, the only Nash equilibrium in the game.[91] When 'iterated' encounters are totally featureless and anonymous, players are unable to develop reputations, divine patterns of behaviour and learn from experience. Where this occurs, no pure strategy Nash equilibrium will arise.[92] The question is then, if pure strategy Nash equilibria are the foundation of conventions, how can conventions spontaneously emerge?

B. Breaking Symmetries

The answer is that conventions emerge spontaneously because life is not a symmetric game. People who are caught up in coordination problems modelled by iterative games such as Hawk-Dove do not regard each other as members of a homogenous mass. Instead, they become sensible of some feature that distinguishes them from their opponents in any round of the game. Game theorists describe these distinguishing features as 'asymmetries'. Asymmetry recognition is crucial because it is only once players come to recognise some individuating feature that they can begin to recognise patterns of behaviour, develop reputations and reason inductively from past experience.

Another important insight of modern game theory is that any asymmetry will do, no matter how apparently irrelevant it is to the game. As Hargreaves Heap and Varoufakis demonstrated empirically, creating the necessary distinguishing feature in a population may be as simple as labelling one group of players red and the other blue.[93] Mutual recognition of any asymmetry, no matter how arbitrary, enables the players to 'condition their behaviour on some feature of their opponent',[94] which, in turn, allows for the emergence of two new pure strategy equilibria.[95] In this case, the two pure strategy equilibria are: 'Play Hawk if Red Player and Dove if Blue Player' and vice versa.

These new pure strategy equilibria constitute proto-conventions which, to use Sugden's metaphor, compete with each other like seedlings in a crowded plot.[96] In repeated play, one will come to triumph at the expense of the others because some critical mass of players will, sooner or later, fancy that they can discern some

[91] Hargreaves Heap and Varoufakis (n 79) 215–16; Robert Sugden, 'Salience, Inductive Reasoning and the Emergence of Conventions' (2011) 79 *Journal of Economic Behavior & Organization* 35, 38.

[92] Skyrms describes this as the 'curse of symmetry': Brian Skyrms, *Evolution of the Social Contract* (Cambridge, Cambridge University Press, 1996) 63.

[93] Hargreaves Heap and Varoufakis (n 79) 232–34.

[94] Ibid, 229.

[95] For a particularly clear explanation of this concept see McAdams, 'Focal Point Theory of Expressive Law', (n 86) 1691–96.

[96] Sugden, *Economics of Rights* (n 68) 43.

pattern in the chaos.[97] For example, they may come to believe that 'Blue' players tend to be more belligerent than 'Red' players. It is not required that such a belief be inductively valid. Irrespective of its truth, once such a belief begins to spread throughout the population, it becomes a self-fulfilling prophecy. The resulting 'bandwagoning' effect not only vanquishes the competing pure strategy equilibrium, but it also drives out the hitherto dominant mixed strategy equilibrium.[98] The pure strategy equilibrium that remains at the end of this process is a convention in the sense described above.

C. The Role of Salience in Asymmetry Selection

The mutual recognition of *any* mutual asymmetry explains how and why conventions can emerge spontaneously as solutions to coordination problems. Skyrms has explained this phenomenon by drawing an analogy with a column under compression.[99] Although the column may appear perfectly symmetrical, as more weight is added, it will eventually buckle one way or another. Though useful, Skyrms's analogy is not a complete answer to the puzzle. In cases of human interaction, symmetries can only be broken if some critical mass of people come to identify the *same feature* that distinguishes any one player from any other player in any round of the game.

The problem here is not a dearth but a surfeit of potential asymmetries from which to select.[100] In any given interaction between two people, it is possible to identify an almost infinite number of asymmetries. Two drivers approaching each other at an intersection might notice the following differences: one is approaching from a large road and the other from a small road; one is to the left and the other is to the right; one is driving a large vehicle and the other a small vehicle. They may also notice other differences, such as: one is in a blue car and the other is in a red car; one is in a Mercedes and the other is in a Toyota; one is in a two door coupé, the other is in a sedan, and so on.

Given the almost infinite number of potential asymmetries that might distinguish two players, the chances of some critical number of drivers identifying the same feature would seem to be vanishingly slim. If asymmetry recognition were a matter of random transient variation, then one would expect that the emergence of any convention would take an agonisingly long time and that many panels would be damaged in the meantime.[101]

[97] Ibid.

[98] That is, a pair of mixed strategies ceases to constitute a Nash equilibrium in an asymmetric game. See Hargreaves Heap and Varoufakis (n 79) 229. The reason for this is simple to appreciate. If you persist with a mixed strategy in the face of an established convention such as 'give way to the right', you are simply inviting an accident.

[99] Skyrms (n 92) 67–68.

[100] See also Krier (n 73) 155.

[101] Sugden, 'Salience' (n 91) 39.

Fortunately, equilibrium selection is not a random process akin to pulling the lever on a slot machine and hoping that the symbols line up. On the contrary, we appear to be endowed with a sixth sense that enables us to guess the sort of features that *other people* will find material to the resolution of some common problem. Schelling famously asked each member of a group of students to imagine that they were to meet someone in New York City, but had made no prior arrangements and had no means of communication.[102] All that each respondent knew of the other was that she had been given the same instructions. The respondents were then asked to choose a location and meeting time. Given the huge number of potential meeting places in a city the size of New York, one would expect that the chances of any pair of respondents selecting the same time and place would be vanishingly slim.[103] Remarkably, however, of those surveyed, an absolute majority selected the information booth at Grand Central Station as the rendezvous point and virtually all chose midday as the meeting time. Plainly, this result cannot be chalked up to 'dumb luck'.

As Schelling explained, this simple coordination problem demonstrates that people seem to be able to '"read the same message in a common situation"[104] and are thus able to "mutually recognise" some unique signal that coordinates their expectations of each other'.[105] In game theory, features that, for some reason, stand out, are often described as being 'salient', 'prominent' or 'focal points'. According to Schelling, these simple games illustrate the truth that:

> [p]eople *can* often concert their intentions or expectations with others if each knows the other is trying to do the same. Most situations … provide some clue for coordinating behaviour, some focal point for each person's expectation of what the other expects him to expect to be expected to do. Finding the key, or rather finding *a* key – any key that is mutually recognized as the key becomes *the* key – may depend on imagination more than logic; it may depend on analogy; precedent; accidental arrangement; symmetry; aesthetic or geometric configuration, casuistic reasoning, and who the parties are and what they know about each other … It is not being asserted that they will always find an obvious answer to the question; but the chances of their doing so are ever so much greater than the bare logic of abstract random probabilities would ever suggest.[106]

The importance of Schelling's insight is that the riddle of equilibrium selection must be solved empirically, not analytically.[107] Answering the question, 'What would I do if I were her, wondering what she would do if she were me, wondering

[102] Schelling (n 66) 55–56.

[103] In other words, this is a coordination problem in which players must choose between a near-infinite number of potential equilibria.

[104] Schelling (n 66) 54.

[105] Ibid.

[106] Ibid, 57. Friedman gives the example of the numbers 2, 5, 9, 25, 69, 73, 82, 96, 100, 126, 150. Of these numbers, laymen are likely to find '100' focal. However, mathematicians are likely to find '2' salient, because it is the only even prime. David Friedman, 'A Positive Account of Property Rights' (1994) 11 *Social Philosophy and Policy* 1, 5.

[107] See also Sugden, 'Evolutionary Turn' (n 58) 116–17.

what I would do if I were her …', cannot be answered through a priori, rational analysis. The salience of any particular solution need have nothing to do with its objective desirability, however assessed. This, however, is not a cause for concern. When faced with a coordination problem, any choice is a good one as long as it is held in common with others.[108] As Schelling wrote, '[t]he assertion here is *not* that people simply *are* affected by symbolic details but that they *should* be for the purposes of correct play'.[109] If you become separated from your wife in a strange city, 'go with your gut' is, in fact, good advice.

Schelling's insight about the nature of salience applies equally to asymmetry selection in impure coordination problems.[110] The ability of players to fasten upon the same asymmetry is plainly more than a matter of chance. Some asymmetries, for some mysterious reason, appear to stand out to those who are confronted with the same problem.

D. The Simplicity Imperative

Conventions arise spontaneously because members of the relevant population fasten upon some asymmetry that, for some reason, 'sticks out' as material to the resolution of their common problem. Importantly, there is no necessary connection between the salience of an asymmetry and its efficiency or moral desirability.[111] Though conventions 'solve' coordination problems, it does not follow, as Postema has explained, 'that this solution is optimal from anyone's point of view. Not only is it possible for some parties to regard some alternatives as preferable … but it is possible that *all* may agree that the existing conventional arrangement is sub-optimal'.[112]

Why is it that the desirability of a solution, however assessed, is incidental to its salience? The answer to this question lies in the very function of asymmetry identification. Recognition of a common asymmetry allows those faced with a Hawk-Dove-like situation to determine who is to play Hawk and who is relegated to Dove, in respect of any given resource. In other words, it fulfils a role-allocation function. It is therefore essential that the asymmetry on which the relevant convention turns is simple to apply. If, based on the asymmetry in question, it is possible for the participants to be genuinely uncertain about which role they are to play in any given interaction, then neither will have a settled expectation about how the

[108] As Friedman has noted, players 'succeed in the game because of, not in spite of, the bounded rationality of the players': Friedman (n 106) 5.

[109] Schelling (n 66) 98.

[110] Sugden, 'Salience' (n 91) 39.

[111] Robert Sugden, 'Spontaneous Order' (1989) 3 *Journal of Economic Perspectives* 85, 94. In economic terms, there is no guarantee that a convention will be Pareto optimal. This is the lesson of the game known as the 'stag hunt'.

[112] Postema (n 59) 490.

other will behave in the circumstances. Any such uncertainty will rapidly destroy the convention in question. An essential quality of any convention is thus certainty of application.

Sugden illustrates the point by discussing a hypothetical convention that turns on the asymmetry of beauty.[113] Because, as the saying goes, 'beauty is in the eye of the beholder', no convention could turn on individual assessments of beauty. Nor is this how the players would approach the problem. Because the players are attempting to coordinate, they would not base their choices on what they themselves find attractive. They would instead ask themselves what *other people* are likely to find attractive, knowing that the others are asking the same question of them. What is required to answer this question is a convention for interpreting the original convention. This will inexorably lead to the creation of convention that turns on some simple, observable asymmetry, such as height or hair colour. Over time, the original 'beauty convention' will be replaced by one that turns on some proxy that, though a crude approximation of beauty, has the virtue that it can be predictably applied.

A second reason why human interaction selects for simplicity in conventions is because the use of ambiguous proxies allows for cheating.[114] If the relevant convention is that Player A plays Hawk and Player B plays Dove, then people will naturally want to be assigned the role of Player A as often as possible. If it is possible to imitate the characteristics of Player A, that is what people will do. However, the consequence of mass imitation is that every player in every game will be labelled Hawk and the convention will be destroyed. Thus, the conventions that we would expect to survive in any given population would not only be simple to apply but also cheat proof.[115] Once again, this favours crude conventions that turn on some simple, observable, criteria.

The 'simplicity imperative' explains a very important feature of conventions, and one that will be discussed throughout the remainder of this book. The need to prevent interpretive confusion explains why no convention can turn on complex moral or distributive judgments about relative 'need' or 'desert'. Although there may be clear cases in which one could split the rival claimants on moral grounds, there are simply too many instances in which 'reasonable minds may differ'. As with Sugden's beauty example, any putative convention that turned on such a contestable asymmetry would ultimately be replaced by one which, though a crude approximation of the original, is simple to apply.

Sugden has suggested that the gravitational pull exerted by simplicity explains why conventions appear morally arbitrary.[116] However, if this explanation is true,

[113] Sugden, *Economics of Rights* (n 68) 100–1.
[114] Ibid, 99.
[115] Ibid, 166–67.
[116] Ibid, 101.

the most important message to emerge from this analysis is not that conventions *seem* morally arbitrary; it is that they *are* morally arbitrary.[117]

E. Possession and 'Uncorrelated Asymmetries'

Unsurprisingly, the argument defended in this chapter is that possession is the asymmetry that enables any two people to determine who is to play Hawk and who Dove in any dispute over an object of property.[118] More specifically, the argument advanced below is that, in a dispute over some tangible thing, the party who is first to send the recognised claim-staking signal by performing the appropriate act is assigned the role of Hawk.

This explanation of the function of possession has its origins with Hume, who argued that it must occur to people, 'as the most natural expedient, that everyone continue to enjoy what he is at present master of, and that property or constant possession be conjoin'd to the immediate possession'.[119] More recently, Hume's argument has been refined by Sugden.[120] On Sugden's account, the emergence of the possession convention is not attributable to any immanent moral quality, but is explicable on the basis that possession, as an observable fact based on some physical connection between a person and a thing, is both relatively simple to apply and cheat proof.[121] These insights have significant implications for our understanding of possession as a substantive element of the positive law. However, before discussing these insights, it is important to address a potential misunderstanding about the role of possession, and asymmetry selection more generally.

There is a constant, and understandable, temptation to attribute the rise of the possession convention to some structural or strategic advantage that possession confers in the event of conflict. Epstein, for example, has argued that a possessor is more likely to prevail in a fight against an intruder because he can exploit his superior knowledge of his surroundings.[122] Similarly, Hirshleifer has argued that, all things being equal, a resource is worth more to a possessor and, as a consequence, she will fight harder and longer to retain it.[123]

The first difficulty with these explanations is that they are no more than plausible assertions. A possessor may have superior knowledge of a particular territory but, then again, he may not. Even if he does, it does not necessarily follow that

[117] It does not, of course, follow that they are therefore immoral. This is discussed further in Chapter 5.

[118] Hence Skyrms's observation that '[t]he origin of property … lies in broken symmetries': Skyrms (n 92) 79.

[119] Hume (n 40) 323 [3.2.3.4].

[120] Sugden, *Economics of Rights* (n 68) 87–103.

[121] Ibid, 101.

[122] Richard A Epstein, 'A Taste for Privacy? Evolution and the Emergence of a Naturalistic Ethic' (1980) 9 *Journal of Legal Studies* 665, 672–73.

[123] Jack Hirshleifer, 'Privacy: Its Origin, Function, and Future' (1980) 9 *Journal of Legal Studies* 649, 657.

he would be more successful in a fight. Likewise, the notion that a possessor values her territory more than an intruder is plausible, but one could think of any number of circumstances in which this is not true. Some have argued that the tenacity of the possessor can be explained by the 'endowment effect', the idea, prominent in behavioural economics, that losses are more painful than gains are pleasurable.[124] While this might be true, the endowment effect cannot explain the mystery of possession because it presupposes that the act of possession confers some entitlement. In other words, it does not explain why possessors think they have something to lose. In any case, if the salient asymmetry reflected a superior chance of prevailing in the event of a fight, then we would expect to find a convention that favoured, for example, the larger of the two competitors.[125]

The important point is that differences in payoffs are not required to explain the possession rule. As biologists have long observed, any asymmetry, no matter how arbitrary, is capable of creating a convention.[126] Maynard Smith and Parker thus describe these distinguishing features as 'uncorrelated asymmetries'.[127] Maynard Smith has explained that:

> there is no *need* for differences in payoff before asymmetries will settle contests. Consequently, it is a logical error, rather than a factual one, to conclude that because, in some particular case, ownership does settle contests, there must therefore be a payoff or resource-holding power difference associated with ownership. There may or may not be such a difference, but its presence cannot be deduced from the fact that ownership settles contests.[128]

One may well wonder why obviously arbitrary asymmetries, such as labelling a player either 'red' or 'blue', have this effect. Hargreaves Heap and Varoufakis offer the following explanation:

> [i]n interactions (like *Hawk-Dove*) in which there is *rational indeterminacy* in the conventional game theoretic sense, people try to condition their behaviour on *any* information that comes to hand, even meaningless information … It is a simple psychological response to uncertainty. Indeed there is much evidence to support the idea that people look for 'extraneous' reasons to 'explain' what are in fact purely random types of behaviour. Of course, once they do so, an initial, random difference in the behaviour of the 'reds' and the 'blues' gets a bandwagon rolling, leading to a stable discrimination that succeeds in minimising costly conflict despite being non-rational … So *ex post*, it will seem to make sense as each player does take the best action given that chosen by the other, even though there is no reason *ex ante* for this selection of actions.[129]

[124] On which see, eg, David Cohen and Jack L Knetsch, 'Judicial Choice and Disparities between Measures of Economic Values' (1992) 30 *Osgoode Hall Law Journal* 737, 749–52; Russell Korobkin, 'The Endowment Effect and Legal Analysis' (2002) 97 *Northwestern University Law Review* 1227, 1259–62.

[125] For a similar observation see Sugden, *Economics of Rights* (n 68) 91.

[126] Hargreaves Heap and Varoufakis (n 79) 229–30.

[127] John Maynard Smith and GA Parker, 'The Logic of Asymmetric Contests' (1976) 24 *Animal Behaviour* 159, 163–64.

[128] Maynard Smith (n 82) 96. Maynard Smith uses the term 'ownership' synonymously with the term 'possession'.

[129] Hargreaves Heap and Varoufakis (n 79) 233–34.

Like a drowning man desperately looking for something to cling to, humans seem to be psychologically predisposed to discern patterns, even though the evidence for them may be weak. However, when faced with a choice between multiple equilibria, the validity of the inference is of no importance. All that matters is that the behaviour on which it is based is noticed by other people too. That some patterns and distinguishing characteristics seem to be particularly noticeable is attributable to the largely mysterious quality of 'salience', which itself seems to be part of the deep structure of our psychological pattern-recognition software.[130]

Whilst it may be that the possession convention can ultimately be traced to some belief that possessors have an advantage over non-possessors in a fight, it is immaterial whether this belief is also true.[131] What matters is the perception, not the reality. As long as a critical mass of people come to believe that possessors will aggressively defend some object, the truth of this belief is irrelevant both to the stability of the convention and to any given person's reason for adhering to it.

F. Lessons for the Law

The claim underpinning this chapter is that the *rule* of the positive law that 'possession creates a relative title' cannot be understood in isolation from the customary possession *convention*. According to this account, the possession convention was so pervasive in life that it was, consciously or otherwise, incorporated into the law's formal system of rights and duties. The simple answer to the question, 'Why do acts of possession create property rights in tangible things?', is that this is what the relevant convention prescribes and the law, holding to the motto 'if you can't beat 'em, join 'em', accepted this as sufficient.[132]

What is most striking about the game-theoretic account of possession is the degree to which it dovetails with the expressive theory discussed in Chapter 3. As the discussion of 'uncorrelated asymmetries' sought to make clear, neither the expressive nor the game-theoretic account explains the significance of possession by an appeal to the possessor's superior ability to exclude others from the disputed resource. On the contrary, both posit that the significance of possession lies in its

[130] Sugden attributes the salience of certain asymmetries, including possession, to their susceptibility to analogy, a quality he describes as 'fertility'. See Sugden, *Economics of Rights* (n 68) 94–95. However, this can only be a partial explanation as it does not explain why some asymmetry *first* appeared prominent to people facing the same coordination problem. See also Hargreaves Heap and Varoufakis (n 79) 242.

[131] Maynard Smith (n 82) 22.

[132] This also demonstrates the powerful and enduring role of custom within the law. See generally Henry E Smith, 'Custom in American Property Law: A Vanishing Act' (2012) 48 *Texas International Law Journal* 507. On the question of whether the state creates or, instead, merely recognises property rights see Richard A Epstein, 'International News Service v. Associated Press: Custom and Law as Sources of Property Rights in News' (1992) 78 *Virginia Law Review* 85, 85; Richard A Epstein, *Design for Liberty: Private Property, Public Administration, and the Rule of Law* (Cambridge MA, Harvard University Press, 2011) 99.

role as a device that sends recognised signals about claims to tangible things. On both accounts, the function of possession is purely *expressive*.

Likewise, both the expressive and game-theoretic accounts reinforce the argument, advanced in Chapter 3, that there is no dichotomy between 'lay' and 'legal' conceptions of possession. A convention will never spread throughout any given population if it turns upon an asymmetry that people have difficulty identifying and applying. The asymmetry which distinguishes any two contestants must be, at the very least, one which both recognise. Consequently, any convention that depends upon an esoteric and uniquely legal conception of possession, comprehensible only to those with legal training, could never survive in the broader population. While this does not prove that there is no uniquely legal conception of possession, it does demonstrate that such a conception is bound to fail in its most basic function of resolving a coordination problem.

Finally, the most salutary aspect of the spontaneous order explanation concerns its implications for natural rights-based explanations of the possession rule. Hegel and Locke, amongst others, attempted to explain the possession rule on the basis that it gives expression to some basic moral principle. The claim made above was that all such accounts fail as *explanations* of the possession rule in so far as they attribute its existence to its unique moral qualities. There is simply no reason to believe that possession's salience as a solution to a coordination problem has anything to do with its intrinsic moral properties. In a passage that anticipated Schelling's work on focal points with remarkable accuracy, Hume himself recognised that, 'there are, no doubt, motives of public interest for most of the rules, which determine property; but still I suspect, that these rules are principally fix'd by the imagination, or the more frivolous properties of our thought and conception'.[133]

One might object that the foregoing has only demonstrated that the salience of a solution to a coordination problem is not *invariably* related to its moral appeal. Thus, it remains possible that possession's prominence can be attributed to some inherent moral quality that is unique to it. However, anyone who advances this argument faces the daunting prospect of explaining why the possession rule is not confined to humans.[134] Zoologists have demonstrated that bees, baboons and even butterflies adopt what Maynard Smith described as the 'bourgeois' strategy of playing Hawk if possessor and Dove if non-possessor.[135] Confrontations in the animal world over resources ranging from territory to potential mates are, even amongst species capable of inflicting serious injury, often highly stylised and seldom fatal.[136] Contrary to what we might expect, such disputes are 'settled by prior ownership,

[133] Hume (n 40) 323 [3.2.2.4] n 71.

[134] For an overview see Jeffrey Evans Stake, 'The Property 'Instinct'' (2004) 359 *Philosophical Transactions of the Royal Society* 1763.

[135] Maynard Smith (n 82) 97–99.

[136] J Maynard Smith and GR Price, 'The Logic of Animal Conflict' (1973) 246 *Nature* 15, 15.

and need not depend on perceptions by the contestants of differences in fighting ability'.[137] Unless we credit butterflies with a sense of self-ownership or free will, it is difficult to deny that the salience of possession has little, if anything, to do with its intrinsic moral significance and is instead largely attributable to a genetic predisposition shared by insects and humans alike.

VI. From Conventions to Norms

A. Explaining the Normative Quality of Conventions

If there is one fundamental lesson to emerge from game theory and the study of conventions, it is that the emergence of order from chaos can be explained by the repeated interaction of self-interested individuals pursuing their own best interest. Nevertheless, there is something missing from this account: its failure to reflect our subjective experience of rule-compliance.[138]

To echo Finnis's criticism, people are not walking utility calculators whose every decision is assessed in accordance with a complete and transitive set of individual preferences conveniently represented in a payoff matrix.[139] On the contrary, people comply with many duty-imposing rules because they feel that it is what they *ought to do* in the circumstances. Likewise, people generally disapprove of contraventions of such rules even when they are not on the receiving end. What is missing from the account given so far is how and why conventions come to have the status of 'norms', viz. rules that, in people's subjective experience, have a legitimacy that transcends cost–benefit analyses or the fear of punishment.[140]

Hume also asked this question. He attributed the emergence of the 'artificial virtue' of justice to enlightened self-interest. Conventions, such as those that 'bestow stability on possession', emerge spontaneously because it is in people's self-interest that they do so. Having explained this, Hume's next task was to explain, '*[w]hy do we annex the idea of virtue to justice, and of vice to injustice?*'.[141] Why, for example, does the act of queue-jumping attract the opprobrium of both those in the queue and of general bystanders who happen to witness it? As Hume noted,

[137] Maynard Smith (n 82) 98.
[138] See also Eric A Posner, 'Law, Economics, and Inefficient Norms' (1996) 144 *University of Pennsylvania Law Review* 1697, 1709.
[139] Finnis (n 80) 67–69.
[140] This working definition of 'norm' does not claim to be definitive. On this topic see also Robert D Cooter, 'Decentralized Law for a Complex Economy: The Structural Approach to Adjudicating the New Law Merchant' (1996) 144 *University of Pennsylvania Law Review* 1643, 1656–7; Robert D Cooter, 'Against Legal Centrism' [Book Review of Robert C Ellickson, *Order Without Law: How Neighbours Settle Disputes* (Cambridge MA, Harvard University Press)] (1993) 81 *California Law Review* 417, 426; Posner (n 138) 1699. The obvious comparison is with Hart's concept of the 'internal aspect': HLA Hart, *The Concept of Law*, 2nd edn (Oxford, Oxford University Press, 1994) 56–57.
[141] Hume (n 40) 320 [3.2.2.23].

a purely self-regarding explanation of this phenomenon only seems plausible in relatively small societies in which one can readily observe the corrosive effect of such breaches.[142] He wrote that:

> when society becomes more numerous, and has encreas'd to a tribe or nation, this interest is more remote; nor do men so readily perceive, that disorder and confusion follow upon every breach of these rules, as in a more narrow and contracted society. But tho' in our actions we may frequently lose sight of that interest, which we have in maintaining order, and may follow a lesser and more present interest, we never fail to observe the prejudice we receive, either mediately or immediately, from the injustice of others; as not being in that case either blinded by passion, or byass'd by any contrary temptation.'[143]

Why is it that, even in very large societies, we condemn, in normative terms, non-complying conduct even when it has no direct or appreciable effect on our interests? Hume's answer was to posit the existence of an innate tendency towards what he called 'sympathy':

> when the injustice is so distant from us, as in no way to affect our interest, it still displeases us; because we consider it as prejudicial to human society, and pernicious to every one that approaches the person guilty of it. We partake of their uneasiness by *sympathy*; and as every thing, which gives uneasiness in human actions, upon the general survey, is call'd *vice*, and whatever produces satisfaction, in the same manner, is denominated *virtue*; this is the reason why the sense of moral good and evil follows upon justice and injustice ... Thus *self-interest* is the original motive to the *establishment* of justice: But a *sympathy* with *public* interest is the source of the *moral* approbation, which attends that virtue.[144]

Sugden has presented an updated version of Hume's account which, in most respects, closely tracks that of Hume. However, he dissents from Hume's belief that the normative dimension of conventions is ultimately attributable to 'sympathy', the innate psychological predisposition to place oneself in another's shoes and to take pleasure from his pleasure and pain from his pain.[145] Sugden argues that this explanation is psychologically implausible and that it is possible to explain the normative character of conventions at the level of individual interactions and individual interests.[146]

Imagine that I am approaching a roundabout and that another car appears on my left. According to the convention 'give way to the right', I expect the driver to slow. However, he fails to slow and we narrowly avoid an accident. In failing to

[142] Ibid, 320 [3.2.2.24].
[143] Ibid.
[144] Ibid, 320–21 [3.2.2.24].
[145] The concept of 'sympathy' is central to Hume's scheme of moral philosophy. See generally David Fate Norton, 'Hume, Human Nature, and the Foundations of Morality' in David Fate Norton (ed), *The Cambridge Companion to Hume* (Cambridge, Cambridge University Press, 1993) 148, 165; JL Mackie, *Hume's Moral Theory* (Abingdon, Routledge & Kegan Paul, 1980) 120–1.
[146] Sugden, *Economics of Rights* (n 68) 171.

abide by the established convention, he has imperilled both of us. As a matter of common experience, it is easy to appreciate why I will feel anger and resentment towards the other driver.[147] The more difficult question is why some bystander, not involved in the interaction, will also condemn the reckless driver's action in distinctly moral terms. According to Sugden, this has nothing to do with the bystander's sense of fair play, but her appreciation that the intersection problem is a form of iterated game and that, as a consequence, the convention-breaker may well be her 'opponent' in a subsequent round. His reckless behaviour thus poses a direct threat to her interests.[148] If we follow some convention, then we will have a reason, rooted in self-interest, to condemn any and all breaches of it. As Sugden writes of the possession convention:

> once a person has resolved to follow the convention, his interests are threatened by the existence of mavericks who are aggressive when the convention prescribes submission. Or in plainer English: provided I own *something*, thieves are a threat to me. So even if the conventions of property tend to favour others relative to me, I am not inclined to applaud theft.[149]

It is not clear, at least for the purpose of this discussion, that there is any great inconsistency between Sugden and Hume. In particular, there is no reason to regard Hume's appeal to 'sympathy' as a reference to anything more than our ability to ask the question, 'What if everyone behaved like that?'.[150] Consistently with his explanation for the spontaneous emergence of conventions, 'sympathy' may simply describe a psychological propensity, ultimately rooted in individual self-interest, to disapprove of behaviour, including our own, that is destructive of the conventions from which we benefit.[151]

What is important is that, given that any convention is better than no convention at all,[152] people's tendency to approve of conforming action and disapprove of non-conforming action can be explained independently of the moral content of the convention itself. As Sugden writes, 'a convention of property may become a generally accepted norm even though it cannot be justified in terms of any external standard of fairness'.[153]

That is not to say the content of a convention cannot accord with some theory of morality, it is simply that any resemblance will be accidental.[154] The morality that grows up around conventions is a sort of instrumental morality that Sudgen

[147] Ibid, 149.
[148] Ibid, 156.
[149] Ibid, 159.
[150] See, in particular, Hume (n 40) 319 [3.2.2.22].
[151] See further Mackie (n 145) 84–85; Norton (n 145) 167–68.
[152] Although, as Sugden notes, it is not invariably true that, relative to the state of nature, all conventions make everyone better off. Sugden, *Economics of Rights* (n 68) 167.
[153] Ibid, 159.
[154] Robert Sugden, 'Normative Expectations: The Simultaneous Evolution of Institutions and Norms' in Avner Ben-Ner and Louis Putterman (eds), *Economics, Values, and Organization* (Cambridge, Cambridge University Press, 1999) 73, 85; Sugden, *Economics of Rights* (n 68) 172; Sugden, 'Spontaneous Order'(n 111) 95–96.

describes as a 'morality of co-operation',[155] but will here be referred to as 'conventional morality'. Hume captured its essence when he wrote that:

> justice establishes itself by a kind of convention or agreement; that is, by a sense of interest, suppos'd to be common to all, and where every single act is performed in expectation that others are to perform the like … 'tis only upon the supposition, that others are to imitate my example, that I can be induc'd to embrace that virtue.[156]

B. Defending Hawk-Dove

The normative quality of any given convention is not dependent upon its substance. In the realm of conventional morality, the 'wrong' of breaching a convention consists in, to paraphrase Hume, 'failing to perform the like'. The implication of this insight is that, consistently with the arguments made throughout this chapter, it is possible to explain the undeniable 'ought' quality that attends the possession rule without resorting to moral theories, or theories of natural law, which seek to explain its normativity in terms of the inherent moral significance of the act of possession, whatever that may be.

This explanation of the normative quality of conventions has another important implication. That is, that one's obligation, as a matter of 'conventional morality', to follow some established convention transcends any pragmatic reason that may have motivated people to observe it in its infancy. Irrespective of the nature of the asymmetry on which they happen to turn, conventions develop a normative life of their own.

This point is particularly important given Rose's recent criticism of Hawk-Dove as a plausible model of emergent property rights. The essence of Rose's objection is that, if non-possessors defer to possessors because they fear the latter's aggression, then Hawk-Dove, predicated as it is on the fear of violent reprisals, cannot explain the legal concept of ownership. She writes that:

> [b]ut here is the rub: possession is not *property*. The critical point about property is that the non-owner show respect for the owner's property even when the non-owner has little reason to fear the owner's defence – that is, when the owner is not actually in possession, or when the owner is an obviously weaker party who could not repel invasion. When a non-owner defers to the owner under those circumstances, something other than fear is keeping her from moving in and stealing the car or the bicycle or whatever.[157]

Rose goes on to observe that:

> [t]he core attribute of property is precisely that the non-owner respects the owner's claim even when it is *not* defended. There is no question but that for some non-owners,

[155] Sugden, *Economics of Rights* (n 68) 173.
[156] Hume (n 40) 320 [3.2.2.22].
[157] Rose (n 81) 282.

> rational fear is the only impediment to larceny. But that is not what makes a property regime work. By and large, in a functioning property regime, most non-owners are not larcenists, and they do not like larcenists. That set of sensibilities is what makes property regimes function: you do not guard your things all the time, because the "world" of non-owners respects your ownership.[158]

Much of what Rose writes here is perfectly consistent with the arguments advanced in this book. In particular, she is right to emphasise the distinction between the fact of possession and the jural concept of ownership and that the observance of property rights is not, for the most part, dependent upon the fear that non-owners have of owners.[159] Nevertheless, these observations do not expose any fundamental shortcoming in Hawk-Dove as a model for emergent property rights.

Rose's argument suffers from two shortcomings. The first is a misunderstanding of the relevant convention. The convention, at least amongst humans if not butterflies, is that possession creates some form of entitlement. That entitlement, once created, is not dependent upon some form of ongoing physical control.[160] That this is true is demonstrated by one of Rose's own examples. As was noted in Chapter 3, during winter, residents of Chicago observe an extra-legal rule, according to which the person who clears and marks a kerb-side parking space is entitled to its exclusive use until the snow thaws.[161] What is notable about this rule is that the entitlement persists despite the absence of any physical control on the part of the 'shoveller'. All that matters is that, by placing some incongruous object, such as chair,[162] in the cleared space, the resident has staked her claim in the manner that the convention prescribes.

This misunderstanding about the nature of the convention is again attributable to the persistent, but unnecessary, tendency to believe that the salience of possession is attributable to the fighting advantage that physical control confers upon the possessor.[163] As the discussion of 'uncorrelated asymmetries' demonstrated, this need not be the case. All that is required is that some critical number of people hold a belief, irrespective of its truth. Once this belief becomes common knowledge, the outcome 'possessor takes the prize' becomes a self-fulfilling prophecy. All that matters is that, like a cinema patron placing her jacket on the back of her seat, the 'possessor' has staked her claim in the accepted manner.

The second, and more important, shortcoming concerns Rose's failure to appreciate why conventions, irrespective of their substance, become norms. The

[158] Ibid, 283.

[159] Merrill and Smith also argue that the success of a system of *in rem* duties depends, in large measure, on the extent to which it reflects extra-legal norms of common morality. Thomas W Merrill and Henry E Smith, 'The Morality of Property' (2007) 48 *William and Mary Law Review* 1849, 1854, 1894. Importantly, the account offered here makes no claim about whether those extra-legal moral intuitions are actually morally justified.

[160] Rose is not alone in this misunderstanding. See also Posner (n 138) 1716.

[161] Rose, 'Possession as the Origin of Property' (n 2) 81.

[162] Robert C Ellickson, 'The Inevitable Trend toward Universally Recognizable Signals of Property Claims: An Essay for Carol Rose' (2010) 19 *William & Mary Bill of Rights Journal* 1015, 1025–26, 1029.

[163] For an example see Rose (n 81) 282.

essence of Rose's objection to Hawk-Dove is that it fails to explain the existence of a 'property ethic' that transcends fear of violent reprisals. As was discussed above, the possession rule's strong normative dimension has nothing to do with people's initial belief, however accurate, that possessors are either particularly bellicose or especially adept fighters. Instead, the 'property ethic' is a particular manifestation of the conventional morality that emerges around any successful solution to a coordination problem. The reason I do not approve of the theft of some millionaire's unattended briefcase is the same reason that I do not approve of people sneaking through red lights when the police are otherwise engaged. I regard this behaviour as 'wrong'. And I regard it is as wrong because, at the deeper level that Hume called my capacity for 'sympathy', I understand that such behaviour is ultimately corrosive of the conventions from which I benefit.

VII. Conclusion

Chapter 3 advanced a definition of possession that emphasised its expressive function. It was argued that what is important about the concept of possession is not the degree of control that some person exercises over some thing, but whether the relationship between a person and a thing sends a recognised signal to others about the possessor's intention to claim it for herself. In this chapter, it has been argued that the convention-based accounts of Hume and, more recently, Sugden, give us reason to believe that this is true. In game-theoretic terms, possession breaks the symmetry between two people competing over a scarce resource and allows for the spontaneous emergence of a property convention that then becomes a property norm. Possession's significance in the law can thus be explained on the Humean basis that fundamental legal norms evolve from the bottom up and are not imposed from the top down. The law protects possession because the law adopted, almost without modification, the spontaneously emergent convention according to which 'possessor trumps non-possessor'.

Because application of the possession rule determines who gets the prize, we are resistant to the idea that it is morally arbitrary and picks winners and losers without regard to relative merit or desert. For this reason, we will always be tempted to ask, '*But what is so special about possession*?' The argument made in this chapter is that attempting to solve the possession riddle by seeking a meaningful answer to this question is doomed to failure. Contrary to, for instance, the natural law tradition, we cannot explain *why* the possession rule, as opposed to some other allocative mechanism, performs the role of allocating things to people. In game-theoretic terms, possession is 'salient' and, crucially, there is no reason to believe that its salience is attributable to its peculiar instrumental desirability or to some immanent moral quality that is unique to it.

The convention-based argument does not claim to explain the entirety of the morality of property. On the contrary, it is but one small part. It is undeniably true that, for example, certain material things are inextricably linked to one's sense of personhood.[164] This very important element of property cannot be explained by an appeal to 'conventional morality'. Likewise, the argument made here is, strictly speaking, purely agnostic on the merits of philosophical arguments *qua* philosophical arguments. It simply insists that they cannot explain the origin of the possession rule. Whether one is a philosopher or a lawyer, the key to understanding possession is to appreciate that it is, first and foremost, a spontaneously emergent convention.

[164] Margaret Jane Radin, 'Property and Personhood' (1982) 34 *Stanford Law Review* 957, 969.

5

Possession and Fairness

I. Introduction

In Chapter 4, it was argued that the initial emergence and subsequent spread of the possession convention cannot be explained by a moral quality that is peculiar to the act of possession. Building on Sugden's account, it was argued that the simplicity imperative makes all conventions blind to distributive and other such ethical considerations, however obvious they may appear to be in some interactions.

That conventions are strictly *amoral* does not, however, mean that they are also *immoral* or otherwise unfair. The primary argument advanced in this chapter is that, if we abandon the pretence that any allocative rule can reliably pick deserving or meritorious winners, fairness simply requires that no person or class of people can be systematically excluded from benefitting from the rule. To continue with the game-theoretic nomenclature, a basic allocative rule will be fair if it is possible for any given member of a population to be assigned the role of Hawk in any given contest over a scarce resource. This, so it is argued, is precisely what the possession rule allows.

Building on Hayek's account of law as a spontaneously emergent phenomenon, it is also argued that, because conventions generate widely held expectations about the resolution of common coordination problems, the positive law should, where possible, incorporate them into its formal system of rights and duties. Where, as is the case with possession, the extra-legal convention is tolerably fair, the argument for convergence between custom and law becomes even more compelling.

II. Hume's Guillotine and Locke's Proviso: Epstein's Partial Defence of the Possession Rule

A. The Problem of Unilateral Acquisition

In his celebrated paper, Epstein uses the following, simple, example to illustrate the predicament that lies at the heart of any system of private property:

> [a] beautiful sea shell is washed ashore after a storm. A man picks it up and puts it in his pocket. A second man comes along and takes it away from him by force. The first man

sues to recover the shell, and he is met with the argument that he never owned it at all. How does the legal system respond to this claim? How should it respond?[1]

As Epstein notes, every system of property must decide '[w]hat principles decide *which* individuals have ownership rights … over *what* things'.[2] Whilst this is obviously true, a paradox at the heart of any system of private property rights makes settling on these basic principles surprisingly difficult. On the one hand, no system of property could rely on mutual consent in order to get 'up and running'.[3] The basic allocative rule must instead turn on a unilateral, non-consensual act because, in addition to prohibitive bargaining costs and holdout problems,[4] parties in the state of nature face the basic problem that there is, by definition, no accepted initial allocation of rights from which to bargain.[5] Even in the unlikely event that agreement were reached, the bargain could not bind unborn members of subsequent generations who did not consent to it,[6] thus necessitating endless rounds of renegotiation.

On the other hand, unilaterally acquired rights raise other problems. While a non-consensual model avoids the catastrophic transaction costs and strategic behaviour of the consent-based model, as a general philosophical matter, it seems impossible to explain why any nominally duty-imposing act should bind others in the absence of their consent.[7] Epstein explains the dilemma in the following terms:

> [t]he essence of any property right is a claim to bind the rest of the world; such cannot be obtained, contra Locke, by [any] unilateral conduct on the part of one person without the consent of the rest of the world whose rights are thereby violated or reduced. First possession runs afoul of this principle; so does the labor theory. Indeed the point is a

[1] Richard A Epstein, 'Possession as the Root of Title' (1979) 13 *Georgia Law Review* 1221, 1221 ('Root of Title').

[2] Ibid.

[3] Locke appreciated this problem, writing that, '[b]y making explicit consent of every commoner necessary to any one's appropriating to himself any part of what is given in common, children or servants could not cut the meat, which their father or master had provided for them in common, without assigning to everyone his particular part'.: John Locke, *Two Treatises of Government and A Letter Concerning Toleration* (Ian Shapiro ed, New Haven, Yale University Press, 2003) 112 §29 ('*Two Treatises of Government*').

[4] See Richard A Epstein, 'Holdouts, Externalities, and the Single Owner: One More Salute to Ronald Coase' (1993) 36 *Journal of Law & Economics* 553, 562 ('Holdouts, Externalities, and the Single Owner'); Richard A Epstein, *Design for Liberty: Private Property, Public Administration, and the Rule of Law* (Cambridge MA, Harvard University Press, 2011) 73 ('*Design for Liberty*').

[5] This is not to say that an initial bargaining point cannot emerge spontaneously. As was noted in Chapter 4, an 'initial distribution' will emerge where the marginal utility of each new asset equals the marginal cost of its acquisition and retention. However, because this initial allocation ultimately depends on force, or the threat of force, it simply replicates the problem of unilateralism. As Umbeck has argued, force is the only allocative mechanism that does not ultimately depend on consent: John Umbeck, 'Might Makes Rights: A Theory of the Formation and Initial Distribution of Property Rights' (1981) 19 *Economic Inquiry* 38, 39–40.

[6] See also NW Sage, 'Original Acquisition and Unilateralism: Kant, Hegel, and Corrective Justice' (2012) 25 *Canadian Journal of Law and Jurisprudence* 119, 125.

[7] For a discussion of this point see Allan Gibbard, 'Natural Property Rights' (1976) 10 *Noûs* 77, 78; Lisa M Austin, 'Possession and the Distractions of Philosophy' in JE Penner and Henry E Smith (eds) *Philosophical Foundations of Property Law* (Oxford, Oxford University Press, 2014) 182, 191–92; Sage, above n 6, 121–22.

> matter of principle perfectly general, and it applies moreover to any and every theory that uses individual actions as the source of entitlements against the collectivity at large. Property may look to be an individualistic institution, but the very nature and definition of the right seems to require some collective social institution to lie at its base. No "natural" act can legitimate a social claim to property.[8]

To return to Epstein's example, the problem for the first shell collector is that he cannot demonstrate why, in the absence of consent, his unilateral act of placing the shell in his pocket should have the effect of placing the second collector under a strict duty of non-interference in respect of it. Epstein argues that his inability to do so is a manifestation of Hume's famous 'guillotine',[9] according to which any move from a factual premise to a moral conclusion is invalid because it depends upon an unarticulated value judgement that is not part of the formal structure of the argument.[10]

Systems of private property thus appear to be stuck in the following bind. In choosing between consent and unilateral acts, they must choose between a starting point that is morally pristine but, due to insuperable transaction costs, impracticable, and one that is viable but, being dependent on unilateral assertions of right, creates duties that no one has any moral obligation to respect.

B. Bypassing Locke's Proviso

The problem of unilateralism appeared to trouble Locke himself. While Locke argued that the unilateral act of mixing one's labour with some object creates a morally justifiable right to it, he diluted that entitlement by subjecting it to a significant qualification. Locke wrote that: '[f]or his "labour" being the unquestionable property of the labourer, no man but he can have a right to what that is once joined to, *at least where there is enough, and as good left in common for others*'.[11] This caveat, which has become known as Locke's 'proviso',[12] appears almost platitudinous and, in daily life, is often invoked in more quotidian forms such as, 'don't hog all the food' or 'leave some for your sister'. As a qualification driven by distributive concerns, the proviso is a substantial and jarring caveat in a theory in which rights to external things are morally justified because they are an extension of one's God-given right of self-ownership.[13]

Of the various criticisms that can and have been made of the proviso, three are pertinent here. The first and most obvious is: who gets to decide whether there

[8] Epstein, 'Root of Title' (n 1) 1228.

[9] Ibid, 1240.

[10] David Hume, *A Treatise of Human Nature*, (David Fate Norton and Mary J Norton eds, Oxford, Oxford University Press, 2000) 302 [3.1.1.27].

[11] Locke (n 3) 111–12 §27. Emphasis added.

[12] See, amongst others, Robert Nozick, *Anarchy, State, and Utopia* (New York, Basic Books, 2013) 175–82; Jeremy Waldron, *The Right to Private Property* (Oxford, Oxford University Press, 1988) 209–18

[13] Locke (n 3) 111 §27.

is enough and as good left for others? As there is no government in the state of nature, there is no obvious entity with the institutional competence to make such a determination. Even if such an institution did exist, how could it ever obtain, except in particularly stark cases, enough information to answer the question posed by the proviso? If sufficient information could only be obtained after the purported creation of the right, could it be declared void *ab initio* by application of the proviso, even though such an ex post declaration would upset what appeared to be a settled distribution of rights?

Secondly, as Harris has identified,[14] although a theory of just *acquisition* may require something like the proviso,[15] a theory of just acquisition does not entail a just theory of *property*. Adherence to the proviso, or something like it, only ensures that a unilateral act of acquisition does not constitute a wrong to anyone else. In Hohfeldian terms, it simply gives one a 'liberty' to acquire. One cannot, however, move from the premise, 'In acquiring X, I do you no wrong', to the conclusion, 'Because I do not wrong you in acquiring X, you *therefore* come under a duty to me with respect to X'. This is a non sequitur. Because the proviso can only justify the creation of *liberties* and not the imposition of *duties*, it gets us no closer to justifying a system of property *rights*.

Thirdly, the proviso has the potential to act as a loose thread that, if tugged on hard enough, can unravel an entire jumper. If some resource is so abundant that acquisition by A does not make B, C and E any worse off, then it is not clear that it needs to be a 'thing' for the purposes of property law. As Merrill has observed, '[t]he "things" to which property attaches are scarce resources that humans find valuable; and they are valuable because they are things that people want. Property does not attach to things that are so plenteous [that] they are not scarce, or to things that no one wants'.[16] If Locke's theory is that one can only legitimately acquire a property right in a resource that is so plentiful that acquisition by A does not leave others worse off, a state of affairs that we may doubt,[17] then his theory of property ought to be rewritten as follows: 'mixing one's labour with some resource creates a morally justifiable right to it, but only if that right is redundant because the resource is so abundant that no one would bother to fight you for it anyway'. The problem is that when a resource becomes sufficiently scarce that force, or the threat of force, becomes worthwhile, Locke's proviso negates the legitimacy of the right precisely when it is most needed.[18]

[14] JW Harris, *Property and Justice* (Oxford, Clarendon Press, 1996) 202–3. See also Gerald F Gaus and Loren E Lomasky, 'Are Property Rights Problematic?' (1990) 73 *The Monist* 483, 490.

[15] Nozick (n 12) 178.

[16] Thomas W Merrill, 'Property and the Right to Exclude II' (2014) 3 *Brigham-Kanner Property Rights Conference Journal* 1, 4.

[17] See David Schmidtz, 'When Is Original Appropriate *Required*?' (1990) 73 *The Monist* 504, 504–5; Epstein, 'Holdouts, Externalities, and the Single Owner' (n 4) 561–62.

[18] As Wenar has remarked, '[a]s for "enough and as good" provisos, they will prevent potentially onerous duties being generated only at the price of prohibiting the acquisition of any scarce good': L Wenar, 'Original Acquisition of Private Property' (1998) 107 *Mind* 799, 810.

To illustrate with Epstein's shell example, Locke's proviso would prevent A, the first possessor, from placing B, the latecomer, under a duty of non-interference with respect to the seashell because B could legitimately complain that, on that particular island, there are insufficient seashells to go around. If application of the proviso negates the legitimacy of A's property right, then how, in the absence of such a right, do we determine who gets the shell? The answer is unlikely to be that A and B will agree to share it. Instead, it is more likely that the allocative problem will be resolved either by violence or the threat of violence and the shell will go to the more ferocious or intimidating of the two. As will be recalled from Chapter 4, if such allocative confrontations are repeated in symmetric contests, the competitors will adopt a mixed strategy, playing the passive 'Dove' strategy with probability x% and the aggressive 'Hawk' strategy with probability 1-x%. Though stable, this equilibrium is plagued by the ever-present threat of violence and will inevitably result in a certain number of Hawk–Hawk confrontations in which each competitor may suffer a serious injury, or worse. While some have argued that the proviso, or something like it, is essential to any morally justifiable system of private property,[19] it is difficult to see why a return to this sort of violent and anarchical world is preferable to a settled system of private property even if, by allocating the shell to A at the expense of B, such a system makes allocative decisions that violate Locke's proviso.

C. Cutting the Gordian Knot

As was argued in Chapter 1, private property describes a system of unilaterally acquired rights of non-interference that create exclusive use-liberties over resources that count as 'things' for the purposes of that system. As discussed above, the paradox at the heart of the system is that the existence of transaction costs means that no system of property could depend on liberty-holders voluntary submitting to duties. However, the problem of unilateralism means that no liberty-holder can become a duty-ower in the absence of her consent. So, how to break this impasse? Epstein argues that we do not need to. The virtue of the possession rule is that, though bedevilled by the problem of unilateralism, it is accepted by duty-owers as determinative. He writes that:

> [w]ithin this viewpoint it is possible to show the unique place of first possession. It enjoyed in all past times the status of a legal rule, not only for the stock examples of wild animals and seashells, but also for unoccupied land. In essence, the first possession rule has been the organizing principle of most social institutions, and the heavy burden of persuasion lies upon those who wish to displace it.[20]

[19] Joseph William Singer, 'Original Acquisition of Property: From Conquest & Possession to Democracy & Equal Opportunity' (2011) 86 *Indiana Law Journal* 763, 764, 775.

[20] Epstein, 'Root of Title' (n 1) 1241.

Epstein arrives at the pragmatic conclusion that, '[i]t may be an unresolved intellectual mystery of how a mere assertion of right can, if often repeated and acknowledged, be sufficient to generate the right in question. As an institutional matter, however, it is difficult in the extreme to conceive of any other system'.[21]

III. Is Possession Fair?

A. Efficiency versus Fairness: The Problem of Initial Allocation

Epstein's 'qualified defence'[22] of the possession rule thus amounts to the following: if we wish to have a system of private property, then we need a rule that allocates objects of property to right-holders. Given that no one can satisfactorily explain why unilateral acts create binding duties *in rem*, the best allocative rule that we can have is the allocative rule that we have got: 'better the devil you know'.

His argument is thus subtly different from that offered by theorists of spontaneous order. Epstein cuts the Gordian knot created by this particular 'is-ought' problem by pointing to the status of the possession rule as an accomplished fact. Spontaneous order-based accounts of possession, on the other hand, simply ignore it. As was argued in Chapter 4, conventions do not emerge through consent, but unconsciously through the individual interactions of self-interested actors and they thrive or perish for reasons unrelated to their moral justifiability. Though conventions become norms, their normative dimension, rooted in 'conventional morality', has nothing to do with their substantive content. Their normative content instead comes from the fact that they represent the established way in which people resolve a problem of human interaction. As Sugden explains, '[h]aving become a norm, a convention *becomes* a standard of fairness; but … it does not become a norm *because* it is seen to be fair'.[23]

Importantly, the premise that conventions are strictly amoral does not entail the conclusion that they are also immoral. Though evolutionary forces do not select for morality in conventions, could it nevertheless be that, by happy coincidence, the possession convention is tolerably fair? Before answering this question, it is necessary to answer an anterior question: why should we care if the rule that establishes the initial allocation of rights to some resource is fair?

This question of initial allocation raises the familiar tension between 'efficiency and equity'.[24] If efficiency is a society's only objective then, as Coase

[21] Ibid, 1242.
[22] Ibid, 1238.
[23] Robert Sugden, *The Economics of Rights, Co-operation, and Welfare* (Oxford, Blackwell, 1986) 159.
[24] See generally A Mitchell Polinsky, *An Introduction to Law and Economics*, 4th edn (New York, Wolters Kluwer Law & Business, 2011) 7–11. 'Equity' here refers to general conceptions of fairness and not the body of law developed by courts of Chancery prior to the enactment of judicature legislation.

demonstrated,[25] in a frictionless world, any initial allocation will do. As Epstein has remarked:

> [i]n this zero transactions cost world, it is difficult to form any strong intuitions of what the law should or should not do, how rights should or should not be defined, precisely because nothing of consequence appears to attach to the choices that are made … Where there are no social effects (save perhaps for some purely distributional consequences), our instincts about the merits of legal rules ebb in a sea of indifference.[26]

Given the existence of transaction costs,[27] a society that chooses to prioritise efficiency above all other considerations should seek to 'develop a set of rules that promote the closest possible approximation to the world of zero transactions costs'[28] by replicating the outcome that would be reached if parties could bargain without cost.

One objection to this indifference about the initial allocation of rights is that, as Epstein noted parenthetically, decisions about initial allocations, irrespective of their efficiency, have distributive effects. To continue with the Hohfeldian nomenclature, even in a world of zero transaction costs, the initial allocation redistributes income from the person with the duty, or no-right, to the person with the right, or liberty, by the amount of the least-cost solution to the conflict.[29] Calabresi and Melamed illustrate this by reference to a society that resolves the familiar conflict over noise by favouring those who prefer loud music over those who prefer silence.[30] If transaction costs are sufficiently low, this initial allocation will not determine how many decibels are ultimately produced. However, it will have distributive effects. Even if such a society is initially perfectly equal then, *ceteris paribus*, those who prefer loud music will, due to a fluke of preference, eventually become wealthier than those who prefer silence. This is because, in order to transform a 'liberty' to play loud music into a 'duty not to', silence lovers will have to negotiate a contract in which they pay the music lovers to, for instance, listen to their music through headphones.[31]

But why should those who prefer peace and quiet get the raw end of the distributive deal? In the absence of a compelling desert-based reason for favouring those who prefer music over those who prefer silence, or vice versa, the answer is simply that someone must. If we are to move from anarchy to society or, more

[25] RH Coase, 'The Problem of Social Cost' (1960) 3 *Journal of Law & Economics* 1, 10.

[26] Epstein, 'Holdouts, Externalities, and the Single Owner' (n 4) 555–56.

[27] It should always be recalled that Coase's objective was, of course, to point out that we do not live in a frictionless world and that the existence of transaction costs means that decisions about initial allocation will often become, de facto, decisions about final allocation. See Coase, above n 25, 15–16, 19.

[28] Epstein, 'Holdouts, Externalities, and the Single Owner' (n 4) 556.

[29] Polinsky (n 24) 14.

[30] Guido Calabresi and A Douglas Melamed, 'Property Rules, Liability Rules, and Inalienability: One View of the Cathedral' (1972) 85 *Harvard Law Review* 1089, 1098–99.

[31] And this is to say nothing of the distributive effects on more distant third parties. See generally Richard A Posner, *Economic Analysis of Law*, 9th edn (New York, Wolters Kluwer Law & Business, 2014) 89–90.

modestly, to solve some problem of social conflict, then we need some initial distribution of rights from which parties can bargain, rather than fight, to their preferred solution. Importantly, the move from anarchy to a system of settled property rights is not zero-sum. Indeed, if we follow Hume's analysis, discussed in Chapter 4, the move is better for everyone.[32] There is some reason to doubt this claim. We can, for example, imagine that some particularly ferocious individuals fared better in the state of nature than in society.[33] Nevertheless, whether it is Pareto efficient, the move from anarchy to property would presumably satisfy the less demanding Hicks-Kaldor standard of efficiency,[34] and any distributional concerns are better addressed by redistributing the gains from trade than by attempting to achieve a society's preferred 'equity goals' through the initial allocation of rights.[35]

Despite this, one might imagine a situation in which the basic allocative mechanism creates a pattern of initial entitlements that runs afoul of a principle on which there is strong moral consensus. This basic point has been made of the reciprocal and normatively inert conception of causation that underpins the Coase theorem. Coase stressed that all forms of social conflict involve two necessary but independently insufficiently causes.[36] To borrow his own celebrated example, crops cannot be trampled without cows and cows cannot trample without crops.[37] While our intuitive tendency is to regard the cows as the 'cause' of the trampled crops, this distracts from the more important question: should we have more beef or more brussels sprouts?[38] Whilst Coase's observation is true, the limits of a purely reciprocal conception of causation are easily demonstrated. To take an obvious example, A's fist and B's face are necessary but independently insufficient causes of B being punched the face. Nevertheless, we do not accept that an initial allocation of rights may either place A under a duty *not* to punch

[32] Hume argued that, in moving from anarchy to society, 'every individual person must find himself a gainer, on ballancing the account …' Hume, (n 10) 319 [3.2.2.22]. This is not to say, nor did Hume intend to say, that everyone would benefit equally.

[33] See also Sugden (n 23) 167.

[34] On the distinction between the Pareto and Hicks-Kaldor versions of efficiency see generally Posner, (n 31) 14–15. Unlike Pareto efficiency, which requires that no one be made worse off, the Kaldor-Hicks standard is satisfied if the gains made by the transition from position A to position B are greater than the losses. The Kaldor-Hicks conception thus allows for the possibility that the winners will compensate the losers but does not actually require that they do so. As Posner notes, the Kaldor-Hicks standard represents the default position in economics because the Pareto standard is so demanding that it will always be more of an ideal than a realistic goal.

[35] On this point see generally Polinsky (n 24) 158–62; Steven Shavell, *Foundations of Economic Analysis of Law* (Cambridge, Belknap Press, 2004) 654–55.

[36] Coase, (n 25) 2, 13.

[37] Ibid, 2.

[38] Similarly, Demsetz has remarked that, '[t]he use of words such as "blame", "responsible" and "fault" must be treated with care by the economist because they have no useful meanings in an economic analysis of the problems other than as a synonym for the party who could have most easily avoided the costly interaction': Harold Demsetz, 'When Does the Rule of Liability Matter?' (1972) 1 *Journal of Legal Studies* 13, 28.

B or, alternatively, allow A the liberty to punch B.[39] Even if either starting point will ultimately result in the same number of assaults, our strongly held moral beliefs about bodily integrity prevent us from accepting as legitimate a starting point in which B must pay A *not* to punch him in the face.

Whether it is efficient and whether any distributive concerns can be mitigated through redistribution, we may also reject a convention that, in creating an initial allocation, systematically discriminates against people on the basis of some morally arbitrary characteristic. This is an ever-present danger because, as was discussed in Chapter 4, conventions arise and thrive because the asymmetry on which they turn is salient, simple to apply and relatively cheat proof. Consequently, it is perfectly possible for a convention to become entrenched even though it contravenes a moral principle on which there is a strong social consensus. Hargreaves Heap and Varoufakis explain that:

> evolutionary theory predicts that the slightest asymmetries will engender a convention even though it may not suit everyone, or indeed even if it short-changes the majority. It may be discriminatory, inequitable, non-rational, indeed thoroughly disagreeable, yet some such convention is likely to arise when antagonistic social interaction (like *Hawk-Dove*) is repeated.[40]

McAdams gives the example of a property convention that turns on the asymmetry of sex such that, in a contest between a man and a woman, the man is always assigned the role of Hawk.[41] Even though it conspicuously and persistently benefits men at the expense of women, its simplicity and resistance to cheating make it a plausible candidate for a convention of property. That people may actively resent it on moral grounds does not make it unstable. Once a convention has become established, it becomes resistant to individual acts of rebellion because everyone does better by conformity than by defiance.[42] As McAdams elaborates:

> [w]hether you are a male or a female, if all other players play the strategy specified for their sex, your best response is to play the strategy specified for your sex. As with all conventions, once it arises, it will not pay for an individual to deviate. If a woman tries to play Hawk against men, who expect women to play Dove, she will simply endure the worst outcome (as will the men with whom she interacts). The result is a convention in which all property winds up in the hands of men. The same point can be made by using race roles instead of or in addition to sex roles, or any other immediately observable distinguishing traits.[43]

[39] Merrill and Smith remark that, 'If A punches B in the nose, we do not see B's nose as having contributed causally to the fist-nose interaction': Thomas W Merrill and Henry E Smith, 'The Morality of Property' (2007) 48 *William and Mary Law Review* 1849, 1861.

[40] Shaun Hargreaves Heap and Yanis Varoufakis, *Game Theory: A Critical Text*, 2nd edn (New York, Routledge, 2004) 247.

[41] Richard H McAdams, 'Beyond the Prisoners' Dilemma: Coordination, Game Theory, and Law' (2008) 82 *Southern California Law Review* 209, 247.

[42] Such a convention could only be changed by concerted, collective action: Hargreaves Heap and Varoufakis (n 40) 246.

[43] McAdams (n 41) 247.

There is a temptation to dismiss McAdams's 'battle of the sexes' hypothetical convention as a strawman. However, as Hargreaves Heap and Varoufakis demonstrated in their colour attribution experiment, noted in Chapter 4, conventions that track easily identifiable physical characteristics satisfy the simplicity imperative and are thus the very sorts of allocative mechanism that we would expect to see emerge spontaneously. Although such a convention is, as Hume argued, both an improvement on the state of nature and provides the basis for a series of welfare-increasing trades, we may nevertheless condemn it on the basis that it creates a morally objectionable initial allocation of rights to scarce things.

B. A Minimalist Conception of Fairness

Although we can assess conventions against standards fairness or morality, we can only ever employ a minimalist standard of fairness. This is so for three reasons. First, as previously explained, no initial allocation of rights could ever be achieved by consent. Although allocation by consent is appealing because it overcomes the philosophical problem of unilateralism, the need for bargaining would generate huge transaction costs and raise insuperable holdout problems. Members of a society that attempted to create an initial allocation by consent would simply replace the philosophical problem of the unilateralism with, as Epstein has remarked,[44] the very real problem of starvation.

Secondly, no allocative mechanism could rely upon case-by-case evaluations of merit or desert. Because the 'simplicity imperative' demands that there be little or no ambiguity in the application of a convention, no robust convention could turn on individual assessments of the most 'deserving' or 'needy' candidate, even if there were a strong social consensus on the answers to such questions in individual interactions. As with Sugden's beauty example, discussed in Chapter 4, the relevant population would rapidly replace the concept of 'need' or 'desert' with some proxy that is a crude approximation of the original concept but can, for that very reason, be applied with little interpretive confusion.

Finally, no convention that solves an impure coordination problem can avoid creating unequal outcomes in *individual* interactions.[45] Though the move from Hawk-Hawk to Hawk-Dove is a Pareto improvement, it is a greater improvement for the party selected to play Hawk than for the party selected to play Dove. The unequal division of spoils is not, however, a defect in the applicable convention, but a consequence of the antagonistic predicament in which the players find themselves.[46]

[44] Epstein, 'Holdouts, Externalities, and the Single Owner' (n 4) 562.

[45] This is not to say that the inevitability of unequal outcomes in individual interactions will lead to unequal outcomes overall. As noted below, a convention of unequal division that is 'perfectly cross-cutting' will, over the run of cases, replicate the distributive outcome of a convention of equal division.

[46] See also McAdams (n 41) 231.

Nor is the problem of unequal division solved by a move to Dove-Dove. A move from Hawk-Hawk to Dove-Dove looks like a better solution for two reasons. First, by dividing the prize in two, it treats indistinguishable parties without distinction. Secondly, it yields the same aggregate gains as Hawk-Dove but does so without the looming spectre of violence. However, as was discussed in Chapter 4, because it is not a Nash equilibrium, Dove-Dove is not a viable convention of property.[47] In any impure coordination problem, it is inevitable that one party must leave disappointed.

C. 'Cross-cutting' Asymmetries and Fairness

Given the limitations noted above, is there a standard of fairness against which an allocative convention should be judged? The argument defended below is that a convention will be *fair*, and thus morally acceptable, as long as no one is systematically excluded from benefiting from it. In the case of the basic allocative rule in property law, the argument can be put in the following way: because the simplicity imperative means that a rule cannot draw distinctions between people based on relative merit or desert, it follows that it ought to treat everyone as equally deserving. Consequently, a convention can be said to be 'unfair' if the asymmetry along which it breaks means that some people are systemically excluded from benefitting from it because, due to some salient but morally irrelevant characteristic, such as sex or hair colour, they are forever doomed to be assigned the role of Dove.

In other words, a convention will be fair if it breaks along an asymmetry that allows any given member of the population to play Hawk at least some of the time. Sugden has described asymmetries that have this property as 'cross-cutting' asymmetries.[48] If the convention is such that any given individual has the same probability of being assigned a particular role as any other individual, then the asymmetry upon which it turns is 'perfectly cross-cutting'.[49]

The notion of a cross-cutting asymmetry can be illustrated by reference to the intersection coordination game, discussed in Chapter 4, that models the simultaneous arrival of vehicles at an intersection. There are numerous conventions that could solve this very common coordination problem, but not all are cross-cutting. The rule 'cars give way to buses' is an example of a convention that is not cross-cutting because those who travel exclusively by car must always adopt the submissive strategy of giving way.[50] In contrast, the rule 'give way to the right' is cross-cutting because there is nothing preventing any given road user from being positioned to the right of any other road user at an intersection.

[47] Rose also notes that a convention of equal sharing would negate one of the great benefits of private property, exclusive resource management: Carol M Rose, 'Psychologies of Property (and Why Property Is Not a Hawk/Dove Game)' in JE Penner and Henry E Smith (eds), *Philosophical Foundations of Property Law* (Oxford, Oxford University Press, 2014) 272, 281.

[48] Sugden (n 23) 157.

[49] Ibid.

[50] Ibid.

Cross-cutting asymmetries are important in Sugden's account because they explain why certain conventions come to have moral force.[51] He argues that, as long as any given member of a population has a chance of being assigned the role of Hawk in any given encounter, everyone will have a reason to condemn those who defy the convention by playing Hawk when it demands that they play Dove. If someone tells me that he never yields at an intersection irrespective of whether the other vehicle is approaching him from the left or right, I will condemn his behaviour because, '[i]t is bound to occur to me that some day I might meet a fool like him approaching from my left'.[52]

On the account presented here, cross-cutting asymmetries are significant, but for a different reason. The significance of a cross-cutting asymmetry such as 'give way to the right' is that, because any given person can find himself on either side of the relevant fault-line, a convention that turns on such an asymmetry guarantees a minimum level of fairness by ensuring that no one is, due to some arbitrary characteristic, doomed to play Dove in every encounter.[53]

Possession satisfies this minimalist conception of fairness because the fact of possession is, as Sugden himself has noted,[54] cross-cutting. It is cross-cutting because there is nothing to prevent any given individual, regardless of her personal attributes, from being the first person to perform the recognised claim-staking act and, in so doing, being assigned the role of Hawk and de facto owner of the resource. Because possession turns, not on who a person *is*, but on what he *does*, the possession rule does not condemn anyone to the fate of being a perennial Dove in a world of Hawks.

This is not to deny that there are potential fairness objections to the possession convention. As noted above, because no convention can reliably assess the merits of rival claimants, an ideal convention would be one that treated each as equally deserving. This is one of the virtues of the Dove–Dove solution. Given, however, that a convention of equal sharing is not, for the reason noted above, a viable convention of property, the next best solution is a Hawk–Dove convention that turns on a perfectly cross-cutting asymmetry. Although, in individual interactions, one party must leave empty handed, such a convention would, given a sufficiently large number of interactions, replicate a convention of equal division.

However, because the possession convention depends on the outcome of a race to perform the requisite physical act,[55] it will not, in practice, be perfectly cross-cutting. It is obviously not true that, for instance, someone with a physical

[51] Ibid, 157–59.

[52] Ibid, 157. Sugden's example is predicated on the existence of a road rule that obliges those entering an intersection to give way to the right.

[53] Traffic examples are particularly apt to this discussion. As Owen has noted, a traffic light is, in its simplest form, a randomising mechanism that combines the fairness of a mixed strategy with the efficiency of a pure strategy. See Guillermo Owen, *Game Theory*, 4th edn (Bingley, Emerald Group Publishing, 2013) 179.

[54] Sugden (n 23) 158.

[55] The racing analogy is relatively common. See, eg, Thomas W Merrill, 'Accession and Original Ownership' (2009) 1 *Journal of Legal Analysis* 459, 463.

disability has an equal chance of being allocated the role of Hawk, particularly when the convention requires the performance of a physically demanding act, such as mortally wounding a fox or harpooning a whale. To the extent that the possession convention is not, for this reason, perfectly cross-cutting, it departs from our ideal in which morally indistinguishable parties are treated without distinction. Likewise, because one's ability to take possession of some object of property may depend upon the fluke of one's natural endowments or disabilities, it is perhaps not precisely the convention of property that would be agreed to by those bargaining behind a veil of ignorance.[56]

However, the fairness argument being defended here does not aim to demonstrate that the possession rule creates an ideal distribution of resources. The primary virtue of the possession rule is that, in creating a first cut of entitlements, it prevents, as Hume argued,[57] social implosion and provides the basis for welfare-increasing trades. Although almost everyone gains by a move from anarchy to a settled system of property rights, there is no guarantee that the mechanism that makes this possible will be morally attractive. Indeed, because evolutionary pressures select for simplicity and cheat-resistance, there is every possibility that it will not be. What is significant about possession is that, unlike a convention that fastens on some easily identifiable but morally irrelevant characteristic, be it gender, race, or whatever, there is no de jure restriction that prevents any given person from being assigned the role of Hawk in any encounter over an object of property. Because it simply requires that one be the first to perform the requisite possessory act, the possession convention avoids the moral faux pas of, in effect, telling people that they must forfeit a resource because of who they are.

If the possession rule fails some conception of distributive justice because it favours the able bodied over the disabled or those with sight over the blind then, given the possible alternative mechanisms, the solution is not to discard the possession rule, but to design redistributive mechanisms that bridge the gap between the ideal distribution dictated by some thought experiment and the world as it actually is.[58]

IV. The Place of Conventions in the Law

A. Hayek and the Danger of 'Divergence'

The above section argued that incumbency is not the possession rule's only virtue.[59] Because it is cross-cutting, it is also tolerably fair. So far, this chapter has offered

[56] John Rawls, *A Theory of Justice* (Cambridge MA, Harvard University Press, 2009) 118–19.

[57] Hume (n 10) 330 [3.2.4.1].

[58] A point noted in Ronald Dworkin, 'What Is Equality? Part 2: Equality of Resources' (1981) 10 *Philosophy & Public Affairs* 283, 291.

[59] Epstein, 'Root of Title' (n 1) 1242.

a defence of a particular emergent convention in the law of property. The remainder of this chapter argues that there are systemic benefits to be gained from incorporating emergent conventions into the positive law more generally.

Epstein has written of the possession rule that, '[t]he rule that possession lies at the root of title is one that a court can understand and apply; absent a better alternative it becomes therefore an attractive starting point for resolving particular disputes over the ownership of particular things'.[60] Although it is undoubtedly important that a rule be intelligible to a court, this is not the primary advantage of the possession rule, or any rule that tracks a conventional solution to a problem of social conflict. Possession's primary virtue is instead that, as a salient convention, it can be understood and applied by laymen *without* the assistance of specialists or the need for judicial intervention. This basic point, emphasised throughout this book, was captured by Ackerman's observation that:

> [e]very day, Layman is obliged to make countless decisions as to whether one thing or another belongs to him or somebody else. Yet it is a rare thing indeed for him to find it profitable to obtain carefully considered legal advice before making this decision. Indeed, most of the time Layman negotiates his way through the complex web of property relationships that structures his social universe without even perceiving the need for expert guidance.[61]

The reason why non-specialists can navigate their way through the web of property transactions which, as both Ackerman and Penner note,[62] are the stuff of daily life, is that the basic rules, 'possession creates entitlement', 'keep off' etc, are simple and salient. In game-theoretic terms, rules that track salient, extra-legal norms will reliably achieve their most basic goal of avoiding Hawk–Hawk miscoordination events. This sort of 'piggybacking' also has efficiency advantages. As Ellickson has noted,[63] one important cost that Coase omitted from his discussion is that of acquiring information about the law. As any lawyer knows, determining who has the right, or liberty, and who has the duty, or no-right, in respect of some asset or conduct can be complex and time consuming.[64] Because spontaneously emergent conventions turn on distinctions that naturally 'stick out' to those confronted with a particular problem, rules that piggyback on these conventions minimise these 'entitlement-determination'[65] costs and, in doing so, remove a potential barrier to the efficient allocation of resources.

[60] Ibid, 1229.

[61] Bruce A Ackerman, *Private Property and the Constitution* (New Haven, Yale University Press, 1977) 116.

[62] Ibid, 97; JE Penner, *The Idea of Property in Law* (Oxford, Clarendon Press, 1997) 30.

[63] Robert C Ellickson, *Order without Law: How Neighbors Settle Disputes* (Cambridge MA, Harvard University Press, 1994) 281. For Coase's list of transaction costs see Coase (n 25) 15.

[64] Indeed, as his study demonstrated, even those with formal legal training may have a poor working knowledge of the law; Ellickson (n 63) 50–51.

[65] Thomas W Merrill, 'Trespass, Nuisance, and the Costs of Determining Property Rights' (1985) 14 *Journal of Legal Studies* 13, 23.

This is not to say that rules which piggyback on emergent conventions will necessarily be optimal from any external perspective. Moreover, it is not an argument that the law should never seek to improve upon customary solutions to coordination problems. Ellickson has argued that, at least within close-knit groups, there are many instances in which, 'lawmakers interested in the resolution of humdrum disputes that arise *within* a group are unlikely to improve upon the group's customary rules'.[66] However, one could conceive of extra-legal rules that are morally repugnant, inefficient or otherwise undesirable, in which case the law ought to harness its own form of prominence to create an alternative convention.[67]

Be that as it may, the danger inherent in designing rules that diverge substantially from prevailing extra-legal conventions is that, just like the Académie française's futile attempts to banish 'le weekend' from demotic French, those rules will simply be ignored by those whose behaviour they are intended to guide.[68] If there is one lesson to be drawn from the work of law and society scholars, it is that the state is not the exclusive source of 'rules'.[69] Scholars such as Ellickson and Bernstein have demonstrated that communities are perfectly able to regulate their affairs by recourse to an entirely extra-legal code of rules.[70] As Ellickson concluded in his study of the cattlemen of Shasta County, 'some spheres of life seem to lie entirely beyond the shadow of the law'.[71]

It is possible to go further than this and argue that a substantial divergence between legal rules and conventional rules not only results in legal futility, but also has the potential to confound the legitimate expectations of those who are formally subject to the law's jurisdiction but whose behaviour is not necessarily guided by it. This sort of argument has previously been made by Hayek.

Hayek regarded 'the law', in contrast to legislation, as the collection of spontaneously emergent rules, standards, customs etc that people rely upon in their dealings with one another.[72] The law, on his account, is a 'going order which nobody has

[66] Ellickson (n 63) 283.

[67] The paragon example is Sweden's decision, implemented at 5:00 am on 3 September 1967, to switch from driving on the left to the right-hand side of the road. The established law, and underlying convention, was changed to harmonise Sweden's driving rules with those of its neighbours. The change was also desirable because most Swedes drove left-hand drive cars, which made executing right-hand turns dangerous. Revealingly, the convention was successfully changed despite a strong preference for the status quo amongst Swedish drivers. On law's expressive power see Richard H McAdams, *The Expressive Powers of Law: Theories and Limits* (Cambridge MA, Harvard University Press, 2015) 63; Richard H McAdams and Janice Nadler, 'Testing the Focal Point Theory of Legal Compliance: The Effect of Third-Party Expression in an Experimental Hawk/Dove Game' (2005) 2 *Journal of Empirical Legal Studies* 87, 97–98.

[68] For a similar observation see Merrill and Smith (n 39) 1854.

[69] Ellickson (n 63) 138–47.

[70] See, eg, Ellickson (n 63); Lisa Bernstein, 'Opting out of the Legal System: Extralegal Contractual Relations in the Diamond Industry' (1992) 21 *Journal of Legal Studies* 115.

[71] Ellickson (n 63) 283.

[72] FA Hayek, *Law, Legislation, and Liberty: A New Statement of the Liberal Principles of Justice and Political Economy* (London, Routledge and Kegan Paul, 1973) vol 1 'Rules and Order', 72–73. Hayek's view of law thus departs from the positivist tradition, according to which the question o whether a norm constitutes a 'law' depends upon its source or pedigree. See John Gardner, 'Lega Positivism: 5 1/2 Myths' (2001) 46 *The American Journal of Jurisprudence* 199, 199.

designed, an order that has formed itself without the knowledge and often against the will of authority, that extends beyond the range of deliberate organization on the part of anybody'.[73] Given his conception of law, Hayek believed that role of courts should simply be to enforce the set of expectations engendered by those spontaneously emergent norms. A judge must determine whether the parties:

> have conformed to expectations which the other parties had reasonably formed because they correspond to the practices on which the everyday conduct of the members of the group was based. The significance of customs here is that they give rise to expectations that guide people's actions, and what will be regarded as binding will therefore be those practices that everybody counts on being observed and which have thereby become the condition for the success of most activities.[74]

What ought to be decisive in any dispute is not whether the impugned action was:

> expedient from some higher point of view or served a particular result desired by authority, but only whether the conduct under dispute conformed to recognized rules. The only public good with which [a judge] can be concerned is the observance of those rules that individuals could reasonably count on.[75]

As long as parties can resolve any dispute by application of in-group norms and do not have recourse to the legal system,[76] no problem of confounded expectations is likely to occur. However, should a dispute end up in court, any substantial divergence between the conventional basis on which the parties conducted their affairs and the positive law, which a judge is bound to apply, may lead to an outcome that is not only unexpected but also unjust to the losing party. Even if, at least according to standard accounts,[77] this sort of divergence might not strictly amount to a failure of the rule of law, it nevertheless has the potential to diminish the law's claim to authority in the eyes of those who are subject to it.[78]

This 'divergence' concern is not always a decisive argument for retaining conventional or customary arrangements. Hayek himself acknowledged that 'we have always done it this way' is not a sufficient reason to persist with a customary rule that is demonstrably undesirable.[79] However, it does provide another, cumulative, reason to retain conventional rules, particularly when, as was argued of the possession rule, they are tolerably fair.

[73] Hayek (n 72) 119.

[74] Ibid, 96–97. Hayek's concept of a custom is almost identical to that of a convention.

[75] Ibid, 87.

[76] Indeed, as Bernstein has demonstrated, keeping in-group disputes out of the courts can itself be a substantive in-group norm. See Bernstein (n 70) 124–26, 134–35.

[77] See, eg, Joseph Raz, *The Authority of Law: Essays on Law and Morality*, 2nd edn (Oxford, Oxford University Press, 2009) 214–18; Lon L Fuller, *The Morality of Law* (New Haven, Yale University Press, 1964) 39.

[78] Raz argues that, '[t]he notion of legitimate authority is presupposed by that of effective authority' (n 77) 9. It is not clear that the law has 'effective authority' if people do not rely on its norms to resolve disputes, other than as a last resort in instances when the customary norms do not give them their preferred outcome.

[79] Hayek (n 72) 88–89. Although Hayek argued that change should only be made by legislation because, unlike judicial decision, legislation operates prospectively: at 89.

B. The Role of Possession in Land Registration Regimes

The enduring power of extra-legal conventions in the positive law and the complex relationship between emergent and made orders is powerfully illustrated by the continuing relevance of possession in jurisdictions that have moved to a comprehensive system of land registration. Although, in such systems, title to land is created by the administrative act of registering prescribed documents,[80] possession remains relevant in at least two circumstances.

First, disputes in which neither party claims as registered proprietor will be decided in favour of the party who can establish title by a prior act of possession. That is, prior possession is sufficient for the purpose of maintaining an action in trespass or ejectment against any third party who does not claim as, or through, the registered proprietor.[81] This point has been articulated by Hope J, who explained that:

> if A was the registered proprietor of an estate in fee simple in land and X remained in possession for twenty years, X would not obtain effective title as against A, but he would obtain a title against all the world save A and those claiming through him. If Y dispossessed him, I should have thought that X would be entitled to bring an action of ejectment against him; and indeed, [X] could do this whether he had been in possession for twenty years or for some lesser period.[82]

Secondly, many Australian jurisdictions also recognise adverse possession as an exception to the indefeasibility of titles created by the statutory process of registration.[83]

Australia is not the only jurisdiction that continues to recognise the significance of possession in real property law. The United Kingdom's legislative scheme provides that transferees of registered interests take subject to the unregistered interests of those who are, to use the legislative phrase, in 'actual occupation' of the land.[84] Moreover, as in many Australian jurisdictions, the United Kingdom's statute also recognises a modified version of the adverse possession doctrine.[85]

[80] *Breskvar v Wall* [1971] HCA 70; (1971) 126 CLR 376, 385 (Barwick CJ). It should be noted that not all systems of land registration are identical. For instance, the UK legislation creates a system of 'registration of title' and recognises numerous 'overriding interests' which, as is also noted below, either override first registration or registered dispositions. See generally Robert Edgar Megarry et al, *The Law of Real Property*, 8th edn (London, Sweet & Maxwell, 2012) chapter 7.

[81] See, eg, *Spark v Whale Three Minute Car Wash Pty Ltd* (1970) 92 WN (NSW) 1087, 1105 (Slattery J); *Newington v Windeyer* (1985) 3 NSWLR 555, 563–64 (McHugh J).

[82] *Spark v Meers* [1971] 2 NSWLR 1, 13.

[83] Although not all jurisdictions achieve this end through the same mechanism. Compare, for example, *Transfer of Land Act 1958* (Vic) s 42(2)(b) with *Real Property Act 1900* (NSW) s 45D(1). For an overview see Fiona Burns, 'Adverse Possession and Title-by-Registration Systems in Australia and England' (2011) 35 *Melbourne University Law Review* 773, 792–803.

[84] *Land Registration Act 2002* (UK) Sch 3, para 2. See generally EH Burn and J Cartwright, *Cheshire and Burn's Modern Law of Real Property*, 18th edn (Oxford, Oxford University Press, 2011), 1104–13.

[85] Ibid, Sch 6. Significantly, the UK scheme requires that the registered proprietor must be notified of any application by the adverse possessor who is seeking to become registered under the Act. See generally Megarry et al (n 80) 1494–512 [35-070]–[35-095].

It is not immediately apparent why possession should continue to play such an important role in jurisdictions in which prospective purchasers no longer need to trawl through chains of title deeds and can establish the identity of those with an interest in land by a simple computer search.[86] Given the widely held belief that the doctrine of adverse possession is morally dubious,[87] and may even amount to state-sanctioned land theft,[88] one might expect that many jurisdictions would happily consign it to the dustbin of history. So why does it live on? A solution to this puzzle is suggested below and, once again, the answer concerns the salience of possession.

C. The Power of Salience and the Danger of Divergence

Burns has written that, 'in a title-by-registration system, possession is no longer the bedrock of land law … As possession declines as the normative principle, so the legitimacy of registration is amplified because the only way of dealing with the land is through alteration of the register'.[89] As the discussion in the previous section demonstrated, Burns is not correct to say that alteration of the register is the only way of dealing with registered land. While alteration of the register is the only way of dealing with a registered *interest* in land, it does not prevent someone from selling, gifting, devising or otherwise alienating a 'possessory title' to registered land.[90] Just as importantly, while registration regimes have undoubtedly reduced possession's formal role in real property law, they have not sapped it of its normative force.

As the decisions in *Pye* and *Abbatangelo*, discussed in Chapter 3, demonstrate, possession has retained its salience as a means of making a property claim in jurisdictions with sophisticated registration systems. Whether that claim is ever formalised through registration, the audience accepts that possession confers an entitlement on the person who performed the requisite act. It thus seems likely that, even if the possession rule is eliminated from the *law* of property, it will not be eliminated from the *practice* of property. The consequence of attempting to purge the law of the possession norm will simply be to create a 'formal' and an 'informal' system of rights that operate in parallel, though not necessarily consistently. The essentially Hayekian argument for retaining formal recognition of the possession rule is thus that it prevents substantial divergence between the formal

[86] See generally Lynden Griggs, 'Possessory Titles in a System of Title by Registration' (1999) 21 *Adelaide Law Review* 157.

[87] *JA Pye (Oxford) Ltd v Graham* [2002] UKHL 30; [2003] 1 AC 419, 426 (Lord Bingham) ('*Pye*').

[88] Larissa Katz, 'The Moral Paradox of Adverse Possession: Sovereignty and Revolution in Property Law' (2010) 55 *McGill Law Journal* 47, 60.

[89] Fiona Burns, 'The Future of Prescriptive Easements in Australia and England' (2007) 31 *Melbourne University Law Review* 3, 22.

[90] *Asher v Whitlock* [1865] LR 1 QB 1, 6 (Cockburn J). See also *Allen v Roughley* [1955] HCA 62; (1955) 94 CLR 98, 145 (Taylor J).

law of property and the norms that actually guide people's behaviour in respect of objects of property.

This is not necessarily a decisive argument. As was also noted above, one can conceive of some imperative that justifies the law's departure from a customary solution and it is possible that the conclusiveness of the register is such an imperative. Nor is this to deny that there is a complex interplay between legal and customary understandings of property, such that the former comes to influence the latter.[91] However, even accepting this, the more general point is simply that salient solutions to coordination problems are not easily ignored or dislodged. Although, as Posner has argued,[92] a register will often, although not invariably,[93] represent an improvement over the possession rule, it may well be that the sheer prominence of possession as a means of announcing a claim to a tangible thing is such that it cannot be completely excluded from our, or perhaps any, system of property.[94]

V. Conclusion

This chapter commenced by considering Epstein's famous essay, in which he defended the possession rule on the qualified basis that 'the devil you know is better than the devil you don't'. The account offered above went substantially further than this partial defence. It was argued that, not only does the possession convention have the distinct advantage of incumbency, it is also fair because the asymmetry on which it turns ensures that no one is systemically excluded from playing 'Hawk' in any given encounter over an object of property. Perverse as it may appear, the moral arbitrariness and distributive blindness of the convention actually help to ensure that it satisfies a minimal standard of fairness.

What is more, because possession is the salient solution to the coordination problem created by scarcity, incorporation of the possession convention into the positive law's system of formal rights and duties ensures that, unless divergence is justified on moral or instrumental grounds, the law will not confound widely held normative expectations about the proper resolution of some question of mine and thine.

[91] As Pottage has argued, modern registration regimes appear to have changed, quite fundamentally, the way in which we conceive of property in land: Alain Pottage, 'The Measure of Land' (1994) 57 *Modern Law Review* 361, 363.

[92] Eric A Posner, 'Law, Economics, and Inefficient Norms' (1996) 144 *University of Pennsylvania Law Review* 1697, 1716.

[93] The benefits of such a system must be weighed against the costs of creating and maintaining it. See Douglas Baird and Thomas Jackson, 'Information, Uncertainty, and the Transfer of Property' (1984) 13 *Journal of Legal Studies* 299, 303–8. This issue is discussed further in Chapter 7.

[94] See also Thomas W Merrill, 'Possession as a Natural Right' (2015) 9 *New York University Journal of Law and Liberty* 345, 364.

Chapters 3, 4 and 5 of this book have set out what has been described as 'the expressive theory of possession'. Chapter 3 argued that the concept of possession refers to those acts and symbols that, within a given population, constitute an understood and accepted means of staking a claim to some object of property. Chapter 4 argued that the possession *rule* of the positive law is, first and foremost, an extra-legal *convention* that generates widely held expectations about how people are to behave when faced with a particular coordination problem. Contrary to the natural law tradition, the emergence of the possession rule cannot be attributed to some moral quality that is peculiar to it. However, as was argued in this chapter, that the possession has *amoral* origins does not mean that it is therefore *immoral* or otherwise unfair. Chapters 6 and 7 will complete this investigation into possession by discussing the implications of applying this account to three notoriously difficult issues in personal property law. Chapter 6 will consider the group of cases generally referred to as the 'finders' cases' and, finally, Chapter 7 will consider the issues of theft and good faith purchase.

6

Losing, Finding and the Limits of Possession

I. Introduction

In Chapter 3 it was argued that possession describes the family of signals that, within a population, constitute recognised and accepted ways of reducing objects of property to private ownership. One may wonder why the possession rule persists in such an unadulterated form in societies in which so little is *res nullius*.[1] One explanation, advanced in Chapter 5, is that possession's remarkable salience is such that, even in the presence of sophisticated registration systems, it will always remain an accepted way of announcing a property claim.

Though little remains unowned, there is one event that necessitates the existence of some mechanism for assigning new names to objects of property that have already been reduced to private ownership. Every society, no matter how urbanised, must have some means of dealing with the inevitable fact that people lose things. Although lost objects do not become *res nullius*, there must be some settled rule for peaceably filling the vacuum caused by the absence of the owner so as to prevent lost property from becoming, in Donaldson LJ's words, 'subject to a free-for-all in which the physically weakest would go to the wall'.[2] Whether the owner is ultimately found, the law must, as Auld LJ remarked, look 'for a substitute owner'.[3] The question is, how should the law go about selecting such a person?

Though a lost object does not become 'ownerless' in the strict sense, there is a very real sense in which it returns to the commons. Consequently, one might assume that the problem of losing and finding should be solved by application of the possession rule, according to which the first person to send the appropriate claim-staking signal would acquire a property right to the lost object. Because the title so acquired would be relative and not absolute, application of the possession rule would create a 'substitute owner' but without preventing the original owner from reclaiming the lost chattel from its finder. As discussed below, courts

[1] For a similar observation see Joseph William Singer, 'Starting Property: Approaches to Teaching Property' (2002) 46 *Saint Louis University Law Journal* 565, 570.

[2] *Parker v British Airways Board* [1982] QB 1004 (CA), 1009 ('*Parker*'). See also *Tamworth Industries Ltd v Attorney-General* [1991] 3 NZLR 616 (HC), 621 (Eichelbaum CJ) ('*Tamworth*').

[3] *Waverley Borough Council v Fletcher* [1996] QB 334 (CA), 345 ('*Waverley*').

claim that disputes over lost objects are resolved by determining which of the two competing parties can show prior possession.[4] The orthodox position is that when two people, neither of whom claims as or through the owner, are in a dispute over a lost chattel, that dispute will be decided in favour of the party whose root of title is based on an earlier act of possession.

The question for this chapter is whether, based on the expressive account of possession developed in the previous three chapters, this explanation of the 'finders' cases' is true. The answer given below is that it is not. The attempts, both judicial and academic, to explain the law's response to the problem of loss as a manifestation of the possession rule are both artificial and unconvincing. Although no compelling moral or instrumental case has been made for departing from the possession rule as determinative in disputes over lost chattels, it is clear that, at least in cases in which one party claims as an 'occupier', such disputes are resolved by a collection of non-possessory rules which turn on facts about the location of the find. While efforts to integrate these finding-specific rules into a general theory of possession have been motivated by a desire to rationalise the law, the only effect of shoehorning these *sui generis* rules into an ever more artificial concept of possession has been to further distort the basic concept.

II. The Rules in Outline

A. Occupiers, Possessors and Owners: (Another) Brief Note on the Nomenclature

Before commencing the substantive analysis, a brief note should be made about the terminology used below.

The term 'owner' is used to refer to the right-holder who has lost the chattel in question. This term is not intended to suggest that she has the best possible right to the lost chattel. It simply denotes that her right remains superior to that of either of the competing finders. For obvious reasons, the owner never appears 'on stage' in disputes over lost objects.

As will become apparent from the discussion below, most disputes over a lost object are between a finder and someone with some form of control over the land on which it was found. The question is: what to call such people? Although one is tempted to describe them as 'possessors', this suggests that they have an estate or interest in the land on which the chattel was found. However, it is not clear whether the relevant rules include people, such as contractual licensees, who have no proprietary interest. To prevent this peripheral issue from derailing the more important discussion, those who have some form of control over the land on

[4] See, eg, *Parker* (n 2) 1008 (Donaldson LJ).

which a lost chattel is found, whether or not they also have a property right in it, will be referred to by the generic appellation 'occupier'. Although the term 'occupier' is not entirely free of ambiguity, it is hoped that its use will avoid the sort of semantic distractions discussed in Chapter 2.

Because the rules on finding have been thoroughly discussed,[5] the overview given here will be brief. Before commencing, one important point must be reemphasised about the structure of the summary given below. Hickey, for instance, argues that the term 'finders' cases' is a misleading taxonomical category because it suggests a distinction without a difference.[6] If one believes that cases on finding can be explained as particular manifestations of the possession rule, then there is no reason to distinguish cases on finding from those on the acquisition of original rights to things, such as foxes and whales, that are, in fact, *res nullius*. However, this is not the argument that will be made in this chapter. Instead, it will be argued that 'finding' is a distinct taxonomical category within the law of property because, where one of the parties to the dispute is an occupier of the land on which the lost chattel was found, the law employs unique rules that turn, not on recognised claim-staking signals, but on one of the party's status as an occupier. Consequently, the brief outline offered below will distinguish between fact scenarios in which one party claims as an occupier and those in which neither party does.

B. Finder vs Non-Occupier

The simplest case of finding is that of an uncontested find. If I see a $20 note lying on the footpath and I pick it up and place it in my wallet, I will acquire a relatively good property right to that note by virtue of that very simple act of claim staking. If someone other than the owner takes it from me, I can sue in conversion.

The authority for this proposition is *Armory v Delamirie*,[7] in which Pratt CJ held that a chimney sweep's boy who found a ring was entitled to maintain trover against the goldsmith to whom he had delivered it for the purpose of obtaining a valuation. Pratt CJ held that, 'the finder of a jewel, though he does not by such finding acquire an absolute property or ownership, yet he has such a property as will enable him to keep it against all but the rightful owner, and consequently may maintain trover'.[8] As Patteson J stated in the equally famous case of *Bridges v Hawkesworth*, '[t]he general right of the finder to any article which has been lost as against all the world except the true owner, was established in the case of *Armory v Delamirie*, which has never been disputed'.[9]

[5] Most notably by Hickey, whose account is discussed in detail throughout this chapter. See Robin Hickey, *Property and the Law of Finders* (Oxford, Hart Publishing, 2010) ('*Law of Finders*').

[6] Ibid, 72. See also *Gray v Official Trustee in Bankruptcy* [1991] FCA 216; (1991) 29 FCR 166, 172 (Heerey J) ('*Gray*').

[7] *Armory v Delamirie* (1721) 93 ER 664; (1722) 1 Str 505 ('*Armory*').

[8] Ibid, 664.

[9] *Bridges v Hawkesworth* [1843–60] All ER Rep 122 (QB); (1852) 21 LJQB 75, 77 ('*Bridges*'). See also *Bird v Fort Frances* [1949] 1 WLUK 28 (HC); (1949) 2 DLR 791, 793 (McRuer CJ).

In *Bridges* itself, the plaintiff, a commercial traveller, found a parcel containing £55 in bank notes lying on the floor of the defendant's shop. The plaintiff handed the notes to the defendant with instructions that they be returned to their owner. The defendant advertised the find but no one came forward to claim it. Three years later, the plaintiff requested that the defendant return the notes, even offering to reimburse him for the expense incurred in advertising the find. When the defendant refused, the plaintiff commenced proceedings. The plaintiff lost at first instance but succeeded on appeal to the Court of Queen's Bench.

Although, to borrow Goodhart's neat phrase, *Bridges* has had a most 'distinguished posthumous career',[10] it was, in fact, a very simple case decided by a straightforward application of the possession rule enunciated in *Armory*. Patteson J held that the plaintiff succeeded because there were:

> no circumstances to take it out of the general rule of law, that the finder of a lost article is entitled to it as against all parties except the real owner; and we think that rule must prevail, and that the learned Judge was mistaken in holding that the place in which they were found makes any legal difference.[11]

As Goodhart and, more recently, Hickey, have demonstrated,[12] subsequent analyses of *Bridges* have mistakenly focused on the fact that notes were found in the 'public' part of the shop. This misunderstanding was apparently caused by Patteson J's remark that the notes, 'were never in the custody of the defendant, nor within the protection of his house before they were found'.[13] This remark led Lord Russell CJ, in the subsequent case of *South Staffordshire Water Co v Sharman*, to conclude that the decision in *Bridges* turned on the location of the find and to hold that the decision was therefore something of an anomaly that 'stands by itself, and on special grounds'.[14] If Lord Russell were correct, not only would it follow that *Bridges* would have been decided differently had the notes been discovered in a private part of the shop but, even more significantly, it would also have established that the status of one of the disputants as the occupier of the land on which the find was made is a relevant, if not decisive, factor in such cases.

Lord Russell's analysis was, however, based on a misreading of the decision. Justice Patteson's remark was not intended to highlight the importance of the location of the find. As Patteson J made explicit in the extract above, the place of find was irrelevant to the resolution of the dispute. His reference to the 'protection of his house' was instead, as Hickey has demonstrated,[15] a reference to the law of innkeepers. At common law, an innkeeper was strictly liable for loss or damage to his guests' goods. The corollary of an innkeeper's liability was his superior right, enforceable against third parties, to things which were *infra hospitium*, 'within

[10] AL Goodhart, 'Three Cases on Possession' (1928) 3 *The Cambridge Law Journal* 195, 196.
[11] *Bridges* (n 9) 78.
[12] Goodhart (n 10) 197–8; Hickey (n 5) ch 2.
[13] *Bridges* (n 9) 78.
[14] *South Staffordshire Water Co v Sharman* [1896] 2 QB 44 (QB), 47 ('*Sharman*').
[15] Hickey (n 5) 30–32.

the protection of his house'. When Patteson J remarked that the notes were not within the protection of the shopkeeper's house, he was simply making clear that the defendant could not oust the plaintiff's claim as finder on the basis that the notes were *infra hospitium*.

Although never overruled, *Bridges* is now a dead letter.[16] As the discussion below demonstrates, no modern judge presented with the facts in *Bridges* would resolve it as Patteson J did. Nevertheless, the decision demonstrates that, at least until 1851, disputes over lost chattels were resolved by a straightforward application of the possession rule. The plaintiff succeeded in *Bridges* simply because he was the first person to signal his intention to claim the notes for himself, subject to the superior entitlement of the owner who lost them.

In summary, even if the possession rule no longer resolves disputes between a finder and occupier, it continues to resolve disputes over lost items where neither party to the dispute claims as the occupier of the land on which they were found.

C. Finders vs Occupiers

(i) The 'Attached/Under' Rule

Different rules apply in disputes between a finder and the occupier of the land on which it is found. In these situations, there is not one rule, but two. The outcome turns not only on whether one of the parties claims as occupier, it also depends on whether the chattel was attached to, or buried beneath, the surface of the land.

If the lost chattel was attached to, or buried beneath, the surface of the land, then the claim of the occupier will invariably trump that of the finder. To recall the Hohfeldian nomenclature discussed in Chapter 2, the fact that the lost chattel is physically attached to, or subsumed under, the land is an 'operative' rather than a merely 'evidential' fact.

The origin of the 'attached/under' rule is the decision in *Elwes v Brigg Gas Company*,[17] described by Auld LJ in *Waverley* as the 'foundation of the modern rule'.[18] In *Elwes*, the defendant lessee found an ancient canoe buried beneath the surface of the soil. Despite being ignorant of the canoe's existence, it was held that the plaintiff, as lessor, had a superior right to possession. Chitty J reasoned that if the canoe:

> ought to be regarded as a chattel, I hold the property in the chattel was vested in the Plaintiff, for the following reasons. Being entitled to the inheritance under the settlement of 1856 and in lawful possession, he was in possession of the ground, not

[16] Ibid, 52.
[17] *Elwes v Brigg Gas Company* (1886) 33 Ch D 562 (Ch) ('*Elwes*').
[18] *Waverley* (n 3) 340.

> merely of the surface, but of everything that lay beneath the surface down to the centre of the earth, and consequently in possession of the boat … The Plaintiff then, being thus in possession of the chattel, it follows that the property in the chattel was vested in him. Obviously the right of the original owner could not be established; it had for centuries been lost or barred, even supposing that the property had not been abandoned when the boat was first left on the spot where it was found. The Plaintiff, then, had a lawful possession, good against all the world, and therefore the property in the boat. In my opinion it makes no difference, in these circumstances, that the Plaintiff was not aware of the existence of the boat.[19]

Although, as is discussed below, Chitty J's reasoning is far from convincing, the 'attached/under' rule has been applied in several subsequent cases and now constitutes the orthodoxy.[20]

(ii) The 'On/Unattached' Rule

A different rule applies in disputes between occupiers and finders where the lost chattel is not attached to, or under, the land. In such cases, the occupier will only succeed if she can demonstrate an intention to control property lost on her premises. In *Sharman*, decided just ten years after *Elwes*, Lord Russell CJ was asked to decide who, as between a workman and the freeholder, had the better title to two gold rings that the workman found buried beneath mud at the bottom of the pool he had been employed to clean out.

As noted above, Lord Russell CJ erroneously distinguished *Bridges* on the basis that that decision turned on the fact that the notes were found in the public part of the shop.[21] Because the rings were under the surface of the land, *Sharman* was resolved by a direct application of the 'attached/under' rule, the authority relied upon being Pollock's formulation of the rule in his *Essay on Possession*.[22] Although this was sufficient to resolve the case, Lord Russell, with whom Willis J agreed, went on to observe that:

> [i]t is somewhat strange that there is not more direct authority on the question; but the general principle seems to me to be that where a person has possession of house or land, with a manifest intention to exercise control over it and the things which may be upon or in it, then, if something is found on that land, whether by an employee of the owner or by a stranger, the presumption is that the possession of that thing is in the owner of the locus in quo.[23]

[19] *Elwes* (n 17) 568–9.
[20] See *Sharman* (n 14) 46–47 (Lord Russell CJ); *City of London Corporation v Appleyard* [1963] 1 WLR 982 (QB), 986–7 (McNair J) ('*Appleyard*'); *Waverley* (n 3) 350 (Auld LJ).
[21] *Sharman* (n 14) 47.
[22] Ibid, 46–47.
[23] Ibid, 47. By including things both 'upon or in' the land, Lord Russell extended, whether inadvertently or otherwise, the scope of the principle enunciated by Pollock.

This 'manifest intention to control' rule was subsequently confirmed by the Court of Appeal in *Parker*, in which the plaintiff, an outbound passenger, found a gold bracelet lying on the floor of the British Airways executive lounge at Heathrow Airport. The plaintiff handed the bracelet to an employee of the defendant but requested that it be returned to him should the owner not be found. Though the owner was never found, the defendant did not return the bracelet but sold it for £850. After hearing of the sale, the plaintiff successfully sued the defendant for the sale price.

Parker should have been an extremely simple case. The plaintiff was the holder of a valid ticket and entitled to use the lounge, so there was no issue of trespass. Likewise, because the bracelet was lying on the floor, the Court of Appeal was not faced with the added complication of the 'attached/under' rule derived from *Elwes*. It is thus unclear why the dispute could not have been resolved by a straightforward application of *Bridges*, a decision which, in turn, rests on the authority of *Armory*, the correctness of which, as Donaldson LJ made clear, was never in doubt.[24]

Nevertheless, in delivering the leading judgment, Donaldson LJ remarked that, '[i]t is astonishing that there should be any doubt as to who is right. But there is'.[25] Purporting to follow Lord Russell's obiter remarks in *Sharman*, Donaldson LJ held that, 'I would accept Lord Russell of Killowen C.J.'s statement of the general principle … provided that the occupier's intention to exercise control over anything which might be on the premises was manifest'.[26] Eveleigh LJ expressly agreed.[27] Donaldson LJ formulated the relevant rule as follows:

> [a]n occupier of a building has rights superior to those of a finder over chattels upon or in, but not attached to, that building if, but only if, before the chattel is found, he has manifested an intention to exercise control over the building and the things which may be upon it or in it.[28]

The defendant airline failed in *Parker* because it had not manifested the necessary intention to control items lost on its premises.[29]

One final matter that requires clarification is who constitutes an 'occupier' for the purpose of this rule. In *Hannah v Peel*,[30] the plaintiff, a soldier, found a brooch lying in a crevice above a window frame in a house that had been requisitioned by the Ministry of Defence. The house was owned, but never occupied, by the defendant. The soldier reported his find and the brooch ended up with the police who, after an unsuccessful attempt to find its owner, handed it, not to the plaintiff,

[24] *Parker* (n 2) 1009.
[25] Ibid, 1008.
[26] Ibid, 1013.
[27] Ibid, 1020. See also the comments of Sir David Cairns at 1021.
[28] Ibid, 1018.
[29] Ibid, 1019 (Donaldson LJ), 1020 (Eveleigh LJ), 1021 (Sir David Cairns).
[30] *Hannah v Peel* [1945] KB 509 (KB) ('*Hannah*').

but to the defendant. The defendant subsequently sold the brooch and the plaintiff successfully sued in detinue. As Birkett J observed, the dispute was very simple:

> [a]s to the issue in law, the rival claims of the parties can be stated in this way: The plaintiff says: "I claim the brooch as its finder and I have a good title against all the world, save only the true owner." The defendant says: "My claim is superior to yours inasmuch as I am the freeholder. The brooch was found on my property, although I was never in occupation, and my title, therefore, ousts yours and in the absence of the true owner I am entitled to the brooch or its value."[31]

After a thorough review of the authorities, Birkett J concluded that:

> [t]he defendant was never physically in possession of these premises at any time. It is clear that the brooch was never his, in the ordinary acceptation of the term, in that he had the prior possession. He had no knowledge of it, until it was brought to his notice by the finder. A discussion of the merits does not seem to help, but it is clear on the facts that the brooch was "lost" in the ordinary meaning of that word; that it was "found" by the plaintiff in the ordinary meaning of that word, that its true owner has never been found, that the defendant was the owner of the premises and had his notice drawn to this matter by the plaintiff, who found the brooch.[32]

Because the freeholder was never in occupation, *Hannah* does not conform to the archetypal model of an 'occupier vs finder' dispute. Hickey has remarked of Birkett J's judgment that:

> [i]n effect, what *Hannah v Peel* decides is that *possession* of land, as opposed to ownership or occupation, is a necessary prerequisite to any claim against a finder of goods, at least where the claimant has not otherwise established some title to the find, for example, by delivery or assumed duty.[33]

While Hickey is correct to say that *Hannah* decides that merely having a freehold right is insufficient to trump the rights of a finder, it is not, however, clear that this is also true of 'occupation'. We simply do not know because this question did not arise on the facts. As Birkett J made clear, the defendant, 'was never physically in possession of these premises at any time'.[34] Whether or not mere occupation, as opposed to possession, is sufficient to trump the rights of a finder could only be answered if there were a dispute between a finder and someone who was in occupation as a mere licensee, such as a guest at a hotel. Unfortunately, there is no reported case that decides this question.

Given that, in deciding for the plaintiff, Birkett J professed to be following the decision in *Bridges*,[35] we can confidently say that, in a dispute between finder and a non-occupying owner, the possession rule continues to apply.

[31] Ibid, 513.
[32] Ibid, 521.
[33] Hickey (n 5) 41–42.
[34] *Hannah* (n 30) 521.
[35] Ibid.

III. Are these Rules Possessory?

A. The 'Attached/Under' Rule

According to the analysis above, if neither of the parties claims as occupier, disputes over lost chattels will be resolved in favour of finders by a straightforward application of the possession rule. Moreover, as the decision in *Hannah* makes clear, the simple possession rule, derived from *Armory*, will also apply in disputes between finders and owners where those owners do not also 'occupy'. A more difficult question, and the primary question for this chapter, is whether the rules that govern disputes between occupiers and finders are really manifestations of the possession rule. Before answering this question, it is necessary to consider the judicial and academic attempts to bring these rules within the possessory fold, beginning with the 'attached/under' rule.

An occupier will prevail over a finder if the chattel in question is attached to or under the land on which it was found. One should begin by noting that, as a matter of basic land law, it is not clear why this should be. The rule appears to be an outgrowth of the doctrine of fixtures, to which Chitty J made reference in *Elwes*.[36] This view is supported by Auld LJ's remark about *Elwes* that as 'Goodhart concluded in his celebrated article … the lessor "was the possessor of the boat because he was in possession of the ground," to which I add what is implicit in that conclusion, *because the boat had become permanently fixed in the ground*.'[37]

This cannot, however, be correct. The consequence of concluding that the boat had become 'permanently fixed in the ground' must be that the boat had ceased to exist as a chattel because it had merged with the realty. If this were true, then two things would follow. First, *Elwes* would not have been a case of finding at all. The lessor would have succeeded simply because the boat formed part of the 'land' to which he held the reversion. Secondly, to hold that a lost chattel has become a fixture would have the perverse consequence of foreclosing on the title of the owner.[38] Whilst destruction of the title of the owner is unproblematic in the case of a pre-historic boat, it is the worst possible outcome in more mundane cases in which the owner may be in a position to reclaim the lost chattel.

If, on the other hand, the lost item does not become a fixture and retains its identity as a chattel, then there appears to be no legal reason for favouring the lessor. It will be recalled that in *Elwes*, Chitty J held that, before leasing the land, the lessor was:

> in possession of the ground, not merely of the surface, but of everything that lay beneath the surface down to the centre of the earth, and consequently in possession of the

[36] *Elwes* (n 17) 657.

[37] *Waverley* (n 3) 341. Emphasis added.

[38] This criticism is also made in Ben McFarlane, *The Structure of Property Law* (Oxford, Hart Publishing, 2008) 157–58.

> boat ... The Plaintiff then, being thus in possession of the chattel, it follows that the property in the chattel was vested in him.[39]

But was the lessor in possession of everything beneath the surface? The only authority cited by Chitty J in support of this proposition was *Regina v Rowe*,[40] in which it was held that a canal company had sufficient title to the iron found at the bottom of its canal to enable the accused to be indicted for larceny. Pollock CB held the canal company's right to the iron, 'was of the same nature as that which a landlord has in goods left behind by a guest. Property so left is in the possession of the landlord for the purpose of delivering it up to the true owner; and he has sufficient possession to maintain an indictment for larceny'.[41]

Apart from the obvious point that the authority for Chitty J's proposition is very slight, it is also not very persuasive given the facts in *Elwes*.[42] This is because, as Hickey has demonstrated,[43] Chitty J overlooked the fact that the outcome in *Rowe* was expressly based on Pollock CB's conclusion that the canal company was under a legal obligation, analogous to that of an innkeeper, to return items lost in the canal to their owners. Clearly, no analogous duty arose on the facts in *Elwes*.

The more important point is that Chitty J's conclusion does not, as a matter of basic land law, follow from his premise. As was discussed in Chapter 1, the *ad coelum* principle, to which he appears to refer in the extract above, provides that the concept of land in English law has three dimensions. As a consequence, trespassory protection is not confined to interferences that occur at ground level but extends to acts of boundary crossing that occur both above and below the surface of the earth. Contrary to what Chitty J appears to suggest, it does not follow from this principle that any object that happens to fall within the territorial boundaries of that three-dimensional column is therefore 'realty'. Were it otherwise, the doctrine of fixtures would be redundant. Likewise, it would also mean that if A conveyed his freehold title to B, B would be entitled to everything, whether a chattel or otherwise, that happened to be on the land at the time of the conveyance. This, as McFarlane also observes, cannot be correct.[44]

More particularly, although the removal of a chattel from freehold land would, in the absence of permission, constitute a trespass to land, it does not follow that the freeholder therefore has a property right in whatever it is that the trespasser has removed. Imagine that I accidentally hit a cricket ball over my neighbour's fence. While I will commit a trespass if I attempt to retrieve the ball from her backyard without asking her permission, my neighbour's right to exclude me from her land does not, without more, give her any entitlement to my ball as a chattel.

[39] *Elwes* (n 17) 568.
[40] *Regina v Rowe* (1859) 169 ER 1180; Bells CC 93 ('*Rowe*').
[41] Ibid, 1181.
[42] The decision in *Regina v Rowe* was mentioned briefly in Oliver Wendell Holmes, *The Common Law* (Boston, Little, Brown and Company, 1948) and followed in *Hibbert v McKiernan* [1948] 2 KB 142.
[43] Hickey (n 5) 33.
[44] McFarlane (n 38) 158–59. See also *Moffatt v Kazana* (1969) 2 QB 152.

This conclusion does not change depending upon whether the ball lands on my neighbour's roof or becomes buried beneath her compost heap. In the absence of a consensual transfer, she will only acquire a right to the ball if she takes possession of it or if, as a matter of law, it becomes a fixture. Quite apart from the fact that an inadvertent act such as hitting a ball over a fence would never satisfy a test that turns on the affixer's objectively ascertained intention to merge a chattel with land,[45] to apply the fixture rule to cases of finding would, as noted above, have the unwelcome consequence of destroying the owner's title.

Given this, is there some other orthodox basis on which to justify the 'attached/under' rule in *Elwes*? The most influential explanation is that given by Pollock, who wrote that:

> [t]he possession of land carries with it in general, by our law, possession of everything which is attached to or under that land, and, in the absence of a better title elsewhere, the right to possess it also. And it makes no difference that the possessor is not aware of the thing's existence.[46]

The question for Pollock was whether the principle to emerge from *Elwes* was unique to those cases of finding in which the lost chattel was buried beneath the surface of the land, or whether it could instead be explained as a particular manifestation of the general possession rule. He argued that:

> [i]t is free to any one who requires a specific intention as part of *de facto* possession to treat this as a positive rule of law. But it seems preferable to say that the legal possession rests on a real *de facto* possession, constituted by the occupier's general power and intent to exclude unauthorized interference.[47]

Pollock's account of *Elwes* was, as noted above, adopted without qualification by Lord Russell CJ in *Sharman*,[48] whose statement of principle was, in turn, approved by the English Court of Appeal in *Parker*.[49] For present purposes, the relevant question is not whether it represents the orthodoxy, but whether it is convincing.

One shortcoming with Pollock's explanation of *Elwes* is that, as Hickey has argued, it was based on a 'general theory of possession, which was not expressly considered or invoked by the court'.[50] As far as the present account is concerned, its more significant shortcoming is that, if possession describes a signal by which someone informs others of his intention to stake a claim to some thing, one cannot possess that thing whilst being entirely ignorant of its existence.

This problem will be discussed in greater detail below. For present purposes, it is sufficient to make the following observation about *Elwes*. When Chitty J

[45] *Holland v Hodgson* (1871–1872) LR 7 CP 328, 334–35 (Blackburn J); *Melluish (Inspector of Taxes) v BMI (No 3) Ltd* [1996] AC 454 (HL), 473 (Lord Browne-Wilkinson).

[46] Frederick Pollock and Robert Samuel Wright, *An Essay on Possession in the Common Law* (Oxford, Clarendon Press, 1888) 41.

[47] Ibid.

[48] *Sharman* (n 14) 46–47.

[49] *Parker* (n 2) 1013–14 (Donaldson LJ).

[50] Hickey (n 5) 37.

remarked that, '[i]n my opinion it makes no difference, in these circumstances, that the Plaintiff was not aware of the existence of the boat',[51] he was not assuming, as Pollock suggested, that the plaintiff's *animus possedendi* was established by his general 'intent to exclude unauthorized interference'.[52] As far as Chitty J was concerned, the lessor's intention simply did not enter into the matter because, as was discussed above, his Honour appeared to believe that, as a matter of land law, everything beneath the surface of the soil *was in fact the soil*. Although, as a matter of law, Chitty J was wrong to think so, this is nevertheless the best, if not the only, explanation for his decision.

There is also another reason to believe that the 'attached/under' rule has little, if anything, to do with a simple application of the possession rule. That is, courts appear to regard it as a *sui generis* rule justified by instrumental considerations that have nothing to do with possession. In *Waverley*, the defendant, with the aid of a metal detector, found a medieval brooch buried nine inches beneath the surface of the soil in a public park in Surrey. Auld LJ, with whom Ward LJ and Sir Thomas Bingham MR agreed, resolved the dispute in favour of the plaintiff council by application of the 'attached/under' rule.[53]

Counsel for the defendant attacked the 'attached/under' rule as an unprincipled and arbitrary way of distinguishing between the claims of occupiers and finders.[54] In defending the rule, Auld LJ did not justify it by an appeal to the orthodox principle that 'possession is a root of title'. Instead, his Honour highlighted its supposed rationale. Reprising comments made by Donaldson LJ in *Parker*, Auld LJ argued that the explanation for the rule is to be found in the law's concern to prevent those who commit trespass by interfering with land from profiting from their wrong.[55] Putting aside the merits of this, and the other, instrumental concerns discussed below, Auld LJ's comments at least suggest that courts do not view the 'attached/under' rule in possessory terms.

B. The 'On/Unattached' Rule

Where there is a dispute between a finder and an occupier, but the lost item is not attached to or under the land, an occupier will only succeed if he has manifested an intention to control the land and the things that may be on it. Although this rule differs in substance from the 'attached/under' rule, those who seek to explain it as a manifestation of the possession rule nevertheless face the same basic obstacle. That is, they must explain how someone can have an intention in respect of some object despite being completely ignorant of its existence. This notion is obviously

[51] *Elwes* (n 17) 569.
[52] Pollock and Wright (n 46) 41.
[53] *Waverley* (n 3) 350. Auld LJ was also prepared to find that the council had manifested the intention to control items lost on its property: at 350.
[54] Ibid, 344–45.
[55] Ibid, 345.

incompatible with a theory of possession according to which the very function of the possession rule is to signal one's intention to stake a claim to some tangible thing. Even if one does not subscribe to this view of possession, the idea that one can possess in ignorance is one that many find unsatisfactory.[56]

Courts and commentators have attempted to walk this conceptual tightrope by arguing that there are circumstances in which an occupier's intention, though not express, is nevertheless 'manifest'. In *Parker*, Donaldson LJ remarked that:

> [i]t was suggested in argument that in some circumstances the intention of the occupier to assert control over articles lost on his premises speaks for itself. I think that this is right. If a bank manager saw fit to show me round a vault containing safe deposits and I found a gold bracelet on the floor, I should have no doubt that the bank had a better title than I, and the reason is the manifest intention to exercise a very high degree of control. At the other extreme is the park to which the public has unrestricted access during daylight hours. During those hours there is no manifest intention to exercise any such control. In between these extremes are the forecourts of petrol filling stations, unfenced front gardens of private houses, the public parts of shops and supermarkets as part of an almost infinite variety of land, premises and circumstances.[57]

Likewise, Eveleigh LJ commented that:

> I would be inclined to say that the occupier of a house will almost invariably possess any lost article on the premises. He may not have taken any positive steps to demonstrate his *animus possidendi*, but so firm is his control that the animus can be seen to attach to it. It is rather like the strong room of a bank, where I think it would be difficult indeed to suggest that a bracelet lying on the floor was not in the possession of the bank. The firmer the control, the less will be the need to demonstrate independently the *animus possidendi*.[58]

This view has also been advanced by Pollock.[59] Likewise, in discussing *Bridges*, Holmes wrote that, '[t]here can be no *animus domini* unless the thing is known of; but an intent to exclude others from it may be contained in the larger intent to exclude others from the place where it is; without any knowledge of the object's existence'.[60] In Hohfeldian terms, Pollock and Holmes treated the location of the find as an 'evidential' rather than an 'operative' fact. Unlike in the case of the 'attached/under rule', the relevance of the location of the find is that it provides evidence from which a court may infer the existence of the 'operative' mental fact, namely the occupier's *animus possidendi*, or lack thereof.

This issue has been more recently discussed by Hickey. Although Hickey claims that Pollock's and Holmes's 'physical control plus intention' theory of possession

[56] See generally Richard A Epstein, 'Possession' in Peter Newman (ed), *The New Palgrave Dictionary of Economics and the Law* (London, Palgrave Macmillan, 1998) 62, 65.
[57] *Parker* (n 2) 1019.
[58] Ibid, 1020.
[59] Pollock and Wright (n 46) 39.
[60] Holmes (n 42) 222.

is a novelty borrowed from Roman law,[61] he argues that it can nevertheless help to explain, perhaps even to rationalise, the modern law's apparent preoccupation with the circumstances of the find. On Hickey's account, the circumstances of the find are relevant, but not because they determine which of several discrete rules must be applied in order to resolve a dispute over a lost chattel.[62] Rather, they are relevant because they justify raising a presumption in favour of an occupier which relieves him of the usual obligation to prove the mental fact of his intention by adducing evidence of it. Hickey writes that:

> [p]ut shortly, disputes between possessors of land and finders are to be resolved according to which of the parties can show a prior right by virtue of possession. This always depends on the possessor of land's ability to oust the claim of the finder by proving the twin possessory elements of control and intention, but sometimes we remove from him the burden of proving the latter because it is so obvious as to speak for itself. The apparent rule giving a possessor of land a better right to goods attached to his land is no more than the most widely recognised example of this evidentiary concession.[63]

Before discussing whether this explanation is correct, something must first be said about the function of presumptions in the law. Presumptions are not substantive rules of property law, but adjectival rules that form part of the law of evidence. As Swadling explains:

> [p]resumptions properly-so-called form part of the law of proof. Generally speaking, facts can be proved by admission, judicial notice, or evidence. In the absence of admission and judicial notice, the general rule is that facts must be proved by evidence, the burden of proving those facts lying on the party alleging them to have occurred. Very occasionally, however, proof by evidence of one fact, the "basic" or "primary" fact, gives that party to the litigation the benefit of another fact, the "secondary" fact, without any need to adduce evidence in proof. In such cases, the fact is proved by presumption. The burden then lies on the other party to adduce evidence to rebut the presumption. If they do not, the tribunal of fact must find the secondary fact proved.[64]

Proof of the second fact by presumption is justified because, in the absence of actual evidence to the contrary, it represents a state of affairs that one would expect to obtain given by proof of the primary fact.[65] Because presumptions are merely starting points, they must yield to actual evidence to the contrary. An 'irrebutable presumption' is an oxymoron. A presumption that cannot be rebutted by evidence to the contrary is not a method of proof but a substantive rule of law.[66]

[61] Hickey (n 5) 34–37.
[62] Ibid, 46–47.
[63] Ibid, 52.
[64] William Swadling, 'Explaining Resulting Trusts' (2008) 124 *Law Quarterly Review* 72, 74.
[65] Ibid. See also *Calverley v Green* [1984] HCA 81; (1984) 155 CLR 242, 264 (Murphy J). Although, as Ullmann-Margalit correctly notes, the proposition that X is very likely given proof of Y is only a piece of practical wisdom that does not, of itself, justify why the law allows a party to prove X by a presumption rather than by evidence. See Edna Ullmann-Margalit, 'On Presumption' (1983) 80 *The Journal of Philosophy* 143, 157–58.
[66] Swadling (n 64) 75.

On Hickey's account, rules concerned with the circumstances of the find can be reconciled with the general possession rule because they are not substantive but evidential in nature. To borrow Swadling's terminology, these rules describe the 'primary facts' that, if proved by evidence, allow the 'secondary' mental fact about intention to be proved by presumption rather than by evidence.

If this explanation is true, then it must be possible to conceive of facts that, if proved, are capable of rebutting the presumption. Serious doubt is thrown on this by the decision in *Chairman, National Crime Authority v Flack*.[67] In *Flack*, the respondent was the lessee of a house in Sydney, to which her son had free access. The police, who suspected the son of drug offences, searched the house and discovered a briefcase containing $433,000 in cash concealed at the back of a cupboard. The uncontested evidence was that the respondent was not only unaware of the existence of the suitcase but was horrified when its presence was brought to her attention.[68] Pursuant to statutory powers, the appellant seized the suitcase as evidence. Sometime later, the respondent sought an order for the delivery up of the suitcase and its contents based on her prior possession.

Because the owner of the suitcase, presumably the respondent's son, never lost it, *Flack* was not a traditional case of finding. However, as was expressly noted, this made no difference to the applicable principles.[69] Following the Court of Appeal in *Parker*, a majority of the Court found for the respondent on the basis that, as the occupier of a private home, she had manifested the necessary intention to control items on her premises, whether or not she was aware of their existence.[70] Foster J delivered a powerful dissent, arguing that the presumption generated by the circumstances of the find was rebutted on the facts. His Honour wrote that:

> I return to the finding which I have made, namely that had her son, or anyone else, sought Mrs Flack's permission to leave this case and its contents in her custody or possession, this permission would have been refused. That is, I am satisfied that she would never voluntarily have taken possession of the briefcase and contents nor assented to them passing into her custody or control. In these circumstances, I ask myself how can it be presumed simply from her status as householder that she had these goods in her possession? To make that assumption on the basis that her occupation and control of her premises as a householder necessarily manifested an intention on her part to exercise control over them would be to fly in the face of a contrary finding of fact. The presumption, which is not irrebuttable, must yield to the finding. To put the matter another way, is it reasonable that Mrs Flack, who clearly manifested shock and horror when confronted with the presence in her home of these goods, and who, quite clearly, would not have countenanced their presence had she known of

[67] *Chairman, National Crime Authority v Flack* [1998] FCA 932; (1998) 86 FCR 16 ('*Flack*').
[68] Ibid, 19–20 (Foster J).
[69] Ibid, 27 (Heerey J).
[70] Ibid, 25–27 (Heerey J), 30–31 (Tamberlin J).

> them, be nevertheless entitled or obliged, by the presumption relied upon, to assume possession of them? This would be to impose upon her possession of unwanted goods.[71]

As this passage makes clear, the majority's decision in *Flack* makes it difficult to conceive of circumstances in which the presumption could be rebutted. Although, as a matter of law, it is possible to defend the outcome on the basis that the intention is general and does not apply to specific chattels, the result strongly suggests that the location of the find, at least as far as private houses are concerned, is not regarded by courts as giving rise to an evidential presumption. Instead, like the 'attached/under' rule, it is treated as a substantive rule of law.

C. Is the Presumption Justifiable?

A final observation should be made about the desirability of the presumption. As was noted above, allowing a party to prove a fact by presumption rather than evidence is only justified because there is reason to believe that the secondary fact is likely to be true given proof of the primary fact. Thus, if Hickey's explanation of these cases is preferable to the 'discrete rules' account offered here, there must be some reason to believe that occupiers have some intention in respect of chattels that have been lost on their land.

The deficiency in Hickey's account is that it does not overcome what might be described as the basic 'argument from ignorance'. The fundamental problem is that knowledge is the *sine qua non* of an intention of any sort. Take the example of people who occupy land as a private home. While it is true that such people have a generalised intention to exclude everyone but invitees, without knowing who those non-invitees actually are, it is not possible to extrapolate from this reasonable claim, substantiated by the existence of door locks, to the further claim that they also have an intention to control objects of whose very existence they are ignorant.

Occupiers of private homes have no intention in relation to such things because, unlike lawyers attempting to rationalise cases on finding, they simply have no reason to consider the possibility until a find is brought to their attention. To ask whether occupiers have an intention in respect of items which, unbeknownst to them, someone has lost on their premises is, to borrow the phrase made famous by Donald Rumsfeld, to enter the realm of the 'unknown unknown'. To test the matter in another way, in how many homes does one see a basket labelled 'lost property'? If we are in the realm of the 'unknown unknown', then the attempt to justify an occupier's superior entitlement to lost chattels on the ground of a presumptive belief about his intention is to use a presumption to prove a fiction.

[71] Ibid, 22.

Even Tamberlin J, who formed part of the majority in *Flack*, recognised the artificiality of attempting to bring these rules within the possession fold. His Honour wrote that:

> [T]he notion of a person intending to exercise possession or control over an article of which he or she was at all relevant times unaware is somewhat artificial. In some respects it is analogous to a legal "fiction" in the sense that it is a statement which on its face is false but is recognised as having utility in the application of legal principles … However, its proper characterisation in my view, is rather that of a rebuttable presumption of fact. The presumed intention of a housekeeper to extend the protection of her home to everything in it, is a concept which has been applied in the authorities and serves a useful purpose in resolving disputes between claimants to possession where there might otherwise be an unexplained gap or vacancy in the possessory chain. The presumption is designed to assist in the development of a coherent doctrine of possession. In his text, Professor Fuller specifically refers to fictions of applied law, such as the fiction of 'finding' in an action of trover. It provides assistance in dealing with the difficult questions which can arise in deciding which of two competing parties, if any, has the better claim to possession of an article.[72]

Although legal fictions may have uses, it should always be remembered that they are nevertheless just that: fictions. Whilst the fiction of the occupier's intention might bring a certain taxonomical simplicity to the law of property, it does so only at the cost of an ever-more artificial and strained concept of possession.

D. Conclusion

The previous section considered whether there is one rule that applies to cases of finding or several, discrete, rules. It was concluded that, although it may be taxonomically elegant to explain the cases discussed above as nothing more than particular manifestations of the possession rule, this is the least plausible reading of them. The better view is that cases of finding turn on a set of discrete rules, the applicability of which depends on the identity of the litigants and the circumstances of the find.

When a dispute over a lost chattel is between two parties, neither of whom claims as the occupier of the land on which it was found, the dispute will be resolved by a straightforward application of the possession rule. However, this is not true of disputes between a finder and an occupier. Despite valiant attempts to argue otherwise, the resolution of these cases cannot be explained in terms of priority of possession. Rather, they depend on discrete rules that turn on the circumstances of the find, including the nature of the premises and the location of the lost chattel at the time of finding. If such cases did turn on possession, they would invariably be resolved in favour of the finder for the simple reason that she was the first party to signal her intention to stake a claim to the lost chattel.

[72] Ibid, 30.

If the foregoing analysis is true, then one interesting, though clearly unintended, consequence follows. If, in some cases, occupiers succeed against finders by dint of their status as occupiers, then we must amend the list of ways in which one can acquire an original property right in a chattel, discussed in Chapter 1. In addition to possession, natural increase and so on, we must add that occupiers of land will acquire original rights to chattels that have either become attached to or subsumed under land or lost on land that constitutes 'a private home'. Given that there is a *numerus clausus* of property rights, but no equivalent restriction on the ways in which such rights can be created, this amendment, though perhaps undesirable and almost certainly accidental, can seemingly be made without contravening any basic rules of property law.

Finally, and perhaps most importantly, what is never explained is why both courts and commentators feel it necessary to justify the outcome of these 'finder vs occupier' disputes by an appeal to the possession rule. As Krier and Serkin remark, these conceptual gymnastics have resulted in common law judges making, 'a proper spectacle of themselves as they struggled to determine who, as between locus owner and finder, was the prior possessor of the item in question'.[73] But to what end? Just as there is no apparent benefit in persisting with the fiction that a bailor-at-will has 'constructive possession' of the bailed goods, no obvious goal is achieved by explaining these cases of finding on the equally artificial grounds of the 'prior possession' of the occupier. Although, as Hickey argues,[74] the existence of discrete rules may seem taxonomically unsatisfactory, it is not as unsatisfactory as the attempts to explain them as examples of the possession rule in action. Hickey has justifiably criticised the tendency of the courts to 'bend and augment basic concepts, to propose qualifications to established rights in pursuit of the elusive policy'.[75] However, the 'bending and augmenting of basic concepts' is precisely what his account requires.

IV. Instrumental Justifications

A. Introduction

Courts have often justified the rules on finding on the ground that they serve useful instrumental purposes. As noted above, the 'attached/under' rule was justified on the ground that it prevents trespassers from benefitting from their wrongdoing. Perhaps the paramount instrumental consideration is the desirability

[73] James E Krier and Christopher Serkin, 'The Possession Heuristic' in Yun-chien Chang (ed), *Law and Economics of Possession* (Cambridge, Cambridge University Press, 2015) 149, 162.
[74] Hickey (n 5) 47.
[75] Ibid, 161.

of returning the lost chattel to its owner.[76] Indeed, Eichelbaum CJ has remarked that, '[t]he ultimate object of the law in this area must be to enhance the prospects that the lost article will be reunited with its owner'.[77] Although it is conceivable that these considerations may justify the creation of rules that are peculiar to cases of finding, no one has yet proposed a compelling reason for departing from the possession rule as the simplest and most effective means of resolving disputes over lost chattels.

B. Benefitting from Wrongdoing

Take, first, the concern about trespassers benefitting from their wrongdoing. Is this concern sufficiently serious as to justify a departure from the possession rule such that the claim of a finder ought to be subordinated to that of the occupier of the land on which the lost chattel was found? There are several arguments that suggest that it is not.

The first is simply that the law already has an adequate response to acts of trespass; the tort of trespass. If an act of trespass causes loss, then the right-holder can sue for damages. If the right-holder is compensated, or indeed suffers no loss, why does it matter that the tortfeasor may also have benefited from his breach of duty by acquiring a relative title to a lost chattel? In particular, those who defend this policy-motivated departure from the possession rule must justify why the conduct of the finder warrants an exception to the fundamental principle that damages in tort are only to be awarded for losses that the right-holder has actually suffered.[78]

One response to this argument is that, but for the rule that favours an occupier, he will have suffered a loss, namely the value of the lost chattel to which the finder claims a right. However, this is to beg the question. Determining whether the finder or occupier has a superior entitlement to the lost object is the very question that the court is being asked to decide. Indeed, the more realistic view is that the effect of the 'attached/under' rule is simply to confer upon an occupier a right to a chattel which, but for the actions of the finder, may well have remained undiscovered.

A better argument is that there are indeed instances at common law in which a tortfeasor is obliged to pay damages measured, not by the victim's loss, but by the quantum of his gain.[79] So, for example, in cases that have traditionally come

[76] Ibid, 94; DR Harris, 'The Concept of Possession in English Law' in AG Guest (ed), *Oxford Essays in Jurisprudence* (Oxford, Oxford University Press, 1961) 69, 82–83.

[77] *Tamworth* (n 2) 623.

[78] *Livingstone v Rawyards Coal Co* (1880) 5 App Cas 25 (HL), 39 (Lord Blackburn).

[79] See generally James Edelman, *Gain-Based Damages: Contract, Tort, Equity and Intellectual Property* (London, Bloomsbury Publishing, 2002) 113–18.

under the headings of 'wayleaves'[80] and 'mesne profits',[81] trespassers have been ordered to pay a sum reflecting the benefit they obtained through acts of trespass, without proof of loss to the victim. Likewise, in personal property law, there are cases in which those who wrongfully detain goods have been ordered to pay damages measured by a reasonable hire fee, irrespective of whether the victim suffered any loss.[82]

Two related points should be made in response. First, the awards made in these cases effected 'restitution' and not 'disgorgement'.[83] Their effect was not to strip the tortfeasor of any gain that he may have made through the commission of his wrong, but to reverse a transfer of value that came from the plaintiff and was received by the defendant in breach of duty.[84] As a consequence, a wrongdoer ordered to pay restitutionary damages may still make a profit.

Secondly, English law allows individuals to acquire property rights through acts that constitute tortious, if not criminal, wrongdoing.[85] Most obviously, if I squat on your land without your permission I become a trespasser, but in doing so I acquire a relative title which may, by operation of statute, mature into the best possible right at your expense.[86] Likewise, as is discussed further in Chapter 7, English law allows thieves to acquire ownership rights in the things that they steal. If the law permits those who are not only tortfeasors but also criminals to gain valuable rights from their wrongdoing, what justifies Donaldson LJ's claim that, '[t]he finder of a lost chattel acquires very limited rights over it if he takes it into his care and control with dishonest intent or in the course of trespassing'?[87] No explanation has been given that satisfactorily explains the apparently anomalous treatment of trespassing finders.

[80] *Martin v Porter* (1839) 151 ER 149; 5 M&W 351; *Whitwham v Westminster Brymbo Coal and Coke Co* [1896] 2 Ch 538 (CA), 541–42 (Lindley LJ); *LJP Investments Pty Ltd v Howard Chia Investments Pty Ltd (No 2)* (1990) 24 NSWLR 499, 507–8 (Hodgson J).

[81] *Swordheath Properties Ltd v Tabet* [1979] 1 WLR 285 (CA); (1979) 37 P&CR 327, 330 (Megaw LJ); *Ministry of Defence v Ashman* [1993] 4 WLUK 13 (CA); (1993) 66 P&CR 195, 200–1 (Hoffmann LJ). See also Elizabeth Cooke, 'Trespass, Mesne Profits and Restitution' (1994) 110 *Law Quarterly Review* 420, 422–3.

[82] *Strand Electric and Engineering Co Ltd v Brisford Entertainments Ltd* [1952] 2 QB 246 (CA), 254 (Lord Denning); *Gaba Formwork Contractors Pty Ltd v Turner Corporation Ltd* (1991) 32 NSWLR 175, 188 (Giles J); *Bunnings Group Ltd v Chep Australia Ltd* [2011] NSWCA 342; (2011) 82 NSWLR 420, 471–72 [194]–[199] (Giles JA).

[83] On the difference between the two species of gain-based damages see Edelman (n 79) 65–78.

[84] That is, these are examples of restitution for wrongs, not for unjust enrichment. On this distinction see Andrew Burrows, *The Law of Restitution*, 3rd edn (Oxford, Oxford University Press, 2011) 9–12.

[85] There are some branches of the law, notably the law of fiduciaries, in which wrongdoers are not permitted to retain the fruits of their wrongdoing. However, "that no man shall profit by his wrong" is not a freestanding principle of the law. The erroneous tendency to think otherwise is likely attributable to Dworkin's famous interpretive analysis of the majority's decision in *Riggs v Palmer* 115 NY 506, 22 NE 188 (1889): Ronald Dworkin, *Law's Empire* (Cambridge MA, Belknap Press, 1986) 20.

[86] See *Limitation of Actions Act 1958* (Vic) s 18; *Limitation Act 1980* (UK) s 17.

[87] *Parker* (n 2) 1017. As Roberts has also noted, this passage betrays a basic misunderstanding of the principle of relative title. See Simon Roberts, 'More Lost than Found' (1982) 45 *The Modern Law Review* 683, 687. Roberts was generally critical of the decision, remarking that Donaldson LJ's judgment 'contains rather little that could pass for conventional legal analysis' (at 685). Tellingly, Sir David Cairns expressly declined to offer an opinion on the position of thieves and trespassers: *Parker* (n 2) 1021.

A final objection to the 'attached/under' rule is consequentialist and comprises two, related, points. First, as is discussed in greater detail below, the effect of a rule that invariably resolves disputes between finders and occupiers in favour of the latter is simply to encourage finders to conceal their finds, thus reducing virtually to nil the chances that the lost chattel will be returned to its owner. Secondly, because the 'attached/under' rule provides that finders always lose to occupiers, its consequence is simply to, in effect, punish those finders who are honest enough to publicise their find in the hope that it will result in the lost chattel being reunited with its owner.

C. Facilitating Reunification

Given that the reunification of a lost object with its owner is the most desirable resolution to any case of losing and finding,[88] the question is what, if any, alteration to the possession rule is most likely to facilitate that result? In a dispute between a finder and an occupier, an obvious rule would appear to be one which favoured the occupier, on the simple ground that, as Harris has noted,[89] the owner is most likely to enquire after the lost object at the place of loss. This seemingly commonsense observation explains the distinction, recognised in American law, between chattels that are 'lost' and those that are 'mislaid'. The distinction between these two events is that, in cases of loss, the owner is unaware of becoming parted from her chattel whereas, in cases of mislaying, she has merely temporarily forgotten where she placed it.[90] If a chattel has been 'mislaid', the dispute will be resolved in favour of the occupier on the basis that he is in the best position to return it to its owner. If a chattel has been 'lost' and there is, consequently, no chance of the owner being located, then the law allows the finder to prevail.[91]

However, the solution to the problem of owner reunification is not as simple as the foregoing suggests. As both courts and commentators have observed,[92] a rule that invariably resolves all disputes against finders would undermine the very goal it is seeking to achieve because, as noted above, it would encourage finders to conceal their find, thus eliminating any chance that the lost chattel will be reunited with its owner. Any attempt to ameliorate this problem of misaligned incentives by distinguishing objects that have been 'lost' from those that have been 'mislaid'

[88] This does not apply to cases such as *Waverley* and *Elwes* in which, due to the age of the lost chattel, the trail of ownership has long since gone cold.

[89] Harris (n 76) 82.

[90] Richard A Posner, 'Savigny, Holmes, and the Law and Economics of Possession' (2000) 86 *Virginia Law Review* 535, 556.

[91] RH Helmholz, 'Equitable Division and the Law of Finders' (1983) 52 *Fordham Law Review* 313, 313–14.

[92] *Parker* (n 2) 1017 (Donaldson LJ); *Tamworth* (n 2) 623–4 (Eichelbaum CJ). See also 'Comments: Lost, Mislaid, and Abandoned Property' (1939) 8 *Fordham Law Review* 222, 235–37.

is of no assistance because a distinction that turns on a fact about the unknown owner's mental state at the time of the loss is almost impossible to apply in practice.[93] Epstein is surely correct to conclude of the finders' cases that, 'choosing a sound rule is no easy task because it is difficult to discover which rules create the optimum incentives for the parties'.[94]

In *Parker*, Donaldson LJ sought to create the necessary incentives by formulating a series of duties that are specific to finders. In particular, he held that, '[a] person having a finder's right has an obligation to take such measures as in all the circumstances are reasonable to acquaint the true owner of the finding and present whereabouts of the chattel and to care for it meanwhile'.[95] Two observations should be made about this apparent duty. First, it is unlikely to exist. As Hickey has also noted,[96] not only was Donaldson LJ's formulation unnecessary for the resolution of the dispute in *Parker* and thus obiter, it was also unsupported by any authority.

Secondly and more importantly, it is not obvious that imposing such a duty on finders would improve the frequency with which lost items are returned to their owners. An important fact about the finders' cases, and one so obvious that it almost passes unnoticed, is that disputes between finders and occupiers only occur *because* the finder has done the right thing by publicising his find. Donaldson LJ's supposed duty was irrelevant to the resolution of the dispute in *Parker* for the very reason that the plaintiff voluntarily handed the bracelet to the defendant in the hope that it might be reunited with its owner. Had he not done this, the defendant would have remained ignorant of the bracelet's existence and there would have been no dispute in the first place. One can, of course, respond that it is impossible to infer from the facts in cases such as *Parker* and *Hannah* that people usually publicise their finds. This is quite true. However, we cannot draw the opposite inference either. Given that instances in which a finder conceals his find will never be the subject of a dispute, we simply cannot know.

What one can reasonably say is that people are unlikely to look to the English Court of Appeal to discover the norms that ought to guide their behaviour in these situations. Whether or not people decide to publicise their find will instead depend upon prevailing social expectations as modified by various factors, including the value of the lost item, whether the owner was likely to have had some sentimental attachment to it, the likelihood of locating the owners, and so on. Given this, perhaps Harris was right to observe of the finders' cases that:

> [t]he reported decisions give no clear guidance on the judicial view of the underlying purpose of our possessory remedies in disputes between occupier and finder. It seems that judges subconsciously think more of the question 'Who ought to hold the chattel

[93] Helmholz (n 91) 316–17; Hickey (n 5) 59–60.
[94] Epstein (n 56) 65.
[95] *Parker* (n 2) 1017.
[96] Hickey (n 5) 75. For further criticism see Graham Battersby, 'Acquiring Title by Theft' (2002) 65 *Modern Law Review* 603, 604–5.

in the event of the true owner never appearing?' than of the question 'Is the true owner more likely to discover his chattel if possession is given to one rather than the other?'[97]

D. Are Disputes between Finders and Occupiers Exceptional?

Hickey contends that the present law on finding is perfectly adequate. He argues that there is no need to 'bend and augment basic concepts, to propose qualifications to established rights in pursuit of the elusive policy'[98] because these basic principles do not operate in isolation but are subject to the 'countervailing rules of crime and tort'.[99] The argument defended here is that, *even* if we ignore the role played by rules of general liability, the instrumental concerns discussed above do not provide compelling reasons for departing from the possession rule as the basic mechanism for resolving disputes over lost things. This is, first, because the law has not articulated a compelling reason for treating trespassing finders differently from others who benefit from wrongful conduct. Secondly, while the desirability of reuniting owners with their lost chattels is undoubted, it is almost impossible to determine which rules maximise the chances of this occurring. For the reasons discussed above, when dealing with lost chattels, we can do little better than to appeal to the better angels of our nature.

One final possibility that has yet to be considered is whether a departure from the possession rule is justified on the ground that there is something unique about the relationship between finders and occupiers that makes one party more deserving than the other. A potential basis for distinguishing finders from occupiers has been suggested by Tettenborn. Writing on the decision in *Parker*, he argued that the claim of a finder should be preferred to that of an occupier on the basis that the act of finding can be compared to *specificatio*, discussed in Chapter 1. On Tettenborn's account, the Court of Appeal's decision in *Parker* was correct:

> … both on principle and in law. The point is, as the Proculians wisely saw in the law of *specificatio*, that people who *do* things to property are generally more meritorious than people who merely *have* it. Mr Parker *did* something; he found the bracelet, picked it up, in a sense improved it: against this, British Airways' claim that they merely *had* (nay occupied) the place where Mr Parker found it, is insubstantial indeed.[100]

Tettenborn is here following in the tradition of justifying the outcome in cases on finding by an appeal to reasons that never occurred to the judges who decided them. This aside, his attempt to draw a comparison between finding and

[97] Harris (n 76) 83.

[98] Hickey (n 5) 161.

[99] Ibid.

[100] Andrew Tettenborn, 'Gold Discovered at Heathrow Airport' (1982) 41 *The Cambridge Law Journal* 242, 242.

specification is unconvincing. While someone who turns grapes into wine may attempt to justify his entitlement to the wine on broadly Lockean grounds, this justification does not readily apply to someone who, as Tettenborn himself said, did no more than to pick up a bracelet that was lying on the ground. As with Locke's example of someone who picks up an acorn that has dropped from an oak tree,[101] this is a straightforward example of the possession rule in action and it is difficult to see why, as a matter of morality or desert, this unilateral act should place others under a duty of non-interference. At the very least, *Parker* is not a promising vehicle for the argument that a finder ought to acquire a property right as a sort of reward for useful labour.[102] In any case, and this is not a criticism of Tettenborn's analysis, his argument simply provides another reason to retain the possession rule in such cases.

The reality is that there is no obvious moral or distributive reason for favouring the claims of finders over occupiers, or vice versa. In a contest between a finder and an occupier, the former can always say, 'I found it, not you', to which the latter can always respond, 'Yes, but only because you were on my land' and so on, *ad infinitum*.[103]

Cases on finding are notable because they involve fact patterns that do not support the usual conclusion that a chattel belongs to the occupier of the land on which it is located. In most cases, if I see a barbeque in your backyard, I do not assume that it has been lost. Instead, I draw the obvious inference that you own it. Cases of finding are not like this because they involve an object discovered in an incongruous place and this sense of incongruity leads the finder to conclude that the occupier of the land is not its owner. As with the concept of a 'thing', discussed in Chapter 1, the finder's reasoning tracks extra-legal intuitions about the collections of attributes that commonly clump together. While barbeques naturally go with suburban backyards, prehistoric canoes do not. This intuition about 'what goes with what' is socially useful in so far as those who identify lost items can help to reunite them with their owners.

Despite this, one might still argue that the law ought to favour an occupier when the finder is not an invitee but a trespasser. However, as was discussed above, provided that the trespassing finder compensates the occupier for any loss caused by his breach of duty, there is no obvious reason why the occupier should acquire a title to chattels the existence of which, but for the actions of the finder, she may well have remained ignorant. In sum, it seems impossible to disagree with Birkett J's observation that, in disputes between finders and occupiers, '[a] discussion of the merits does not seem to help'.[104]

[101] John Locke, *Two Treatises of Government and A Letter Concerning Toleration* (Ian Shapiro ed, New Haven, Yale University Press, 2003) 112 §28.

[102] Applying this argument to the facts of *Waverley*, for example, might be more promising.

[103] Helmholz suggests that this equivalence makes 'equitable division' the appropriate solution: Helmholz (n 91) 315, 326.

[104] *Hannah* (n 30) 521.

V. Are the Rules on Finding Desirable?

A. Introduction

If the above is correct, there is no reason for departing from the possession rule in cases of finding. Nonetheless, not only has the law departed from the possession rule, it has replaced it with rules that are equally arbitrary. As counsel for the defendant finder asked in *Waverley*, if a watch is lost on a muddy path, why should the occupier's claim to the watch be stronger than that of the finder simply because, after a day or two, the watch has become covered by a thin film of mud?[105] In response, Auld LJ defended the 'attached/under' rule by reference to the instrumental justifications, discussed above,[106] but also observed that, '[a]s to borderline cases … potential absurdities can always be found at the margins in the application of any sound principle'.[107]

Auld LJ is undoubtedly correct to note that, given the right factual scenario, any rule can appear capricious and absurd. Just as importantly, in the absence of any moral or instrumental reason for favouring one party over another, a rule's arbitrariness ceases to be an objection to its adequacy. If, as is true in cases of finding, rival claims are in a state of moral equipoise, what is crucial is that the tie-breaking rule is capable of being reliably applied across a diverse range of factual scenarios. Auld LJ's dictum might to be reworded to say: 'an absurd rule can be forgiven so long as it produces very few marginal cases'. The primary argument made below is that, while this revised dictum is true of the 'attached/under' rule, it is not true of the 'on/unattached' rule.

B. The 'Attached/Under' Rule

It is possible to conceive of circumstances in which there may be some uncertainty about the application of the 'attached/under' rule. To borrow the example given in *Waverley*, a wristwatch may be only partially buried beneath a muddy path. Nevertheless, instances in which it is unclear as to whether some object is indeed attached to or under the surface of the land must be rare. That there is no reported decision in which a court was confronted with some uncertainty about the application of the 'attached/under' rule is testament to this. Thus, at the very least, the 'attached/under' rule satisfies the certainty of application imperative.

A different sort of objection to the 'attached/under' rule is that, to the extent that it is *sui generis* and not possessory, it does not harness the salience of the possession rule. As was discussed in Chapter 4, salience is the mysterious but

[105] *Waverley* (n 3) 345.
[106] Ibid, 345–46.
[107] Ibid, 345.

empirically observable phenomenon that allows for the spontaneous emergence of solutions to coordination problems. As was discussed in Chapter 5, legal solutions to coordination problems that do not harness extra-legal salience run the very real risk of confounding the expectations that salient conventions create. This danger of 'divergence' creates a powerful argument for ensuring compatibility between legal and extra-legal norms as long as this does not compromise other values that the law may wish to promote.

While the need to prevent divergence is important, it is not of grave concern in the context of the sorts of disputes discussed above because 'occupier vs finder' disputes are extremely rare, a fact attested to by the paucity of decided cases on the topic. Their rarity is easily explained. If a chattel is lost other than in a public place, in the vast majority of cases, one would expect it to be found by the occupier. As the cases discussed above demonstrate, lost chattels are only discovered by invitees or trespassers in unusual circumstances. In the absence of Court of Appeal authority to the contrary, it would be desirable to simply return to the possession rule in all cases of finding. However, given the rarity of such cases, the 'attached/under' rule constitutes a very minor, and thus tolerable, example of divergence in the law.

C. The 'On/Unattached' Rule

As with the 'attached/under' rule, the 'on/unattached' also suffers from this 'salience deficit' and is thus a possible source of unwelcome divergence between custom and law. However, unlike that rule, 'on/unattached' is not redeemed by the simplicity of its application. In contrast to the 'attached/under' rule, the 'on/unattached' rule does not turn on a simple fact about the location of the find. Rather, it turns on whether a mental fact, the *animus possidendi*, can be inferred from the fact of the location of the find. In the Hohfeldian nomenclature discussed in Chapter 2, the location of the find operates as an 'evidential fact' from which the existence of this 'operative' mental fact can be inferred. Quite apart from the objection that one simply has no intention in respect of things of which one is ignorant, the 'on/unattached' rule turns on inferences which themselves depend on contestable assumptions about the significance of the location of the find.[108]

Fortunately, the uncertainty generated by the 'on/unattached' rule is ameliorated by the fact that, in some circumstances, courts do not treat the location of the find as an evidential fact from which one can infer the existence of the requisite intention, but as grounds for the application of a discrete rule. Following *Flack*, it seems inconceivable that a finder could succeed against an occupier in a dispute

[108] This question of the location of the find has been discussed by the courts in terms of points on a continuum, limited by bank vaults at one extreme and public parks on the other. See *Parker* (n 2) 1019 (Donaldson LJ). It is thus interesting to note that, in *Waverley*, Auld LJ would have been prepared to hold that the council had manifested the requisite intention in respect of a public park: *Waverley* (n 3) 350.

over a lost chattel that was found in a family home. This is not, however, because the *animus possidendi* is proved by a genuine presumption. Rather, it is because the courts treat 'occupier of private home prevails over finder' as a substantive rule of law.

What should be emphasised is that the uncertainty created by the 'on/unattached rule' is not justified by the need to arrive at the 'right answer' because, as was argued above, there is no obvious basis on which to prefer the claim of an occupier over that of a finder, or vice versa. Consequently, the only imperative that the relevant rule must serve is certainty in its application. While the 'attached/under' rule appears to satisfy this imperative, the 'on/unattached' rule has the twin vices of being both arbitrary *and* uncertain its application. There is thus a strong argument that it ought to be replaced by one which, though arbitrary, is at least simple to apply. Unsurprisingly, the possession rule recommends itself as the most obvious candidate.

VI. Navigating the Property Universe

A. Can there be Unwitting Possessors?

The primary argument advanced in this chapter is that it is both artificial and unsatisfactory to describe the outcome in a case such as *Elwes* as turning on the plaintiff's prior possession of the lost object. This follows from the central argument advanced in this book, namely that possession is a purposeful act by which one stakes one's claim to a material thing. One cannot, therefore, possess an object unless one is, at the very least, aware of its existence.

A simple objection to this argument is that it is indeed possible to possess something despite being ignorant of its existence. To take a particularly good example, Bell has written that, 'I must surely be in possession of milk or mail that is delivered to my house, even if I am asleep when it arrives'.[109]

While one can appreciate Bell's argument, there are two responses to it. The first is that, as the presence of mailboxes amply demonstrates, people turn their minds to the possibility of receiving mail even though they may not know precisely when it will arrive. Thus, unlike ancient canoes buried beneath the surface of the land, mail and milk do not fall into the realm of 'unknown unknowns'. The second and more relevant rejoinder is that, as is discussed below, this tendency to create an ever broader and more abstract notion of possession unnecessarily overburdens the concept.

[109] Andrew P Bell, *Modern Law of Personal Property in England and Ireland* (Oxford, Butterworths, 1989) 38.

B. Non-Possessory Rules of Thumb

Given that the function of possession is to reduce objects of property to private ownership, it is reasonable to assume that the possession rule plays a reduced role in societies in which so little is *res nullius*. This is not to say that it becomes irrelevant either as a matter of law or custom. As was discussed in Chapter 3, a successful outing to the cinema, for example, still requires that we are cognisant of conventional claim-staking behaviour. Likewise, as was discussed above, the possession rule continues to select a substitute owner where a chattel has been lost and neither of the rival parties claims as the occupier of the land on which it was found.

Nevertheless, the relative rarity of ownerless things has two implications. First, it makes rules on the transfer of rights correspondingly more important. Secondly, it means that, unlike hunters or settlers, we do not assume that the tangible things with which we typically interact are *res nullius* and thus appropriate objects of claim-staking behaviour. If I see a car parked by the kerb, my decision about the duties that I owe, or do not owe, in respect of it does not generally turn on the presence, or absence, of recognisable possessory earmarks. Rather, my default assumption is that a car, unless obviously abandoned, is the sort of thing that belongs to some other legal person, to whom I owe the simple duty to 'keep off'.[110] When one is dealing with cars, laptops and mobile phones, as opposed to whales and foxes, then, to adapt Worthington's description, '[t]he physical reality of the property acts as its own form of notice to the world that someone has interests that merit protection'.[111]

Waldron has written of ownership as an organising idea that a layman is able to 'go about his business' without expert guidance:

> because he knows in an informal and non-technical way which things are "his" and which are not. If something is "his" then (roughly) he determines what use is to be made of it; if not somebody else does. Of course, this is rough and ready knowledge by the standards of legal science. But it is there and it is socially very important: in the case of the overwhelming majority of citizens, it provides the main basis on which they learn to apply the property rules of their society.[112]

Putting aside cases of cinema seats and car spaces in the snow, in highly urbanised societies in which so little is *res nullius*, making this determination about what things either are, or could legitimately become, 'mine' only rarely requires that I answer the question, 'does someone possess this?'

To return to Bell's example, the reason why no one interferes with the mail in someone else's mailbox has nothing to do with whether the occupier of the house

[110] JE Penner, *The Idea of Property in Law* (Oxford, Clarendon Press, 1997) 30, 75; Henry E Smith, 'The Language of Property: Form, Context, and Audience' (2003) 55 *Stanford Law Review* 1105, 1115–17.

[111] Sarah Worthington, 'The Disappearing Divide between Property and Obligation: The Impact of Aligning Legal Analysis and Commercial Expectation' (2006) 42 *Texas International Law Journal* 917, 933.

[112] Jeremy Waldron, *The Right to Private Property* (Oxford, Oxford University Press, 1988) 43.

'possesses' his daily newspaper prior to retrieving it from his mailbox. Instead, people refrain from interfering with other people's mail because they know that mail is not typically an ownerless thing and, when dealing with things that are not *res nullius*, people adhere to a duty of non-interference irrespective of who, if anyone, happens to possess them. While the question of who is in possession of some object at any given time may be relevant to the passage of title and,[113] consequently, standing to sue if tortious interference does occur,[114] it does nothing to alter the general duty of non-interference owed by others in respect of it. Penner has remarked that:

> [w]e all owe the single, general duty not to interfere with property that is not our own. It doesn't matter in the least to my understanding of my own duty in respect of the property of others, and thus the way in which I guide my behaviour in respect of that duty, whether I know who happens to own the individual houses I pass walking down the street. My duty does not change in the least if one of the houses is sold to a new owner. Something that is completely extraneous to the compliance with a duty, such as the knowledge of who owns the particular car I refrain from taking for a joy ride, is not properly comprised in the description of that duty.[115]

Penner's remarks about the irrelevance of the identity of the owner apply equally to the question of who, if anyone, happens to possess a particular thing at a particular time. Where some object is already owned and is not obviously lost or abandoned, the answer to that question neither alters the nature of the duty owed to the right-holder nor anybody's reason for complying with it. Thus, while some might insist that there can be unwitting possessors, the more important point is that, as far as the law of property is concerned, it is not a question that requires an answer. On the contrary, and consistently with the argument made in this chapter, these sort of scholastic enquiries into the nature of possession not only make unnecessary demands of the concept, they also fail to reflect the much simpler practice of property.

VII. Conclusion

Chapters 3, 4 and 5 of this book developed an expressive theory of possession, according to which possession is best understood, not as a factual relationship of control over a tangible thing, but as a series of acts that convey one's intention

[113] Although, in the case of sale, the passage of title does not require manual delivery. However, where there is a purported gift, the issue is more complex. In particular, it depends upon whether a donee's consent is required for title to pass. On this topic see Jonathan Hill, 'The Role of the Donee's Consent in the Law of Gift' (2001) 117 *Law Quarterly Review* 127, 129–33.

[114] Although, as was discussed in Chapter 2, the law, often for entirely sensible reasons, sometimes fudges this issue by deeming that certain people have 'constructive possession' of chattels.

[115] JE Penner, 'Hohfeldian Use-Rights in Property' in JW Harris (ed), *Property Problems: From Genes to Pension Funds* (London, Kluwer Law International, 1997) 164, 170.

to claim an entitlement to a particular thing. This chapter has described the implications of this theory when applied to what is perhaps the most famous group of cases in personal property law, the 'finders' cases'.

The argument advanced in this chapter departed from the orthodox position by insisting that these cases cannot be explained as examples of the possession rule in action. It is true to say that, if neither party claims as occupier, then a dispute over a lost object will be resolved by a simple application of the possession rule. However, if one party claims under the special status of 'occupier', the dispute will instead be governed by a set of discrete rules that turn on the factual circumstances of the find. Because, in such cases, the occupier is ignorant of the very existence of the lost chattel, these rules cannot be reconciled with the idea of possession as a claim-staking act. Just as importantly, by departing from the possession rule in cases of finding, the law has, without instrumental or moral justification, replaced a salient, though arbitrary rule, with one that, at least in the case of the 'on/unattached ruled', is both arbitrary *and* difficult to apply.

Perhaps most importantly, what warrants criticism is the persistent and strained attempt, both on the part of courts and commentators, to explain these rules as manifestations of the possession rule. Although they are attempts at rationalisation, these accounts of the finders' cases have only succeeded in creating an artificial concept of possession that neither simplifies the law nor reflects the way in which people navigate the web of property transactions that forms part of everyday life.

7

Theft, Good Faith Purchase and the Limits of Conventions

I. Introduction

In Chapter 5 it was argued that, although spontaneously emergent conventions are strictly amoral, there is reason to believe that the possession convention is tolerably fair. Despite this, the application of the convention may, on occasion, place the law in invidious positions. This might be because its simple and morally neutral operation permits individuals of questionable merit to be vested with a property right. Alternatively, it may be because it selects two 'Hawks', leading to disputes in which parties, each of whom have complied with the convention, have equally meritorious yet incompatible claims to some object of property.

In this final chapter, these issues will be discussed with reference to two notoriously difficult problems in the law of property: the acquisition of property rights through acts of theft and the position of the good faith purchaser at common law. The argument advanced below is that the issues of theft and good faith purchase do not demonstrate a fundamental flaw in the possession rule. Rather, they highlight, first, the inherent limitations of rules that are, at base, emergent conventions and, second, the necessity of creating rules for resolving the disputes that arise when people wish to deal with the rights created by the possession convention. That the problems of theft and good faith purchase are inevitable does not make them insoluble. It simply means that their solutions must be found in considerations that are unrelated to the basic convention by which a society allocates 'names to things'.

II. Possession and Theft

A. 'Proprietary Overkill'

The account of the possession convention offered in Chapter 4 made two important claims. First, that the rule which allocates 'names to things' was never designed but emerged unconsciously and spontaneously through the interactions of countless people confronted with the same coordination problem. Secondly, that, due to the 'simplicity imperative', any such rule is bound to be blind to fine-grained consideration such as the identity and relative merit of the competing parties. Any rule that turned on an assessment of the parties' bona fides or the relative distributive merit of their claims would be too difficult to apply and, as a consequence, would be replaced by a rule which, though cruder, created fewer interpretive difficulties for those who must apply it. The morally neutral and undiscriminating nature of the possession rule means that it can, and sometimes does, generate property rights in situations in which they appear unnecessary or even undesirable. Hickey has described this phenomenon as 'proprietary overkill'.[1]

This issue of proprietary overkill was raised by Crompton J in *Buckley v Gross*.[2] *Buckley* concerned a dispute over a quantity of tallow that had melted in a fire and reconstituted in the frigid waters of the Thames, whence it was collected by several opportunists. Some of the tallow was then sold to the plaintiff, from whom it was seized by police. Following an order from a police magistrate, the tallow was detained under powers conferred by statute. The police subsequently sold it to the defendant, whom the plaintiff sued for conversion. The Court unanimously found for the defendant, holding that, while the plaintiff's possession would have been sufficient title against a 'wrongdoer', the police were not 'wrongdoers' because the order made by the magistrate under the Act had lawfully extinguished the plaintiff's title.[3] For present purposes, the pertinent aspect of the case was Crompton J's concern about the potential consequences of the possession rule. His Honour wrote that:

> [h]ere, in my mind, the plaintiff's possession was gone. The goods were properly taken from him, and there is no such doctrine as that it will reinvest in him in the manner contended for; otherwise every person who was possessor of goods for any time, however short, might bring an action against any person afterwards found in possession of them, however he may have come by it. That would be pressing too far the doctrine of sufficient title against a wrongdoer.[4]

A similar argument has been advanced by Gordley and Mattei, who argue that the logical consequences of Pollock's view that possession creates a relative title:

> go beyond anything he or an English court would be likely to accept. If Pollock were right, a possessor would have a title which, like an owner's, would not be extinguished when he abandoned the property. Indeed, if Pollock were right, anyone who had been in possession, even for a day, could, until the statute of limitations ran out, claim the property from any current possessor who could not trace title flawlessly from a prior possessor. If that is English law, one should spend one's next vacation taking brief possession of as many English houses as possible in hopes of returning years later and finding them occupied by someone who cannot prove title.[5]

[1] Robin Hickey, 'Possession as a Source of Property at Common Law' in Eric Descheemaeker (ed), *The Consequences of Possession* (Edinburgh, Edinburgh University Press, 2014) 77, 92.
[2] *Buckley v Gross* (1863) 122 ER 213 (QB); 3 B&S 566 ('*Buckley*').
[3] Ibid, 215–16 (Cockburn CJ), 216 (Crompton J), 216–17 (Blackburn J).
[4] Ibid, 216. Emphasis added.
[5] James Gordley and Ugo Mattei, 'Protecting Possession' (1996) 44 *The American Journal of Comparative Law* 293, 303.

Although Gordley and Mattei regard their example as troubling, it is nothing more than a textbook illustration of the principle of relative title. One might respond to their argument by noting that, because the rights created by acts of possession are relative and not absolute, their concern is of little practical significance. While true, this does not answer the broader question of why it is either necessary or desirable for the law to permit this multiplication of rights. In particular, one troubling consequence of the rule that 'possession creates title' is that a wrongdoer can acquire a property right through an act of possession that amounts to theft.

B. Possession and Theft: The Position at Common Law

According to Hickey, the question of whether thieves acquire property rights remained open as late as 1887.[6] However, whatever doubts the law may have entertained in the late nineteenth century have since been resolved by a line of cases concerning statutory powers of seizure and detention exercised by police. These cases definitively demonstrate that possession, however acquired, is sufficient to create a relative property right.

The first in this line of cases was the Court of Appeal's decision in *Webb v Chief Constable of Merseyside Police*,[7] in which the claimant sought the return of £36,000 in cash, or damages for its conversion, which police had seized on suspicion that it represented the proceeds of drug trafficking. The Court of Appeal found for the claimant, holding that, even though the trial judge found that the money represented the proceeds of crime,[8] the police could not retain the money once their statutory powers of detention had expired.[9]

Shortly thereafter, the Court of Appeal gave judgment in what is now the leading case, *Costello v Chief Constable of Derbyshire Constabulary*,[10] in which the appellant sought the return of a car that police had detained pursuant to statutory seizure powers that had expired. Although the Court upheld the trial judge's finding that the car was stolen and that the appellant was fully aware of this fact,[11] it was unanimously held that the police must release it to the appellant on the ground that he was the prior possessor and that the law protects possession no matter how it was acquired. Lightman J, with whom Keene LJ and Walker LJ unreservedly agreed, concluded that:

> [i]n my view on a review of the authorities … as a matter of principle and authority possession means the same thing and is entitled to the same legal protection whether

[6] Robin Hickey, 'Possession Taken by Theft and the Original Acquisition of Personal Property Rights' in Nicholas Hopkins (ed), *Modern Studies in Property Law* (Oxford, Hart Publishing, 2013) vol VII, 401, 404–5, 412–13.

[7] *Webb v Chief Constable of Merseyside Police* [2000] QB 427 (CA) ('*Webb*').

[8] Ibid, 434.

[9] Ibid, 448 (May LJ), 449–50 (Pill LJ).

[10] *Costello v Chief Constable of Derbyshire Constabulary* [2001] EWCA Civ 381; 1 WLR 1437 ('*Costello*').

[11] Ibid, [8] (Lightman J).

> or not it has been obtained lawfully or by theft or by other unlawful means. It vests in the possessor a possessory title which is good against the world save as against anyone setting up or claiming under a better title. In the case of a theft the title is frail, and of likely limited value … but nonetheless remains a title to which the law affords protection.[12]

An issue in *Costello* was the status of the much earlier decision in *Buckley*. As noted above, the plaintiff in *Buckley* could not succeed against the police's successor in title because, as Cockburn CJ concluded, the order made by the police magistrate under authority of the applicable Act divested the plaintiff of his title to the tallow. Cockburn CJ held that:

> [t]he plaintiff, who had nothing but bare naked possession (which would have been sufficient against a wrongdoer) had it taken out of him by virtue of this enactment. As against the plaintiff, therefore, the defendant derives title, not from a wrong doer, but from a person selling under authority of the justice, whether rightly or not is of no consequence.[13]

In *Costello*, Lightman J held that there was nothing in *Buckley* to derogate from the basic principle that possession, however acquired, creates a relative title. On his view, the *ratio* to emerge from *Buckley* was limited to situations in which property seized under a statutory power is subsequently sold. In such cases, 'the transferee obtain[s] the possessory title in defeasance of the thief or receiver'.[14] Lightman J's analysis thus accords with the widely held view that the decision in *Buckley* did not create a substantive exception to the possession rule, but turned on a judicial order made under the authority of a particular statute.[15]

Although Lightman J's decision did not meet with universal approval,[16] Battersby wrote of the case that:

> [t]he decision and the reasoning in *Costello* seem absolutely compelling. The notion of relative title, which is built into our law of property, is reasserted in the most uncompromising way. Possession, however, acquired, will found a title which will prevail against all claimants whose rights are subsequent to those of the possessor, and, conversely, will be defeated only by those who have continuing rights which are prior to those of the possessor.[17]

[12] Ibid, [31].

[13] *Buckley* (n 2) 215; 572. Cockburn CJ's reasoning was subsequently applied by Holroyd Pearce LJ in *Irving v National Provincial Bank Ltd* [1962] 2 QB 73 (CA), 79–80.

[14] *Costello* (n 10) [31].

[15] G Battersby and AD Preston, 'Stolen Goods and the Sale of Goods Act 1893, s. 25(2): A Rejoinder' (1975) 38 *Modern Law Review* 77, 80; Graham Battersby, 'Acquiring Title by Theft' (2002) 65 *Modern Law Review* 603, 608; Robin Hickey, *Property and the Law of Finders* (Oxford, Hart Publishing, 2010) 118–19.

[16] See David Fox, 'Enforcing a Possessory Title to a Stolen Car' (2002) 61 *The Cambridge Law Journal* 27, 29.

[17] Battersby (n 15) 609.

The reasoning in *Costello* was subsequently applied by the Court of Appeal in *Gough v Chief Constable of West Midlands Police*,[18] in which the claimant sought delivery up and damages in respect of various car parts that the police had seized in the belief that they were stolen. The Court held that the police could not retain the goods after its statutory powers of seizure had expired. After reviewing the decisions in *Webb* and *Costello*, Park J, with whom Carnwath LJ and Potter LJ agreed, concluded that such disputes are resolved according to 'common law principles deriving from the law of detinue and conversion',[19] and that 'it is no defence for the police to argue that the former possessor, the claimant in the civil action, is not the true owner of the property'.[20]

C. Asking the Right Question: Theft and the Limits of Conventions

Perhaps unsurprisingly, the outcomes in cases such as *Gough* and *Costello* were not universally applauded. After all, these are cases in which a plaintiff is seeking a court's assistance to enforce the very duty that he himself deliberately transgressed in acquiring the right on which his claim is based. Potter LJ expressed his misgivings by remarking that:

> [w]e are bound by the decisions of this court in *Webb* and *Costello* … Nonetheless, I find it inherently rebarbative that, by means of civil proceedings in detinue based on the superior possessory title of the claimant over property held by the police following seizure in the course of investigating a suspected offence, a person may be held entitled to recover and continue to enjoy property even though the court may be satisfied that he is not the true owner and has acquired the property illegally, albeit the true owner is not identifiable.[21]

Likewise, Hickey, who is critical of these decisions, has written that:

> by definition, the thief's possession is premised on some high degree of disregard for the property of his victim. Any argument in favour of property acquisition by the thief risks being inappropriately insensitive to the continuing property rights of the victim, and the common law would need at least to offer an express account as to why *proprietary* protection is justified notwithstanding the claimant's obvious disregard for the property of another.[22]

According to Hickey,[23] and consistently with the argument made in Chapter 4, proprietary protection is not required in order to address concerns about

[18] *Gough v Chief Constable of West Midlands Police* [2004] EWCA Civ 206; 3 WLUK 48 ('*Gough*').
[19] Ibid, [15].
[20] Ibid.
[21] Ibid, [48].
[22] Hickey, 'Possession as a Source of Property at Common Law' (n 1) 93.
[23] Ibid, 82–83.

violations of a thief's bodily integrity, of the sort proffered by Savigny.[24] Hickey argues that Roman law more sensitively addressed this issue because it allowed a possessor to bring an interdict against anyone who used force to dispossess him, but stopped short of concluding that his possession also made him *dominus*. Possessors who were not also owners could thus not bring the *vindicatio* and, consequently, had no claim against third parties, such as the dispossessor's successors in title. Acts of possession in Roman law, Hickey concludes, resulted in 'obligations, not property'.[25]

Hickey's criticism extends to other public policy-type justifications raised in the cases discussed above. Of the argument, discussed below, that finding for the claimant is necessary in order to prevent what would otherwise be the ultra vires expropriation of property rights, he writes that:

> the argument is flawed insofar it assumes precisely that which is at stake, namely that possession obtained by theft results in the acquisition of a property right by the thief. Unless this premise is correct, it is meaningless to speak of expropriation in this context, for there can be no expropriation without prior subsisting property.[26]

However, consequentialist justifications, such as the 'expropriation argument', only beg the question if we assume that acts of possession do not invariably create a relative title in the object possessed. Hickey argues that, contrary to the decisions in the line of cases discussed above, 'it is far from self-evident that property acquisition is warranted on the authorities, the better view being at least that the common law has declined to commit itself on the matter'.[27] Thus, for Hickey, the question is whether theft and other serious wrongdoing constitutes an exception to the rule that possession is a 'root of title' at common law. Irrespective of whether Hickey's view of the law is correct, the argument advanced below is that this is not the correct question to ask. The question is not, 'does a right come into existence?', but, 'should the court deny the plaintiff relief in the circumstances?' As is discussed below, when framed in this way, the enquiry becomes one of coherence.

There is an important conceptual distinction between these two enquiries. The first is asking whether the plaintiff has actually acquired a property right. The second, by contrast, is not questioning the normal operation of the possession rule. It assumes that the plaintiff has acquired a property right by performing some recognised act of possession. It instead asks whether he should be able to enforce that right against the defendant given the other facts found by the court.[28] The distinction between these two questions is important because, while they may yield the same outcome on given facts, the first inquiry has the potential to create

[24] See also Oliver Wendell Holmes, *The Common Law* (Boston, Little, Brown and Company, 1948) 212–13.

[25] Hickey, 'Possession as a Source of Property at Common Law' (n 1) 83.

[26] Hickey, 'Possession Taken by Theft and the Original Acquisition of Personal Property Rights' (n 6) 108.

[27] Ibid.

[28] See *Tinsley v Milligan* [1994] 1 AC 340 (HL), 374 (Lord Browne-Wilkinson) ('*Tinsley*').

an exception to the possession *rule* that, though seemingly sensible, is undesirable because it is too subtle to be replicated in the underlying *convention* that actually guides people's behaviour.

This replication problem arises because, as has been stressed throughout this book, any convention that is to determine who is to play Hawk and who Dove in any dispute over a tangible object must satisfy the 'simplicity imperative'. Imagine that the law attempted to improve on the possession rule by introducing the following caveat: 'Acts of possession create property rights unless the possessor is also a thief.' Though seemingly desirable, this caveat would fall foul of the simplicity imperative. This is not, as in Sugden's beauty example, discussed in Chapter 4, because the caveat requires people to make a judgment that ultimately depends on individual taste. Rather, it is because determining whether a given possessor is also a thief is too informationally demanding of those who owe property duties.

Imagine that I observe someone in a supermarket car park unlock a car and step inside. According to the simple possession convention, I must defer to her claim to the car because she is in possession of it. However, under the modified possession rule, I am only obliged to treat her as if she is its owner if I also believe that she is not a thief. The question is, what would I have to know to make this determination? First, I would need detailed knowledge about the provenance of the car to establish a chain of title. Secondly, I would also need to know about the existence of any other people with claims to it to establish whether, for instance, the car had been bailed to the present possessor. Finally, I would also need a working knowledge of property and criminal law to determine whether, based on those facts, the present possessor has committed the offence of theft. In a world of perfect information, this would not present a problem. Unlike the problem of assessing beauty, there would, given sufficient information, be no disagreement about whether the present possessor of the car is also a thief. However, in our world of costly and imperfect information, such a rule is simply too onerous to survive as means of allocating 'names to things'. Consequently, even if the law created an exception to the possession rule in cases of theft, people would continue to treat possessing thieves as legitimate right-holders because, absent compelling evidence to the contrary, this is what the less informationally demanding convention prescribes.

This point is consistent with arguments previously advanced by Penner and Smith. As Penner has argued, when one walks through a car park, one's duty to refrain from interfering with any given car does not alter according to whether 'one of the cars has just been sold, so that there is a new owner, or if one of the cars has been lent to the owner's sister-in-law'.[29] To this list we might add that it does not matter that one of the cars in the car park has been stolen. The duty of non-interference that everyone owes has nothing to do with the personal status of the owner but is, instead, mediated by the purely impersonal concept of a 'thing'. Organising a system of property around the concept of an impersonal

[29] JE Penner, *The Idea of Property in Law* (Oxford, Clarendon Press, 1997) 75.

'thing' is, as Smith points out, necessary to contain what would otherwise be unmanageable complexity.[30] If it is true that, as Smith writes, '[t]he things defined by the basic exclusion strategy mediate the relations between often anonymous parties',[31] then it follows that a duty ower's obligation to comply with her duty of non-interference in respect of some car cannot depend on her assessment of whether or not it was stolen.

D. Illegality and Coherence

The simplicity imperative, discussed extensively throughout this book, makes it inevitable that all conventions will, on occasion, pick unmeritorious winners, such as thieves. Because conventions are necessarily blunt instruments, the creation of a judicial exception to the *rule* that 'possession is a root of title' in cases of theft will not prevent thieves from being treated as owners outside the courtroom. Because the exception is too complex to be replicated in the underlying *convention*, it will simply create a cleft between the law and practice of property. However, it does not follow from this that the courts must therefore resolve cases such as *Costello* in favour of the plaintiff. As noted above, the better question is not whether the plaintiff has acquired a property right, but whether the court ought to grant the plaintiff the desired relief. This is a question that raises the concepts of coherence and illegality.

As Grantham and Jensen note, the concept of 'coherence' operates at two levels.[32] At its broadest, a theory of the law will be 'coherent' if it can explain the law as 'the outworking of a single principle'.[33] Economic analysis of law is coherent because, according to this theory, the law both is, and should be, viewed as nothing more than an instrument for maximising social welfare.[34] At the other end of the spectrum, Weinrib's non-instrumental theory of private law is also coherent because, on his account, all questions of liability depend exclusively on the bipolar relationship between the plaintiff and defendant.[35]

[30] Henry E Smith, 'Property as the Law of Things' (2012) 125 *Harvard Law Review* 1691, 1701.

[31] Ibid, 1706. See also Thomas W Merrill and Henry E Smith, 'What Happened to Property in Law and Economics?' (2001) 111 *Yale Law Journal* 357, 359.

[32] Ross Grantham and Darryn Jensen, 'Coherence in the Age of Statutes' (2016) 42 *Monash University Law Review* 360, 360–61.

[33] Ibid, 361.

[34] See, eg, Richard A Posner, *The Problems of Jurisprudence* (Cambridge MA, Harvard University Press, 1993) 360–62.

[35] Weinrib writes that these, '[c]orrelatively structured reasons focus not on either party separately from the other but on the relationship between them as doer and sufferer of the same injustice': Ernest J Weinrib, 'Private Law and Public Right' (2011) 61 *University of Toronto Law Journal* 191, 192. As a consequence, liability can never depend on extraneous considerations such as the depth of the defendant's pockets, the desirability of loss spreading through insurance, and so on. See Ernest J Weinrib, *The Idea of Private Law* (Oxford, Oxford University Press, 2012) 36–38.

In a narrower sense, and one relevant to the analysis below, coherence refers to the absence of internal contradictions within the law.[36] This conception does not demand that a Herculean judge be able to resolve any given dispute by reference to a principle that undergirds the law as a whole.[37] It simply requires that the law's complex and occasionally overlapping web of rules does not contradict itself. At common law, this version of coherence has also been discussed under the rubric of 'illegality' which, as Edelman and Bant have observed,[38] is not concerned with 'criminality' per se, but with the need to prevent one rule from stultifying the operation of another.

The demands of this narrower conception of coherence are neatly illustrated by the decision of the High Court of Australia in *Equuscorp Pty Ltd v Haxton*.[39] Equuscorp concerned an investment scheme in which investors borrowed their contribution from a scheme company. As the marketers of the scheme had failed to comply with certain statutory requirements regarding the issuing of a prospectus, the loans were unenforceable. The question for the Court was whether allowing the lender's assignee to recover the loan by bringing a claim in unjust enrichment, rather than in debt, would undermine the statutory purpose of protecting investors. A majority of the Court held that it would.[40] French CJ, Crennan and Kiefel JJ held that:

> [r]ecovery from the investors would have been recovery from persons whose protection was the object of the statutory scheme … This is a clear case in which the coherence of the law, and the avoidance of stultification of the statutory purpose by the common law, lead to the conclusion that [the assignee] did not have a right to claim recovery of the money advanced under the loan agreements as money had and received.[41]

To take another example, where two people steal a car, the driver does not owe his co-offender a common law duty to take reasonable care when driving it because, as the High Court held in *Miller v Miller*:

> [t]he statutory purpose of a law proscribing dangerous or reckless driving is not consistent with one offender owing a co-offender a duty to take reasonable care. And in a case where two or more are complicit in the offence of illegally using a vehicle, the statutory purpose of the law proscribing illegal use … is not consistent with one offender owing a co-offender a duty to take reasonable care.[42]

[36] Grantham and Jensen (n 32) 363.

[37] Ronald Dworkin, *Law's Empire* (Cambridge MA, Belknap Press, 1986) 245.

[38] James Edelman and Elise Bant, *Unjust Enrichment*, 2nd edn (London, Bloomsbury Publishing, 2016) 158–60, 303.

[39] *Equuscorp Pty Ltd v Haxton* [2012] HCA 7; (2012) 246 CLR 498 ('*Equuscorp*').

[40] Ibid, 522–23 [45] (French CJ, Crennan and Kiefel JJ), 544 [111] (Gummow and Bell JJ).

[41] Ibid, 522–23 [45].

[42] *Miller v Miller* [2011] HCA 9; (2011) 242 CLR 446, 482 [101] (French CJ, Gummow, Hayne, Crennan, Kiefel and Bell JJ) ('*Miller*'). It should be noted that the High Court did not hold that the mere fact of the theft made the existence of a duty of care inherently incoherent. Rather, the particular statute deemed that the plaintiff was also complicit in the offence of dangerous driving and it was this latter offence that made the plaintiff's claim incoherent: at 479–80 [92]–[94].

As these cases make clear, the plaintiff's claim is denied, not because of some extenuating circumstances in the defendant's conduct, but because granting the plaintiff the desired relief would introduce an internal contradiction into the law. The question for present purposes is whether, in the context of theft, granting or denying the plaintiff the relief he seeks would create such a contradiction.

E. Illegality and Property Rights at Common Law

At common law, it has long been established that property rights pass under illegal agreements.[43] Where there has been a transfer of possession under an illegal contract, the possessor, whether a purchaser, bailee or tenant, can rely on her possession to resist an action for recovery of the asset.[44] In *Taylor v Chester*, the plaintiff pledged half a £50 Bank of England note as security for sums incurred, so reads the headnote, 'for wine and suppers supplied to the plaintiff by the defendant in a brothel kept by her, to be there consumed in debauch'.[45] In an action by the plaintiff to recover the half note Mellor J, delivering the decision of the Court, held that:

> [t]he plaintiff, no doubt, was the owner of the note, but he pledged it by way of security for the price of meat and drink provided for, and money advanced to, him by the defendant. Had the case rested there, and no pleading raised the question of illegality, a valid pledge would have been created, and a special property conferred upon the defendant in the half-note, and the plaintiff could only have recovered by showing payment or a tender of the amount due. In order to get rid of the defence arising from the plea, which set up an existing pledge of the half-note, the plaintiff had recourse to the special replication, in which he was obliged to set forth the immoral and illegal character of the contract upon which the half-note had been deposited. It was, therefore, impossible for him to recover except through the medium and by the aid of an illegal transaction to which he was himself a party. Under such circumstances, the maxim 'in pari delicto potior est conditio possidentis' clearly applies, and is decisive of the case.[46]

Though the brothel madame was equally tainted by the illegality, as Mellor J explained, 'the plaintiff could not recover without shewing the true character of the deposit; and that being upon an illegal consideration, to which he was himself a party, he was precluded from obtaining "the assistance of the law" to recover it back'.[47] Lord Browne-Wilkinson has summarised the position at common law in the following terms:

> (1) property in chattels and land can pass under a contract which is illegal and therefore would have been unenforceable as a contract; (2) a plaintiff can at law enforce property

[43] *Singh v Ali* [1960] AC 167 (PC), 176–77 (Lord Denning). This seems to occur irrespective of whether execution of the contract is also accompanied by a transfer of possession. See *Belvoir Finance Co Ltd v Stapleton* [1971] 1 QB 210 (CA), 217 (Lord Denning MR), 220 (Sachs LJ).

[44] *Feret v Hill* (1854) 15 CB 206; 139 ER 400, 407 (Maule J), 408 (Crowder J).

[45] *Taylor v Chester* (1869) LR 4 QB 309.

[46] Ibid, 314.

[47] Ibid, 315.

> rights so acquired provided that he does not need to rely on the illegal contract for any purpose other than providing the basis of his claim to a property right; (3) it is irrelevant that the illegality of the underlying agreement was either pleaded or emerged in evidence: if the plaintiff has acquired legal title under the illegal contract that is enough.[48]

His Lordship's summary of the law suggests that, in cases such as *Costello*, plaintiffs will succeed because all they need demonstrate is that they were in possession of the goods at the time of seizure. As the passage above makes clear, the fact that it emerges in evidence that those goods were stolen is immaterial. However, this apparently simple analysis is made doubtful by two important factors. First, although the implications for property law are not yet clear, Lord Toulson, with whom a majority of the Supreme Court agreed on this point, has recently held that the inflexible 'reliance' test is no longer good law and should be replaced by a discretionary 'range of factors' test.[49] Secondly, and more importantly, cases such as *Taylor v Chester* are concerned with situations in which both parties are tainted by the illegality. This is why courts are content, to borrow Lord Eldon's famous description, to '[l]et the estate lie where it falls'.[50] The maxim *in pari delicto potior est conditio possidentis* cannot apply to the cases discussed above because the police, unlike nineteenth-century brothel keepers, are not party to an illegal transaction.

F. The Demands of Coherence

Cases such as *Costello* place courts in an invidious and embarrassing position because the plaintiff is asking the court to enforce a right that only arose because he deliberately transgressed a duty that he owed to the victim of the theft. Given this, would it be, to borrow the High Court's phraseology, 'incongruous'[51] for a court to grant the plaintiff the relief he seeks? Although this argument has an appeal, the answer must be 'no'. This is not because, as was discussed in Chapter 5, the law routinely allows individuals to acquire rights through acts that constitute wrongs.[52] It is instead because, in cases that play out against the background of a statutory forfeiture regime, the need to ensure coherence between the civil and

[48] *Tinsley v Milligan* [1994] 1 AC 340 (HL), 370 ('*Tinsley*'). See also *Bowmakers Ltd v Barnet Instruments Ltd* [1945] KB 65 (CA), 71 (Du Parcq CJ).

[49] *Patel v Mirza* [2016] UKSC 42; [2017] AC 467, 501–2 [110]. The case concerned a claim in unjust enrichment. For analysis see James Goudkamp, 'The End of an Era? Illegality in Private Law in the Supreme Court' (2017) 133 *Law Quarterly Review* 14.

[50] *Muckleston v Brown* (1801) 31 ER 934, 942; 6 Ves Jr 52, 69.

[51] *Miller* (n 42) 455 [16] (French CJ, Gummow, Hayne, Crennan, Kiefel and Bell JJ).

[52] Think, for instance, of the trespasser who acquires a property right in the land on which he is squatting.

criminal law demands that the plaintiff, no matter how morally unattractive, must prevail.[53]

In *Webb*, May LJ expressed a concern about the need to prevent statutory powers of seizure, used to gather evidence in preparation for a criminal prosecution, from being deployed as de facto powers of expropriation in the absence of a criminal conviction. He argued that:

> [a]lthough from the Chief Constable's perspective the money is the proceeds of crime, from another perspective the court should not, in my view, countenance expropriation by a public authority of money or property belonging to an individual for which there is no statutory authority. There is statutory machinery for the prosecution of those who deal in drugs and for the confiscation upon conviction of the proceeds of their drug dealing. There is statutory machinery for the confiscation upon conviction of the proceeds of other serious crime. There is statutory machinery for the forfeiture of the cash proceeds of drug trafficking which are being imported into or exported from the United Kingdom. There is no statutory power to confiscate the proceeds of drug dealing within the United Kingdom where the person entitled to possession of the money is not convicted of a drug trafficking offence.[54]

Given that the source of the court's power to confiscate the proceeds of crime is statutory, it is a basic requirement of the rule of law that, in the absence of an express statutory power, courts cannot make what amount to confiscation orders in favour of the executive. Battersby has also advanced this argument, praising the Court of Appeal in *Costello* for adhering to 'the constitutional principle that the police have no greater powers than any other citizen except where the law specifically confers greater powers'.[55]

This rule of law issue also raises an issue of coherence, in the narrow sense, between the civil and criminal divisions of the law. This is not, as in some cases, because the granting of a civil remedy effectively undermines the sanction imposed in a criminal trial.[56] The coherence issue that arises in cases such as *Costello* and *Gough* instead concerns the potential for findings of fact made in civil disputes to circumvent the procedural protections afforded to an accused in a criminal trial. As May LJ's judgment in *Webb* makes clear, Parliament has made confiscation orders conditional on the successful criminal prosecution of the accused.

[53] See, eg, *Hall v Hebert* [1993] 2 SCR 159, 179–80 (McLachlin J). See also Ernest J Weinrib, 'Illegality as a Tort Defence' (1976) 26 *University of Toronto Law Journal* 28, 54. On the dangers of introducing notions of punishment into civil disputes, more generally, see James Goudkamp, 'A Revival of the Doctrine of Attainder? The Statutory Illegality Defences to Liability in Tort' (2007) 29 *Sydney Law Review* 445, 451–55.

[54] *Webb* (n 7) 446. For a similar observation in a similar case, see also *R v Collis* [1990] 2 NZLR 287, 293 (Casey J).

[55] Battersby (n 15) 609. A fundamental principle that is usually traced back to Lord Camden's famous judgment in *Entick v Carrington* (1765) 95 ER 807; 19 St Tr 1030.

[56] Goudkamp describes these 'sanction shifting actions': see Goudkamp (n 53) 455. For a particularly good example see *State Rail Authority of New South Wales v Wiegold* (1991) 25 NSWLR 500, 514 (Samuels JA) ('*Wiegold*'). See also *Gray v Thames Trains Ltd* [2009] UKHL 33; 1 AC 1339.

Unlike litigants in civil proceedings, the accused in a criminal prosecution i afforded unique procedural advantages, particularly the benefit of a presumptio of innocence, a more onerous standard of proof and,[57] in some instances, exclusor rules of evidence.[58] If a court exercising civil jurisdiction is to avoid stultifyin the procedural protections of the criminal law,[59] then a finding of fact in a civ action cannot be used to justify withholding relief where doing so would, so far a confiscation orders are concerned, relieve the Crown of the burden of proving th accused guilty beyond a reasonable doubt in a properly constituted criminal tria However 'inherently rebarbative' the outcome in cases such as *Costello* and *Goug* may appear to be, a finding of fact in a civil trial that the claimant is a thief canno in the absence of a criminal conviction, justify a departure from the normal rul that 'first in time is better in right'.

G. Conclusion

Hickey has written of this issue that:

> [o]riginal acquisition rules are important. In the end, they are the rules that wi determine the distribution of resources within a given community. It is plain that this distribution is generally considered just, then rules about how distribution is t be effected must endorse and in the end serve the prevailing principles of justice. community which takes justice seriously should, at the very least, be able to explai and defend the particular rules it invokes about original acquisition, and this include (perhaps especially includes) original acquisition which seems to run counter t normally accepted principles of justice, as prima facie appears to be the case where w reward a thief or other wrongdoer.[60]

While these comments seem reasonable, they are incorrect. As was discussed i Chapter 5, any rule that governs original acquisition will have distributive effect However, it will only determine the actual distribution of property rights withi a given population if transaction costs are so high as to preclude the rights s created from being transferred to higher-valuing users.

More importantly, what the foregoing has sought to demonstrate is tha contrary to Hickey's argument, the problem of rights acquired by thieves doe

[57] On which see generally Paul Roberts and Adrian Zuckerman, *Criminal Evidence*, 2nd edn (Oxfor Oxford University Press, 2010) ch 6.

[58] See, eg, *Evidence Act 1995* (NSW) s 137; *Police and Criminal Evidence Act 1984* (UK) s 78(1).

[59] *Wiegold* (n 56) 514 (Samuels JA).

[60] Hickey, 'Possession Taken by Theft and the Original Acquisition of Personal Property Rights' (n 409–10.

not, in fact, raise an issue about the desirability of possession as a mechanism for creating these initial entitlements. Because, as Hume argued, the rudimentary features of any property regime emerge spontaneously, the basic allocative rule will always be, first and foremost, a convention. As has been stressed throughout this book, conventions, as evolutionary phenomena, are strictly amoral. Any allocative rule that is sufficiently simple to successfully resolve the coordination problem caused by scarcity will, on occasion, pick unmeritorious winners, including thieves. While adherence to an established convention becomes, as was discussed in Chapter 4, an obligation grounded in 'conventional morality', there is no reason to believe that the substance of any such convention will conform to 'normally accepted principles of justice', whatever they may be. Indeed, any rule that is, by its design, sensitive to 'accepted principles of justice' will almost certainly be too complex to answer the most basic questions of mine and thine.

It does not follow, however, that where a possessor is also a thief, his property right must invariably be enforced by a court order in a civil action. Although, through the normal operation of the rule, such a possessor will have acquired a property right capable of being sold, gifted, mortgaged and so on, it is conceivable that a court may regard enforcement of that right as sufficiently 'incongruous' to justify denying the plaintiff his desired relief. The argument made above was that, in disputes such as *Costello*, coherence provides an additional justification for the outcome reached on doctrinal grounds. However, because this argument is peculiar to disputes in which the defendant is an emanation of the Crown, this may not always be so. Imagine, for instance, a 'double theft' case in which a bicycle, stolen by A, is subsequently stolen by B and then sold to C, a good faith purchaser. A coherence-type argument would not alter A's right of recaption against C. Likewise, a simple application of the principle of relative title dictates that A would also succeed against C in conversion. However, in such an action, might a court refuse to grant A relief on the ground that it would be incongruous for the law to vindicate the claims of those who have deliberately subverted the very system whose assistance they now are seeking against a bona fide purchaser?

Whether or not such an argument would succeed, what is crucial to appreciate is that the possession rule is not the issue of substance here. The concerns that are, quite justifiably, raised about rights acquired by theft are not best addressed by impugning the possession rule but by asking whether, bearing in mind the integrity of the law as a whole, the plaintiff is asking the court to pursue contradictory ends.

This chapter has thus far considered the issue of possession and theft. The remainder of the chapter considers a closely related and equally difficult question: how should the law treat those who, in ignorance, acquire property rights from thieves?

III. Possession and Bona Fide Purchase

A. Conventional Expectations

As has been argued throughout this book, the existence of a convention creates expectations about how, in the absence of an explicit agreement, people will behave in the interactions governed by it. In the case of possession, people organise their dealings with 'things' in accordance with the accepted meaning of those interactions between people and objects of property that, within a particular population, amount to 'possession'. The very purpose of a convention is, in short, to create 'conventional expectations'.

Something very much like the notion of 'conventional expectations' lies at the heart of a theory of possession recently proposed by Austin. She argues that the significance of possession is not to be found in moral philosophy but in its function as a rudimentary or de facto register of title.[61] She writes that:

> [o]n my account, possession gives someone a title claim not because possession justifies ownership in some manner – as useful labour, as a reward, etc. – *but because a system of property must conform to the rule of law and this requires a public system of title. In this way possessory title does not point to justification stories for ownership but towards the requirements of the practice of law*.[62]

Austin's theory provides an interesting point of contrast to that of Ihering, discussed in Chapter 4. Unlike Ihering, who argued that the possession rule should be understood as a heuristic that functions as an evidentiary concession to owners, Austin claims that it serves as an evidentiary concession to third parties who, as adherents to the convention, draw the inference of ownership from the fact of possession. She argues that, '[w]hat possessory title rules say, in general, is that you should consider as owner the person who is *acting* as owner; the person acting as owner is the person acting as if she is the rightful possessor by exercising control over the thing in question'.[63]

Whereas the success of Ihering's argument depends upon the truth of the assumption that most possessors are also owners, Austin's explanation turns on the different claim that the law ought to allow people to assume that the person acting as the owner is the owner, even if this is not invariably true. She writes that, 'possessory title rules do not say: the person holding the apple *is* the owner. They are rules addressed to third parties who need to know that things are owned and by whom if they are to follow the law'.[64] Austin's basic claim is thus consistent with

[61] Lisa M Austin, 'Possession and the Distractions of Philosophy' in JE Penner and Henry E Smith (eds), *Philosophical Foundations of Property Law* (Oxford, Oxford University Press, 2014) 182, 189.
[62] Ibid, 190. Emphasis added.
[63] Ibid, 189.
[64] Ibid, 190.

the central argument of this book. If we accept that possession describes those acts that convey a recognised and accepted claim to an object of property, then we must also accept that the receipt of these signals generates corresponding expectations amongst the people to whom they are directed.

This observation about conventional expectations is of limited significance to those who merely wish to avoid breaching property duties, in which case one need only comply with the duty to 'keep off'. However, it is of significance to those who either wish to acquire the right-holder's right or to engage in conduct that requires the grant of a licence from the right-holder. Unlike those who simply seek to comply with their duties, such people need to know the right-holder's identity. On Austin's account, and consistently with the argument made throughout this book, possession is the observable fact that enables potential purchasers and licensees to quickly and cheaply determine the identity of the person with whom they must negotiate.

A challenge to Austin's theory of possession is posed by an observation recently made by Ellickson, who argues that those who are interested in acquiring rights do not, in fact, rely on simple possessory acts, of the sort discussed throughout this book, which signal one's claim-staking intention. He writes that:

> [a]n owner also commonly has reason to communicate much more detailed information to members of a much narrower audience, namely those who wish to engage in a transaction involving a particular asset. An owner of land, for example, may wish to sell it, lease it, mortgage it, or encumber it with a servitude. A transferee involved in one of these sorts of transactions commonly will offer the owner better contract terms if the owner can assure the transferee that third parties who historically have been associated with the resource have previously relinquished to the owner all their rights to it. To provide this sort of title assurance information to transferees, a property claimant typically uses forms of communication that are quite different from the ones a claimant uses to communicate to casual passersby. Title assurance information is much more particularized than an ownership earmark, the audience for title assurance information is far smaller, and the members of that audience have more time and greater incentive to engage in careful research. Beginning in ancient Mesopotamia, states have encouraged the development of recording and registration systems to facilitate the communication of detailed information about the quality of land titles. Unlike an ownership earmark, title assurance information typically is communicated by means of words, indeed, written words.[65]

Ellickson's argument is another manifestation of the 'intensiveness vs extensiveness' linguistic trade-off developed by Smith and discussed in Chapter 3. Because the audience for 'title assurance information', directed to potential purchasers, is much smaller than that for general ownership claims, directed to people generally, the message can be correspondingly more complex. Ellickson is undoubtedly

[65] Robert C Ellickson, 'The Inevitable Trend toward Universally Recognizable Signals of Property Claims: An Essay for Carol Rose' (2011) 19 *William & Mary Bill of Rights Journal* 1015, 1027.

correct to make this observation. No one, for example, would consider purchasing a house from a purported vendor whose only proof of ownership was possession of the front door key. Any potential purchaser would, at the very least, consult the relevant register.

However, Ellickson's claim that those who require title assurance information do not rely on basic possessory earmarks is not universally true. Whether a purchaser ought to rely on a vendor's possession as sufficient evidence of his title instead depends upon an economic calculus that requires the prospective purchaser to weigh the cost of investigating the vendor's title against the value of the transaction.[66] As is discussed below, in high-value transactions, particularly the purchase of real property, incurring these sorts of verification costs will be justified. However, in low-value transactions, it will not be. No one who, for example, purchases a bottle of milk from the corner shop would bother to investigate the quality of the vendor's title because the costs of doing so would exceed the maximum loss she would suffer in the extremely unlikely event that a third party emerged who could prove a superior title to the milk. Where the stakes are so low, the fact of possession is sufficient proof of title.

B. The Good Faith Purchaser at Common Law

The foregoing argument can be condensed into the following: if, by performing the recognised possessory act, someone is behaving as if they are an owner then, in the absence of evidence to the contrary, people are justified in treating them as such.

As noted above, one of the benefits of a system that uses simple possessory signals to disseminate ownership information is that third parties, particularly purchasers, can make quick and cheap determinations about who owns what. The corresponding detriment is that there is nothing to prevent prospective purchasers from relying upon possessory signals that are sent by people, such as thieves, who are themselves in contravention of the convention. The most difficult and important problem created by this trade-off is that of the good faith or bona fide purchaser.

Imagine that B, a reputable provedore, has an enormous black truffle on display in her shop window. C, a chef, purchases it from B. Unbeknown to C, B is a thief who stole the truffle from A. Several days after purchasing the truffle, C receives a letter from A demanding its return. C returns to the store to remonstrate with B, but she is nowhere to be found. Although C has an action in contract against B for breach of the implied warranty to pass good title,[67] B is likely to make herself

[66] For similar observations see Benito Arruñada, 'The Titling Role of Possession' in Yun-chien Chang (ed), *Law and Economics of Possession* (Cambridge, Cambridge University Press, 2015) 207, 216–17; Thomas W Merrill, 'Ownership and Possession' in Yun-chien Chang (ed), *Law and Economics of Possession* (Cambridge, Cambridge University Press, 2015) 9, 31.

[67] See, eg, *Goods Act 1958* (Vic) s 17(a); *Sale of Goods Act 1979* (UK) s 12(1).

difficult to find and, even if she can be found, is probably not worth suing.[68] Putting aside C's claim in contract, the question for the law of property is whether A or C has the better claim to the truffle. Should the law favour the good faith purchaser or the innocent victim of the theft? McFarlane, has described this invidious choice as the 'basic tension of property law'.[69] Given that one party must prevail, which does the law choose?

The law's general, though not invariable, answer is to favour A, the owner. A will generally prevail because, at common law, one cannot pass a better title than one has.[70] Rendered in doctrinal terms, A's claim to the truffle will prevail over that of C for the simple reason that A's title is older, and thus better, than the derivative title that C acquired from B. C cannot resist A's claim on the basis that B was acting as if she were the owner of the truffle, however convincing she may have been.[71] *Nemo dat's* status as a default rule is, as Smith has argued,[72] a fundamental design feature of property law.

Swadling summarises the general position at law by remarking that '[t]he general rule is that property rights survive dispositions by non-owners, even where the recipient is an innocent purchaser for value. Security of ownership almost invariably takes priority over security of transaction'.[73] Despite this, the law recognises a series of exceptions to *nemo dat* that enable purchasers, and others who have relied upon a vendor's possession as proof of his right, to succeed at the expense of existing right-holders.[74] The effect of these exceptions is to underwrite the conventional expectations created by the receipt of widely accepted possessory signals.

Historically, the most prominent exception to the *nemo dat* principle was sales in 'market overt'.[75] This mercantile custom, adopted by the common law, provides

[68] To borrow Lord Salmon's line, '[u]sually the rogue … is not worth the powder and shot': *Moorgate Mercantile v Twitchings* [1977] AC 890 (HL), 907 ('*Twitchings*').

[69] Ben McFarlane, *The Structure of Property Law* (Oxford, Hart Publishing, 2008) 5.

[70] This basic principle is usually rendered in the Latin maxim *nemo dat quod non habet* and is enshrined in *Goods Act 1958* (Vic) s 27; *Sale of Goods Act 1979* (UK) s 21(1).

[71] Note that the Factors Act does not apply in cases of theft because the mercantile agent is not in possession with the owner's consent. See, eg, *Factors Act 1889* (UK) s 2. Relatedly, jurisdictions that have retained the market overt rule recognise exceptions in the case of theft. See *Sale of Goods Act 1895* (SA) s 24; *Sale of Goods Act 1895* (WA) s 24; *Sale of Goods Act 1896* (Tas) s 29.

[72] Henry E Smith, 'The Elements of Possession' in Yun-chien Chang (ed), *Law and Economics of Possession* (Cambridge, Cambridge University Press, 2015) 65, 91.

[73] William Swadling, 'Restitution and Bona Fide Purchase' in William Swadling (ed), *The Limits of Restitutionary Claims: A Comparative Analysis* (London, The United Kingdom National Committee of Comparative Law, 1997) 79, 80.

[74] For an excellent overview of the *nemo dat* principle and its exceptions at common law see ibid, 83–89. See also Judith Nicholson, 'Owning and Owing: In What Circumstances Will the Responsibilities of Ownership Preclude or Postpone the Assertion of the Rights of an Owner?' (1987) 16 *Melbourne University Law Review* 784.

[75] See generally Brian Davenport and Anthony Ross, 'Market Overt' in Norman Palmer and Ewan McKendrick (eds), *Interests in Goods*, 2nd edn (London, Lloyd's of London Press, 1998) 337; JG Pease, 'Market Overt in the City of London' (1915) 31 *Law Quarterly Review* 270, 274–75. The rule was abolished in the UK by the *Sale of Goods (Amendment) Act 1994* (UK). It survives in South Australia, Western Australia and Tasmania: see *Sale of Goods Act 1895* (SA) s 22; *Sale of Goods Act 1895* (WA) s 22; *Sale of Goods Act 1896* (Tas) s 27.

that purchasers acquire an unimpeachable title to goods sold in those markets in which the custom applies, even if they are stolen. Another important exception to *nemo dat* is the double sale rule under the *Sale of Goods Act*, which allows a good faith purchaser to acquire clear title to goods which, unbeknownst to the purchaser, the vendor in possession has already sold.[76] The rationale for favouring the second purchaser is that, by leaving the vendor in possession of the goods, the first purchaser has allowed prospective purchasers to draw an incorrect inference of ownership, or good title, from the vendor's continued possession of the goods.[77] To take another example from the *Sale of Goods Act*, good faith purchasers do not inherit the voidable titles of their vendors.[78] Perhaps the most significant exception to *nemo dat* is the 'currency rule', according to which creditors who receive those chattels that constitute 'money' in good faith and in satisfaction of a debt take free of equities.[79] When a particular chattel passes into 'currency', the rule of the common law is that 'possession alone must decide to whom it belongs'.[80]

Exceptions to *nemo dat* are not confined to sales. Registration systems, beginning with the *Bills of Sale Act 1878* (UK), sought to overcome the problem of 'ostensible ownership' that arises when an owner retains possession of a chattel that he has mortgaged.[81] Because people draw the inference of ownership from the fact of possession, those who deal with a mortgagor in possession, particularly those who extend him unsecured credit, are given a misleading impression of his solvency. So strong is the tendency to draw this inference that, prior to the advent of registration regimes, it was, as Goode observed, 'considered an almost conclusive badge of fraud for the secured creditor to leave his debtor in possession of the security, thus enabling the debtor to get further credit on the strength of his apparent unencumbered ownership'.[82]

To address this problem, Parliament passed various iterations of the *Bills of Sale Act*, obliging mortgagees to register their 'bills', the instruments by which such interests were created. Failure to comply with the registration requirements under the Act rendered the interest void.[83] Modern registration regimes go further and

[76] *Goods Act 1958* (Vic) s 30; *Sale of Goods Act 1979* (UK) s 24. See, generally, MG Bridge, *Personal Property Law*, 4th edn (Oxford, Oxford University Press, 2015), 215–19.

[77] For discussion see MG Bridge et al, *The Law of Personal Property* (London, Sweet & Maxwell, 2013) 368–69 [13-064]; Swadling (n 73) 88. One could also translate this rationale into economic terms by noting that the first purchaser, who could have demanded possession of the goods, was the least-cost avoider.

[78] *Goods Act 1958* (Vic) s 29; *Sale of Goods Act 1979* (UK) s 23.

[79] For the classic statement of the rule see *Miller v Race* (1758) 97 ER 398, 401; 1 Burr 452, 457 (Lord Mansfield).

[80] *Wookey v Pole* (1820) 106 ER 839, 841; 4 B & Ald 1, 7 (Best J).

[81] The classic authority on ostensible ownership is *Twyne's Case* [1774] 76 ER 809; (1601) 3 Co Rep 80. On the concept itself see Douglas G Baird and Thomas H Jackson, 'Possession and Ownership: An Examination of the Scope of Article 9' (1982) 35 *Stanford Law Review* 175; Richard A Epstein, 'Inducement of Breach of Contract as a Problem of Ostensible Ownership' (1987) 16 *Journal of Legal Studies* 1, 2, 10–11.

[82] RM Goode, 'The Modernisation of Personal Property Security Law' (1984) 100 *Law Quarterly Review* 234, 238.

[83] *Bills of Sale (1878) Amendment Act 1882* (UK) s 8.

not only capture retention of title and cognate arrangements,[84] but also leases of goods and other forms of bailment that, because they separate possession from ownership,[85] create a problem of ostensible ownership, whether or not they secure the payment of a debt.[86] The expansion of these regimes has been necessitated, at least in part, by commercial drafting techniques that outflanked, in form if not in substance, older registration requirements.[87] It is significant that, despite the breadth and complexity of modern registration regimes such as the *PPSA*, security interests can still be perfected by the simple expedient of transferring possession of the collateral to the secured party.[88]

C. Good Faith Purchase and the Limits of Conventions

The previous section described the way in which the law resolves, however imperfectly, the invidious problem caused by disputes between owners and good faith purchasers. While there are exceptions in which the law will guarantee the inference of ownership that people draw from the fact of possession, the basic position is that one cannot pass better title than one has.[89] If the law invariably allowed third parties to rely on possession as conclusive evidence of title then, as is the case with cheques and other bills of exchange, all objects of property would be fully negotiable.[90] However, they are not.

A more difficult question is how the law *ought* to resolve the problem created by the good faith purchaser. McFarlane has remarked that the contest between an owner and a good faith purchaser raises an 'impossibly difficult question',[91] and one can see why. The fundamental difficulty arises because, as discussed in previous chapters, any convention that successfully answers the most basic questions of mine and thine must be able to mediate the relationships of a huge number of anonymous parties who know nothing about each other. Consequently, the applicable allocative rule must turn on the conventional meaning of an impersonal possessory act, and not the identity of the person performing it. As was argued in Chapter 5, the depersonalised nature of the possession convention

[84] See, eg, *Personal Property Securities Act 2009* (Cth) s 12(2)(d) ('PPSA').

[85] See, eg, the comments of Lord Wilberforce on hire purchase agreements in *Twitchings* (n 68) 901.

[86] *PPSA* (n 84) s 12(3)(c). See further AJ Duggan and David Brown, *Australian Personal Property Securities Law*, 2nd edn (North Ryde, Commerce Clearing House Australia, 2015) 77–81 [3.33]–[3.39].

[87] See, eg, *Associated Alloys Pty Ltd v CAN 001452106 Pty Ltd (in Liq)* [2000] HCA 25; (2000) 202 CLR 588, 614–18 [60]–[68] (Kirby J); Goode (n 82) 247–8.

[88] *PPSA* (n 84) s 21(2)(b). It has been remarked that, of the various methods of perfection, possession remains the 'oldest and safest method'. Royston Miles Goode and Ewan McKendrick, *Goode on Commercial Law*, 4th edn (London, Penguin, 2010) 680.

[89] *Shogun Finance Ltd v Hudson* [2003] UKHL 62; [2004] 1 AC 919, 934 [14] (Lord Nicholls); William Swadling, 'Rescission, Property, and the Common Law' (2005) 121 *Law Quarterly Review* 123, 130.

[90] Negotiability is used here in the strict sense that good faith successors in title take free of equities. On the two meanings of 'negotiable' see Bridge et al (n 77) 13 [1-026].

[91] McFarlane (n 69) 189.

is desirable in so far as it makes the basic mechanism by which people acquire original rights to scarce things tolerably fair. However, because it instructs third parties to 'consider as owner the person who is *acting* as owner',[92] the rule demands that third parties treat possessors as owners, even if the possessors are later revealed to be rogues who have themselves breached the possession convention. In short, the problem of good faith purchase reveals the limits of rules that are, at heart, simple conventions.

This problem of the irreconcilable expectations generated by the possession rule is illustrated by the truffle example, given above. By taking possession of a truffle lying on the forest floor, A has complied with the applicable convention and is thus entitled to expect that he has acquired a property right in the truffle that is enforceable against all comers. Likewise, C, by purchasing the truffle from a vendor in possession, has also followed the convention but, in doing so, has developed an incompatible expectation.[93] As Savage CJ remarked of the position of the good faith purchaser:

> [p]ossession of personal property is *prima facie* evidence of property … The *bona fide* purchaser, therefore, is justified in considering the fraudulent vendee the true owner – such *bona fide* purchaser as the terms *bona fide* import, having no notice of the fraud; and considering the possessor as the owner, the *bona fide* purchaser is justified in purchasing such property and giving value for it, or in making advances upon it, or incurring responsibility upon the credit of it, or in receiving it in pledge for money or property loaned upon it.[94]

As was discussed in Chapter 5, Hayek thought that the material question in any dispute was whether one party had 'conformed to expectations which the other parties had reasonably formed because they correspond to the practices on which the everyday conduct of the members of the group was based'.[95] The riddle of the good faith purchaser is that, if we apply Hayek's rule to our truffle example, there is no basis on which to distinguish the claims of A and C because each is the product of legitimate expectations generated by adherence to the socially accepted convention.

[92] Austin (n 61) 189.

[93] On the irreconcilable nature of the parties' claims see generally *Bishopsgate Motor Finance Corp v Transport Brakes Ltd* [1949] 1 KB 322 (CA), 337–38 (Denning LJ); Bridge (n 77) 196–97; Douglas Baird and Thomas Jackson, 'Information, Uncertainty, and the Transfer of Property' (1984) 13 *Journal of Legal Studies* 299, 300.

[94] *Root v French*, 13 Wend 570, 572 (NY Sup Ct, 1835). The reference to 'fraudulent vendee' here is to a bankrupt rogue who fraudulently purchased the disputed goods from the plaintiff and then transferred them to the defendant, the good faith purchaser, who received them in partial satisfaction of an existing debt. So, the relationship between the rogue and the defendant was that of vendor-purchaser. For an excellent discussion of the pre-Civil War sales cases see Harold R Weinberg, 'Markets Overt, Voidable Titles, and Feckless Agents: Judges and Efficiency in the Antebellum Doctrine of Good Faith Purchase' (1981) 56 *Tulane Law Review* 1.

[95] FA Hayek, *Law, Legislation, and Liberty: A New Statement of the Liberal Principles of Justice and Political Economy* (London, Routledge and Kegan Paul, 1973) vol 1 Rules and Order, 96–7. Hayek was perfectly aware that judges will, on occasion, be called upon to decide between litigants who have relied upon rules that generate legitimate, though irreconcilable, expectations: at 115.

Nor does Austin's theory of possession provide a solution. She argues that, as a de facto register of title, the possession rule should be understood as a requirement of the rule of law.[96] However, where two parties have developed irreconcilable expectations by conforming to the convention that underpins the relevant legal rule, no fundamental principle of legality or the rule of law provides a basis on which to favour the purchaser at the expense of the owner, or vice versa. On the contrary, all the rule of law seems to require is that such disputes be resolved by a rule that is clear, prospective, stable, and so on.[97]

Given that the problem posed by the bona fide purchaser highlights the inherent limits of conventions, an obvious solution would seem to be the replacement of possession with registration as the means of announcing a property claim. Posner, for example, has written that:

> [a]lthough the possession norm improves the position of parties relative to anarchy, legal rules improve their position relative to the possession norm. The problem with the possession norm is that it does not protect property in which a person has invested resources but cannot overtly possess – for example, large areas of land or chattels that are best used by third parties. The natural solution to this problem is a recording system, such as those used for real estate transactions and security interests in personal property.[98]

Because they hugely reduce the costs of verifying the quality of a prospective vendor's title, registration systems undoubtedly improve the lot of purchasers. Nevertheless, they are not a panacea. This is so for two reasons. First, even in jurisdictions with sophisticated title-by-registration regimes, possession retains its legitimacy as a way of announcing a property claim. As was argued in Chapter 5, the two means of broadcasting ownership claims continue to operate in parallel. Secondly, the benefits of any registration regime must be weighed against its costs. In addition to the cost to the purchaser of consulting the register, one must also consider the cost of both creating and updating it to ensure its accuracy. While registration regimes are an effective and desirable means of publicising ownership interests in objects of property, such as land, that are valuable and seldom transferred,[99] they are, for the reasons noted above, poorly suited to chattels that are relatively cheap and frequently transferred.[100] In low-cost and high-volume transactions, a simple convention, such as the possession rule, remains, whatever its faults, the only viable mechanism for determining who owns what.

[96] Austin (n 61) 190.

[97] Joseph Raz, *The Authority of Law: Essays on Law and Morality*, 2nd edn (Oxford, Oxford University Press, 2009) 214–18. Nor would this analysis change if one subscribed to a 'thicker' conception of the rule of law.

[98] Eric A Posner, 'Law, Economics, and Inefficient Norms' (1996) 144 *University of Pennsylvania Law Review* 1697, 1716.

[99] Baird and Jackson (n 93) 304.

[100] Ibid, 306. See also Steven Shavell, *Foundations of Economic Analysis of Law* (Cambridge MA, Harvard University Press, 2004) 49–50.

D. Beyond the Possession Rule

Should we therefore conclude that, at least where registration systems are inappropriate, bona fide purchase poses an essentially insoluble problem? The answer is 'not necessarily'. As Hume stressed in his theory of property, discussed in Chapter 4, the role fulfilled by the possession rule is simply to enable order to emerge from anarchy by answering the simplest questions of mine and thine. The difficulty is that the simple and conventional structure of the possession rule, necessary for the resolution of the large problem caused by scarcity, creates other, albeit smaller, ones once the rudiments of the system have been established. This is not an indictment on possession. Rather, it is a reflection of the need, once the delineation of the most basic rights has enabled a system of property to get 'up and running', to design rules that solve the more fine-grained problems faced by a mature system that allows right-holders to buy, sell, gift, mortgage and otherwise deal with the rights created by acts of possession.

In some cases, the question of which of the two convention-abiding parties should be favoured can be satisfactorily, though not painlessly, answered. The currency rule provides a good illustration.[101] If a legal system wishes to ensure that certain physical tokens function as means of payment, it is not enough that they be designated as 'legal tender'.[102] It is also essential that creditors who accept these tokens in good faith in satisfaction of a debt receive them free of other potential claims. As Viscount Haldane LC explained:

> [i]f a sovereign or bank note be offered in payment it is, under ordinary circumstances, no part of the duty of the person receiving it to inquire into title. The reason of this is that chattels of such a kind form part of what the law recognizes as currency, and treats as passing from hand to hand in point, not merely of possession, but of property. It would cause great inconvenience to commerce if in this class of chattel an exception were not made to the general requirement of the law as to title.[103]

If creditors paid in chattel money were subject to the claims of others then, at the very least, we would expect notes and coins to circulate at a discount to their face value, reflecting the risk to the creditor that a third party may subsequently emerge and assert a better right to them.[104] Although it is cold comfort for someone who has had a wallet full of cash stolen from her handbag, the need to ensure that certain physical tokens function as stable media of exchange, units of account and stores of value explains why disputes between owners and transferees must be resolved in favour of the latter where the chattel passes into 'currency'.[105]

[101] See generally McFarlane (n 69) 189–90.

[102] Which simply means that, when tendered in satisfaction of a debt, they constitute good discharge of particular sums specified in a particular unit of account. See, eg, *Currency Act 1965* (Cth) s 16; *Reserve Bank Act 1959* (Cth) s 36. See generally David Fox, *Property Rights in Money* (Oxford, Oxford University Press, 2008) 28–29 [1.90].

[103] *Sinclair v Brougham* [1914] AC 398 (HL), 418.

[104] Fox (n 102) 60–62 [2.32]–[2.39].

[105] On the functions of money see ibid, 6–10 [1.19]–[1.30].

Unfortunately, not every problem caused by incompatible 'conventional expectations' can be so neatly resolved. Consider, once again, the paradigm case of stolen chattels sold to a good faith purchaser. One may think that, in a market economy, ensuring security of transactions ought to be the law's priority. Indeed, this was Blackstone's justification for the market overt exception to *nemo dat*. Blackstone explained that:

> property may also in some cases be transferred by sale, though the vendor *hath none at all* in the goods: for it is expedient that the buyer, by taking proper precautions, may at all events secure his purchase; otherwise all commerce between man and man must soon be at an end. And therefore the general rule of law is, that all sale and contracts of any thing vendible, in fairs or markets *overt* … shall not only be good between the parties, but also binding on all those that have any right or property therein.[106]

There are, however, reasons to doubt the desirability of invariably favouring purchasers over owners. The efficient solution to the problem of theft depends upon which of the two affected parties can avoid the problem at least cost. If it could be demonstrated that it is cheaper to prevent theft than it is to verify the quality of a vendor's title, then the law ought to favour purchasers over owners.[107] While some have argued that this is the case,[108] it is not self-evidently true that owners are the least-cost avoiders.[109] If it were, then we would expect a preponderance of legal systems to favour purchasers over owners. However, as Levmore's comparative study demonstrates, no clear majority of systems do so.[110] Moreover, as Weinberg has noted,[111] the relative antiquity of the *nemo dat* rule must count as prima facie evidence that favouring owners over purchasers is tolerably efficient.

Even if it could be demonstrated that owners are the least-cost avoiders, favouring purchasers may have other undesirable effects. Because the good faith purchaser rule reduces title verification costs for prospective purchasers, it also reduces the effective price of stolen goods. If we assume that a fall in price of stolen goods will increase demand for them, then a general exception to *nemo dat* is likely to increase theft.[112]

A different sort of objection is that, whichever party the law favours, property law's 'all or nothing' approach to the problem of good faith purchase fails to

[106] William Blackstone, *The Oxford Edition of Blackstone's Commentaries on the Laws of England: Book II: Of the Rights of Things*, (Oxford, Oxford University Press, 2016) 304.

[107] Harold R Weinberg, 'Sales Law, Economics, and the Negotiability of Goods' (1980) 9 *Journal of Legal Studies* 569, 583–86. This would include analysis of, for instance, which of the two groups can more effectively pool their risks to more cheaply insure against loss.

[108] Epstein (n 81) 13.

[109] Saul Levmore, 'Variety and Uniformity in the Treatment of the Good Faith Purchaser' (1987) 16 *Journal of Legal Studies* 43, 46–47.

[110] Ibid. See also, Alan Schwartz and Robert E Scott, 'Rethinking the Laws of Good Faith Purchase' (2011) 111 *Columbia Law Review* 1332, 1334–35.

[111] Weinberg (n 107) 586.

[112] Ibid, 576–80; Shavell (n 100) 53–54. One might argue that the market overt rule could assist with the problem of theft by physically concentrating the market for stolen goods, thus making detection easier. As Levmore has noted, promoting effective law enforcement, rather than the free exchange of goods, seems to be the most plausible justification for the rule. Levmore (n 109) 55.

incentivise owners and prospective purchasers to invest optimally in precautions. If owners invariably prevail over purchasers, then owners have insufficient incentive to guard against theft. Likewise, if purchasers always prevail over owners, then purchasers have insufficient incentive to inquire into the quality of their vendor's title. In order to overcome this 'double moral hazard', some have proposed the radical approach of abandoning the strict liability of property law in favour of the fault-based liability of tort.[113]

What is the law to do? Though it is perhaps intellectually unsatisfying, the best answer is that a legal system is justified in either favouring owners over purchasers or the reverse. As Levmore has argued,[114] the fact that there is no overwhelmingly favoured solution to this universal problem demonstrates both the extreme difficulty of measuring the behavioural effects of the two competing approaches and the sufficiency of either.

What is more, we should expect the distributive burden of favouring either owners or purchasers to be broadly neutral. Because purchasers become owners, the rule is effectively self-negating. Though exceptions to *nemo dat* appear to favour purchasers, so far as any individual purchaser is concerned, their effect is simply, to borrow McFarlane's apt description, to trade 'retrospective security … for prospective insecurity'.[115] Because most people become owners by purchasing rights from others, participants in a market economy are, as Epstein has noted, placed 'behind the veil of ignorance, not by philosophical stipulation, but as a simple matter of fact'.[116]

Thus, in solving the good faith purchaser puzzle, we are not faced with the additional complication of justifying a system that increases welfare in the aggregate but, in so doing, leaves some individuals worse off. A system that allows for the alienation of property rights increases social welfare and, in the run of transactions, distributes the unavoidable burden created by inconsistent conventional expectations more or less equally. As a consequence, the only imperative that the law must satisfy is to ensure the quick and cheap resolution of disputes between owners and bona fide purchasers.[117] While this imperative favours neither owners nor purchasers, it does exclude the use of a negligence standard as means of breaking the deadlock. Although the use of a fault standard may address a potential moral hazard, in practice, the problem of determining the appropriate standard of care for different goods in different contexts would consume too large a portion of the social surplus created by a system of freely alienable rights.[118] It is thus

[113] Schwartz and Scott (n 110) 1339–40.

[114] Levmore (n 109) 45, 65.

[115] McFarlane (n 69) 189.

[116] Epstein (n 81) 13.

[117] In other words, because neither solution alters relative shares, the only imperative is to select the solution that maximises the size of the pie. For discussion of this point see ibid, 12–15.

[118] Ibid, 14. Those who have proposed a negligence solution concede the expense point but argue that it can be solved by the use of simple proxies, such as the presence of locks, burglar alarms, and so on Schwartz and Scott (n 110) 1357–62.

unsurprising that, at common law,[119] owners do not come under a duty to take reasonable steps to safeguard their property and that no jurisdiction has adopted the tort law solution to the problem of good faith purchase.[120]

E. Conclusion

In disputes between owners and good faith purchasers, a fundamental problem arises because application of the same convention by each party yields diametrically opposed answers. The difficulty of the good faith purchase problem is thus not merely that two people cannot claim an exclusive entitlement to the one asset.[121] It is also that, because each adhered to the socially accepted convention, there is no obvious basis on which to separate their claims. No matter which party the law favours, the loser will always nurse a legitimate grievance.

Because the possession rule caused these disputes, we cannot look to it for their resolution. What the problem of the good faith purchaser demonstrates is the inherent limitation of the simple, conventional mechanism whose role is to get a system of property up and running. Once a baseline of rights has been established, a system that wishes to allow right-holders to trade, mortgage or otherwise deal with those rights must advance beyond the simple convention whose function is to prevent potentially violent and socially corrosive disputes over scarce resources.

Where the nature of the relevant assets makes it viable, the replacement of possession with registration as the source of title information can largely eliminate the problem of inconsistent conventional expectations.[122] In instances in which a register is not practicable, there are defensible bases for breaking the moral deadlock created by the possession rule.[123] This is not to insist that these tiebreaker

[119] See *Twitchings* (n 68) 902–3 (Lord Wilberforce), 925 (Lord Fraser).

[120] This is freely conceded by the proponents of a negligence standard. See Schwartz and Scott (n 110) 1371.

[121] Although the disputed asset could always be sold and the proceeds of sale divided between the owner and purchaser. Interestingly, it seems that Mongolian tribal law is the only system to have adopted a sharing rule. Levmore speculates that the unpopularity of the 'Solomonic solution' is probably attributable to the costs of valuing the disputed asset. See Levmore (n 109) 64–65. Thus, while it may seem a desirable way of resolving a dispute between two morally indistinguishable claimants, equal division ultimately founders on the same rocks as the negligence solution.

[122] Baird and Jackson (n 93) 303.

[123] The existence of a register does not entirely relieve the law of the need to make essentially arbitrary choices between competing parties. To adapt Baird and Jackson's example, imagine a dispute between a chattel mortgagee who failed to register his interest and the purchaser of the encumbered asset who failed to consult the register, ibid, 318–19. Given that it is not obviously cheaper to register a security interest than it is to consult the register, it is not clear why the purchaser should prevail over the secured party. Nevertheless, registration regimes do not have a reliance requirement and a careless purchaser will prevail over a secured party who has failed to perfect his interest. See, eg, *PPSA* (n 84) s 43(1). What is important is simply that there is a rule for resolving these sorts of disputes. Given that the existence of a state-funded register massively reduces a secured party's publicity costs, we can acknowledge that this is an essentially arbitrary choice, while having little sympathy for a secured party who neglected to register or otherwise perfect his interest.

rules are anything other than merely adequate. Nor does pointing out the obvious necessity for such rules provide much comfort for the losing party. It is simply to make the point that, if a system of property wishes to do more than to merely avoid Hawk-Hawk confrontations, it must lift its gaze above the basic mechanism that attaches names to things.

IV. Conclusion

An important argument made throughout this book is that the rule that determines what belongs to whom must turn on an asymmetry that is simple to identify and can be applied in a wide range of circumstances. In our system, the relevant asymmetry is created by those relations between people and things that, within some population, amount to possession. This simplicity imperative means that the application of the rule, and the convention that underpins it, cannot depend upon difficult and informationally intensive judgments, such as whether the person performing the possessory act is a thief or, for some other reason, has a fragile title. It is thus inevitable that, on occasion, the application of the possession rule will place the law in invidious and embarrassing positions. Two such instances, theft and good faith purchase, were considered in this chapter.

The obvious solution to this problem would seem to be the replacement of possession with registration as the source of 'title assurance information'. The problem is that the transition from possession to registration is only viable where the right to the object in question is valuable and infrequently transferred. The argument advanced in this chapter was that, despite this, the law can solve, however imperfectly, the problems created when the possession rule generates incompatible expectations. However, those answers are not to be found in the expressive mechanism by which the law allocates property rights to those who are competent to bear them.

Conclusion

If one were to peruse the leading textbooks on personal property law, real property law or jurisprudence, one would be left with the impression that possession is a uniquely complex and arcane concept, the mysteries of which can only be fathomed by legal scholars, natural law theorists and other members of some priestly intellectual caste. As should be evident from the analysis in this book, it is undoubtedly true that the possession rule does raise conceptual and moral questions that often do not admit of simple or, for that matter, particularly comforting answers. Nevertheless, by concentrating on the most troublesome aspects of the concept, we can easily overlook a simple and important truth about possession; namely, that it is a pervasive and, on the whole, unremarkable feature of life in those societies that recognise private property rights.

When viewed from afar, what is striking about the 'possession puzzle' is that, for all the debate that the concept has generated in textbooks and scholarly journals, it remains true that laymen, with no training in law or philosophy, are perfectly able to 'get it'. Merrill has recently made a similar observation, writing that:

> [w]hen you entered this room you did not have to devote any intellectual effort to perceiving which seats were taken, which had been claimed by someone who intended to return, and which were open. Your brain processed this information without thinking about it. This feature of possession has been obscured by property teachers, who love to dwell on a small number of cases in which claims of possession are contested, such as the dispute between Pierson and Post over who was first to possess the fox. Such cases are fascinating, and we can learn important things about possession by studying them. But the reality is that 99.9 percent of the time, our perceptions are made effortlessly and unconsciously, and are not challenged by others who are processing the same information. Indeed, this is how we successfully navigate through daily life without significant conflict over thousands of items of value that cross our paths.[1]

Merrill's observations accord with the central argument advanced in this book that, despite the persistent scholarly disagreement discussed in Chapter 2, the concept of possession is much simpler than generations of lawyers and law students have been led to believe. On the account presented here, possession does not describe some species of right that is different from the generic property right described in Chapter 1. Nor does it refer to some esoteric and uniquely legal concept that consists of one fact about 'physical control' and a second, discrete, fact about the

[1] Thomas W Merrill, 'Possession as a Natural Right' (2015) 9 *New York University Journal of Law and Liberty* 345, 358.

putative possessor's intention. Rather, on the account presented in this book, possession refers to any act, earmark or symbol that, as a matter of an extra-legal convention, is recognised by members of a particular population as a legitimate way of staking a claim to an object of property.

In particular, what is crucial to appreciate is that, contrary to standard formulations, the efficacy of these particular acts, symbols and earmarks does not depend upon a possessor's 'physical control' in the sense of his ability to exclude others. On the contrary, all that matters is that, in a community in which property rights are respected as a matter of course, the 'possessor' has staked his claim in the prescribed way.

The account developed in this book does not attempt to undertake the essentially anthropological exercise of exhaustively describing those particular relations between people and things that amount to 'possession' in particular communities. The point stressed is simply that what amounts to possession in the law cannot be neatly separated from what amounts to possession in custom. As was discussed in Chapter 4, the possession *rule* of the positive law is, first and foremost, an extra-legal *convention* that has been applied by, and incorporated into, the common law. Thus, whether some act amounts to possession remains a question of social fact. As the discussion of *Popov v Hayashi* in Chapter 3 sought to make clear, the extra-legal nature of this enquiry does not fundamentally change simply because, in disputes that end up before the courts, this determination is made by a judge who will, depending on her determination, make legally binding orders.

To offer this conceptually neat explanation of the nature of possession is not to deny that there will, at times, be problems generated by uncertainty in its application. This might be because, as in *Pierson v Post*, members of a particular group disagree about whether some particular act amounts to possession. Alternatively, and perhaps more likely, it may be because, as in *Popov*, there is simply insufficient evidence to determine whether the putative possessor performed the requisite act. Nevertheless, it should be emphasised that disagreements, particularly of the sort in *Pierson*, represent the exception and not the rule. As was stressed in Chapter 4, any convention that regularly gives rise to interpretive confusion amongst those whose behaviour is to be guided by it will not survive in the long run. If possession were as confusing as the conflicting academic accounts would have us believe, it would simply cease to be the mechanism that determines elementary questions of mine and thine.

As was briefly noted in Chapter three, the widely held view that possession is a hopelessly ambiguous concept is, at least in part, attributable to the natural tendency of lawyers to view legally significant concepts through the lens of litigated disputes. In common law systems, it is necessary to begin with the decided cases because the *ratio decidendi* to emerge from these decisions *is* the law. Nevertheless, as the 'finders' cases', discussed in Chapter 6, demonstrate, to focus exclusively on difficult cases can lead to the distortion of otherwise coherent concepts. Just as importantly, this focus on the periphery at the expense of the core can also paint an unfairly gloomy picture of their efficacy as behaviour-guiding norms. What must always be remembered is that, as Merrill observed in the extract above, for every *Pierson*, there are countless, quotidian property interactions in which the possession rule functions so effectively that its presence passes unnoticed. This natural tendency to overlook the 'easy cases' reinforces the truth of the methodological claim, made in the Introduction, that in order to understand the nature and function of possession in the law, one must appreciate the extra-legal origins of the rule and its salience in those everyday property interactions in which the positive law is never invoked.

The theory developed in Chapters 3 and 4 made no broad, normative, claims about the possession rule or its ramifications. Indeed, as was discussed in detail in Chapter 4, an important part of this account is that moral arguments about the significance of possession cannot explain why it, as opposed to some other mechanism, came to fulfil the essential function of determining what belongs to whom. To the contrary, it was emphasised that, like all spontaneously emergent conventions, possession is strictly amoral and that its moral desirability is incidental to its ability to spread throughout a population. The moral dimension of a convention is purely conventional. People *ought* to follow the possession convention, not because of its substance, but because it is the established way in which members of a population solve a recurrent coordination problem.

However, while the moral desirability of the possession convention is incidental to its fitness, it does not follow that it is therefore immoral or unfair. The argument advanced in Chapter 5 was that we can go beyond Epstein's minimalist defence of the possession rule. While the arbitrariness of the rule makes it insensitive to distributive and other ethical considerations in any given pairwise contest, it also ensures that no one is systematically excluded from benefitting from it. The blind operation of the rule ensures that it satisfies a minimum standard of fairness. Thus, when one considers all the possible ways in which a system of private property could assign property rights to those capable of enjoying them, possession is not merely tolerable, it may also be desirable.

Moreover, the fact that the application of the possession rule may, at times, place the law in an embarrassing position or generate inconsistent, though equally meritorious, claims does not undermine its role as the dominant allocative rule in property law. Conventions must be simple if they are to be effective and, as the discussion in Chapter 7 sought to make clear, problems of coherence and stultification are not unique to disputes about the acquisition of property rights. Rather, they are an inevitable feature of any complex system of law that must attempt to reconcile often competing moral and instrumental priorities. What must be stressed is that the resolution of difficult questions such as theft and good faith purchase do not implicate the possession rule per se. Rather, they require that the law grapples with questions of efficiency, internal consistency and other instrumental considerations that arise once it has solved the basic problem created by the ineradicable condition of scarcity.

Perhaps what is most remarkable about the possession rule described in this book is its longevity and resistance to change. If this essentially Humean account is correct, the convention that helped order to emerge from anarchy continues to resolve elementary questions of mine and thine over smartphones, electric cars and other things that Hume could scarcely have imagined when he wrote his famous work in 1738.

This is not to deny that, at least in some areas of the law, the role of possession is waning. So, for instance, the old learning on the negotiability of cheques and bills of exchange will soon be of historical interest only. Indeed, one can foresee a not-too-distant future in which chattel money itself becomes obsolete. To borrow Pound's neat phrase, '[w]ealth, in a commercial age, is made up largely of promises',[2] and the vast majority of dealings with what we call 'money' have ceased to be a matter of property law and now fall under the law of contract and debt, in which the concept of possession plays no role.[3] And this is to say nothing of the revolution in payment systems that is set to be ushered in by distributed ledger technologies and the challenges posed by the emergence of virtual and digital assets whose existence, some scholars have argued,[4] undermine the traditional status of the chattel as the paradigm object of property.

Despite the significance of these, and other, changes in law and life, it remains true that we continue to inhabit corporeal bodies and to live in a world full of tangible things capable of being possessed. For so long as our transhuman future remains the subject of science fiction, the concept of possession laid out in this book will continue to remain a fundamental feature of those societies that recognise the right to private property.

[2] Roscoe Pound, *An Introduction to the Philosophy of Law* (Urbana, Project Gutenberg, 2010) 236.

[3] As lawyers have long understood, these changes reflect what Nicholas described as the difference between 'owning and being owed something': Barry Nicholas, *An Introduction to Roman Law* (Oxford, Clarendon Press, 1976) 99.

[4] See, eg, Joshua AT Fairfield, 'Virtual Property' (2005) 85 *Boston University Law Review* 1047, 1075–76.

INDEX

www.ingramcontent.com/pod-product-compliance
Ingram Content Group UK Ltd.
Pitfield, Milton Keynes, MK11 3LW, UK
UKHW020811290926
15470UKWH00003B/1092

9 781509 9299